Sinai

Sinai

Pharaohs, Miners, Pilgrims and Soldiers

Beno Rothenberg

Avinoam Danin, Zvi Garfunkel, Paul Huber,
Martin A. Klopfenstein, Eliezer D. Oren,
Eitan Tchernov, Gerold Walser

Photographs by Helfried Weyer

Joseph J. Binns · Publisher · Washington - New York

Caption to the endpaper:
Bernhard von Breydenbach: *Peregrinatio in Terram Sanctam*
(German edition 21 June 1486).

Editorial Note:
The transcription of Arabic names follows the «Survey of
Egypt» map; hence English pronunciation rules apply.
Ancient Egyptian names occur in the forms customary in the
English Egyptological literature.

Photographs:
Helfried Weyer, Wetzlar, with the following exceptions: 12,
13, 64, 65, 76, 85, 111 Beno Rothenberg, Tel Aviv, 108 Fredy
Knorr, Zurich, 113 NASA 71-HC-107

Front cover: Representation of the
Egyptian goddess Hathor with cow's
ears in the mining temple of Serabit
el Khadim (see Plate 43).

Back cover: Oasis valley of 'Ain
Hudera (see Plates 72 and 78).

Published in the United States 1979
ISBN 089674-002-1
Library of Congress Card Catalog Number 78-53350

Translated by Ewald Osers, revised by
Britta Charleston

Graphical presentation Kümmerly + Frey, Berne
Cartography, photolithography and offset-printing:
Kümmerly + Frey, Berne
© 1979 Kümmerly + Frey, Geographical Publishers, Berne
Printed in Switzerland   ISBN 3-259-08383-9

Contents

MEDITERRANEAN

Sabkhet el Bardawil (Lake Sirbon)

Bur Sa'id (Port Said)

Tell el Farame (Pelusium)
Rumani
Bir el 'Abd
El 'Arish

Bir Qatia
Bir Nagid

Tell el Ahmar
Qantara

Abu Aweigila

Gebel el Maghara

Gebel Halal 892
El Qusaima
Kadesh Barnea
'Ain el Gedeirat

Lake Timsah

Bir Hasana

Khatmia Pass
Bir Gafgafa

Great Bitter Lake

Gebel Yelleq 1094

Gebel Areif el Naqa 934

Small Bitter Lake

Wadi Giddi
Bir Tamada

Giddi Pass

Wadi el Hagg
Ruweiset el Akheider

Col Parker Memorial

S I N A I

Darb el Hagg

Kuntilla

El Suweis (Suez)

Mittla Pass

Nekhel (Nakhl)

Ayun Musa

Qal'at el Gindi

Darb esh Shawi

Ain Sudr

Wadi Sudr

Timna

Gebel Sinn Bishr 618
Gebel Somar

Bir el Themed
Gebel Khashm el Tarif
874
Ras el Naqb

Ras el Sudr

Gebel Bodhya

Elat
'Aqaba (Aila)

'Ain el Fogeiya

W. Sudr
W. Somar
W. el Fogeiya
Wadi el Siq
W. el Shallala

Geziret el Fara'un

B A D I E T   E L   T I H

Gebel Abu Zurub 942
'Ain Yerqa

W. Gharandel

Gebel el Tih Naqb Rakna 1187

Wadi Tayiba

Gebel Umm Rinna 592

Gebel el Egma
'Ain Umm Ahmed

Abu Zenima
Bir Nasib
El Markha
Serabit el Khadim

'Ain el Furtaga

Nuweiba

Maghara

'Ain Hudera

Abu Rudeis

'Ain el Akhdar

Gebel el Gunna

Feiran Oasis

Tell el Mekharet 2070
Sheikh Mohsin

Watia Pass
Sheikh Nabi Sala

Gebel Serbal

Dahab

St. Catherine
Gebel Musa
Gebel Katherina 2642

Gebel Umm Shomer 2585

Gebel Samra 940

El Tor

Gebel Madsus 740

Tiran

Sherm el Sheikh

Ras Muhammad

Abu – Father
'Ain – Spring
Bir – Well
Darb – Track, path
Gebel – Mountain
Ras – Summit, cape
Tell – Hill, hill of ruins
Wadi – Dry river-bed

N

0   25   50 km

0   25 mi

E G Y P T

GULF OF SUEZ

GULF OF ELAT - AQABA

EL HIJAZ

MIDIAN

N E G E V

PALESTINE
EREZ = ISRAEL
DEAD SEA

Gaza
Rafa
Beer-Sheba
Yeroham

E D O M

Wadi el Arish

Introduction
Travellers, Painters, Surveyors and Scholars

The unique character of the Sinai peninsula lies in its striking contrasts, in the fact that it unites within itself incompatible contradictions and, in consequence, displays a particular kind of "earthly spirituality". Sinai is the meeting point of two continents—this is reflected in particular in its flora and fauna—as well as of two disparate worlds: the land of revelation, the "celestial Sinai" of great religions, of ascetics and pilgrims, of monasteries and hermitages, as well as the ancient battlefield between Asia and Africa, the "earthly Sinai" of turquoise and copper mines, of shepherd-warriors, of trade caravans and of wretched settlements. The cradle of monotheism and the scene of decisive historical events —in what is at the same time a dispiriting wasteland and an exciting sandy and rocky desert.

While the "heavenly Sinai" of Biblical tradition has been repeatedly described and depicted by numerous pilgrims and romantics, the "earthly Sinai" has so far been virtually unknown. Explored only by surveyors and cartographers, by naturalists and geologists, the vast Sinai desert remained almost entirely unexplored in terms of cultural history. It was only in recent years, as a result of the archaeological exploration of Sinai by the present author—and by other archaeologists following in his tracks—that this situation has undergone a fundamental change and that the "vast, empty wilderness" is today regarded as a unique settlement area with a wealth of history.

The first scientific exploration in Sinai was conducted in 1816 by the Swiss, J. L. Burckhardt, who spent several weeks in Sinai. Burckhardt, who, dressed as an Arab, set out from Suez with a servant, a Bedouin guide and two camels, was attacked by hostile Bedouin in the desert and did not succeed in reaching 'Aqaba. His account, "Travels in Syria and the Holy Land", London 1822, was not published until after his premature death—at the age of 33, in Cairo—and contains many descriptions of newly discovered landscapes and localities.

In 1822, before the account of that journey appeared, the German zoologist E. Rüppell travelled through the Sinai region and in 1826 produced a map of Sinai—"Das Petraeische Arabien"—in which, for the first time, he proved that the accepted view that the Gulf of 'Aqaba had two bays was mistaken. Rüppell, a man of many gifts, who consulted Burckhardt personally, made repeated journeys in Sinai between 1822 and 1831, mainly in order to study its fauna and to collect samples of its animals; however, he also made astronomical observations and, on behalf of the Egyptian Pasha 'Ali, conducted copper smelting experiments at Bir Nasib. Rüppell succeeded in penetrating into regions which no European had entered before him; his book "Reisen in Nubien, Kordofan und dem peträischen Arabien", Frankfurt 1829, also contains the first drawing of the "Island of the Pharaohs" (Geziret el Fara'un)—the "Island of Emrag"—in the Gulf of Elat-'Aqaba and of the medieval fortress of 'Aqaba. He advised the Pasha against mining the copper ores of Sinai, mainly because of the shortage of firewood for the smelting furnaces in that "most horrendous desert".

An important contribution to the knowledge of Sinai was the account of the French nobleman Léon de Laborde. His Sinai book, "Voyage de l'Arabie Pérée", Paris 1830, is important chiefly for his numerous sketches which, quite apart from their high artistic merit, contain important data on landscapes and ancient remains. Of particular significance was his new map.

Another artist who contributed to our knowledge of Sinai was the Scot, David Roberts, who made a journey to the Holy Land in 1839 and published its "results" in three volumes of magnificent drawings—"The Holy Land, Syria, Idumea, Arabia, Egypt, Nubia", London 1842–1849—including an attempted reconstruction of the temple of Serabit el Khadim. The swelling flood of romantic and adventurous travellers during the first few decades of the 19th century was crowned by the exploratory journey of the American historian and Bible scholar, E. Robinson, who, in 1838, visited Sinai together with the orientalist, E. Smith, within the framework of an extensive study trip to Palestine. Equipped with Burckhardt's report on Sinai and de Laborde's map, the two travelled across the desert. The first volume of

1 Sabkhet el Bardawil—the narrow spit of Lake Bardawil is over 100 km (60 miles) long and leads in a wide arc from the Canal Zone to the south coast of El 'Arish. One of the theories concerning the Exodus from Egypt regards this spit of land as forming the "Reed Sea", i.e. the spot where the sea divided and where the Egyptians, pursuing the fleeing tribes, were destroyed.
2 Date palm plantations and Bedouin camp in the yellow sand dune region on the north coast of Sinai.
3 The sand dunes of the Mediterranean coastal strip. Along the beach, in the troughs of the dunes, where the ground water is within easy reach, date palms flourish.
4 Small Arab vegetable fields near El 'Arish (aerial photograph).
5 Arab fishing boats off the shore of Lake Bardawil.
6 After the men's return from fishing, the nets are cleaned and mended. In the background, one of the fishing villages typical of the Sinai north coast.
7 Arab trader from El 'Arish.
8 Bedouin woman from northern Sinai. The *burga*—a characteristic part of the headdress—often consists of coins, including genuine Maria Theresa dollars.

Robinson's three-volume report, "Biblical Researches in Palestine, Mount Sinai and Arabia Petraea", London 1841, consists in the main of data on the biblical and early Christian features of southern Sinai.

In the 19th century the Sinai peninsula was visited by a whole series of explorers and artists, such as W. H. Bartlett, L. F. C. Tischendorf, C. R. Lepsius, H. Brugsch, A. P. Stanley, and F. W. Holland. However, the first major step forward was made by an official British expedition which, under the leadership of Captain C. W. Wilson and Captain H. S. Palmer, produced a new detailed map of the Sinai peninsula in 1868/1869. Although this survey was designed principally to record the topography of Sinai and its geological features, its springs and wells, its rock drawings and ancient mines, its plants and Bedouin, it was nevertheless hoped that all these would ultimately help "determine the route of the Exodus of the tribes of Israel" and the accurate location of the "Mount of God". For that reason the expedition also produced detailed maps of the two "candidates" for the mountain of the theophany—Gebel Musa and Gebel Serbal. Wilson and Palmer themselves concluded that Gebel Musa was the genuine "Mount of God". The orientalist E. H. Palmer, who was also a member of the "Sinai Survey Expedition", was seeking "the links between sacred history and sacred geography" and therefore, after the conclusion of the official expedition, undertook, on behalf of the "Palestine Exploration Fund", a second Sinai expedition, described in a two-volume work, "The Desert of the Exodus; Journey on Foot in the Wilderness of the Forty Years' Wandering", Cambridge (England) 1871. In August 1882, E. H. Palmer once more returned to Sinai, this time on behalf of the British War Office, in order to win the Bedouin over to Britain's side with the help of 20,000 gold sovereigns. He and his three companions were murdered by Bedouin in the Wadi Sudr.

Romanticism and the quest for the geography of the "heavenly Sinai"—characteristic of Sinai research in the 19th century—continued to be the principal factor in Sinai exploration, as well as its main obstacle. Modern Sinai research started only at the beginning of the 20th century, when the geologists T. Barron, W. F. Hume and J. Ball of the "Survey of Egypt" undertook extensive explorations in Sinai during 1898–1913.

Yet in spite of these efforts and achievements, the Sinai peninsula still remained a virtually empty desert in which only Egyptian turquoise expeditions and Christian pilgrims had left their traces. It was to the Egyptians in Sinai that was dedicated the great work of the English archaeologist Sir Flinders Petrie, who, in 1905/1906, conducted systematic archaeological excavations in the Maghara region and at Serabit el Khadim. Flinders Petrie, the father of modern archaeology, published the results of his enormously important excavations in Sinai—"Researches in Sinai", London—in 1906, but this work still only presents a few Egyptian "islands" in the "vast empty" Sinai desert.

Between the beginning of the present century and the start of the author's researches in Sinai in 1956, British and American archaeologists from time to time continued their specialized research work in the Egyptian turquoise mines in Sinai, visited Saint Catherine's Monastery and published the inscriptions on the rock faces of the *wadis*. However, systematic archaeological exploration and documentation of the whole Sinai peninsula—not romantically on camel-back but by Jeep and Land Rover, with new modern maps and aerial photography, as well as a light aircraft—has been possible only since 1967 and is at present being continued by the author's expedition.

So far, the archaeological map of our expedition in Sinai, from the Suez Canal to the 'Araba, shows over 700 newly discovered sites, which have given rise to an entirely new history of the "earthly Sinai". It is to the description of these cultural-historical connections and to the archaeology of Sinai against the background of the natural conditions of "the wilderness of God" and the perspective of the Old Testament and Christian traditions of the "heavenly Sinai", supported by H. Weyer's magnificent colour photographs, that the chapters of this book are dedicated.

Beno Rothenberg ▷

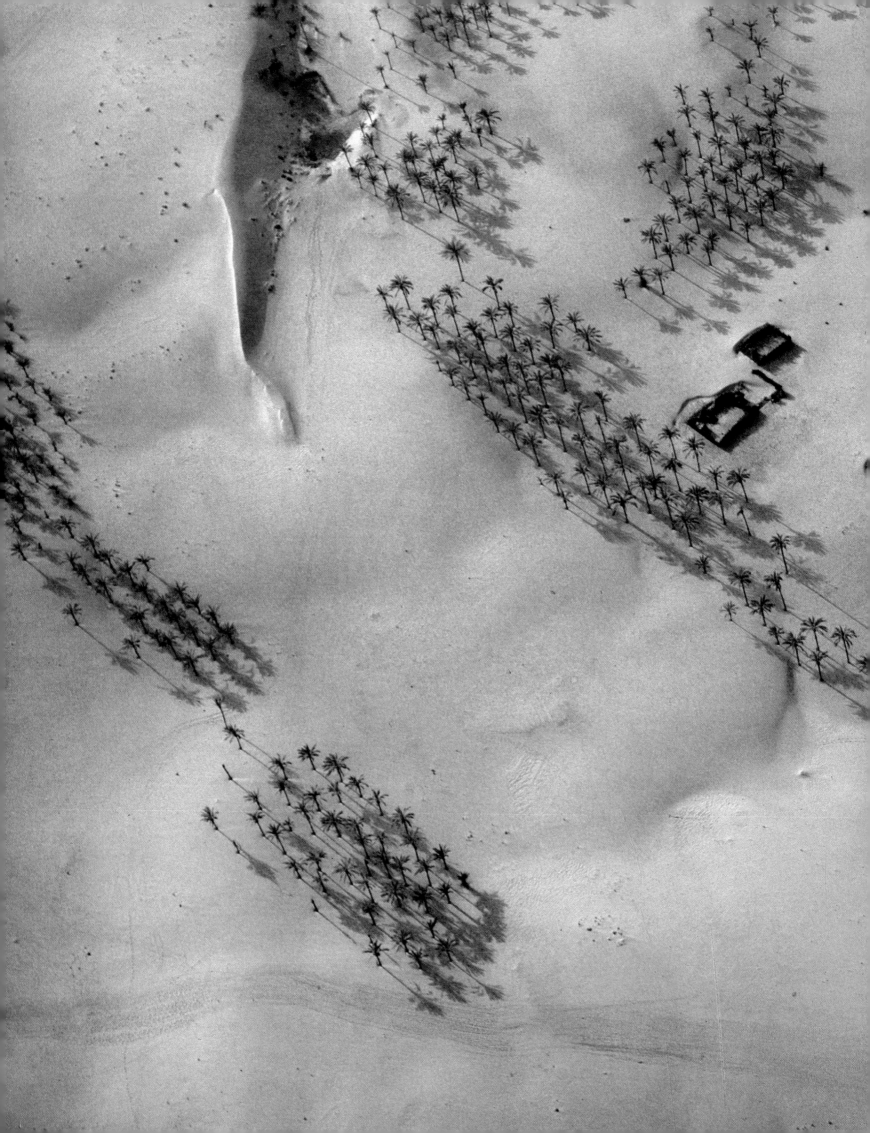

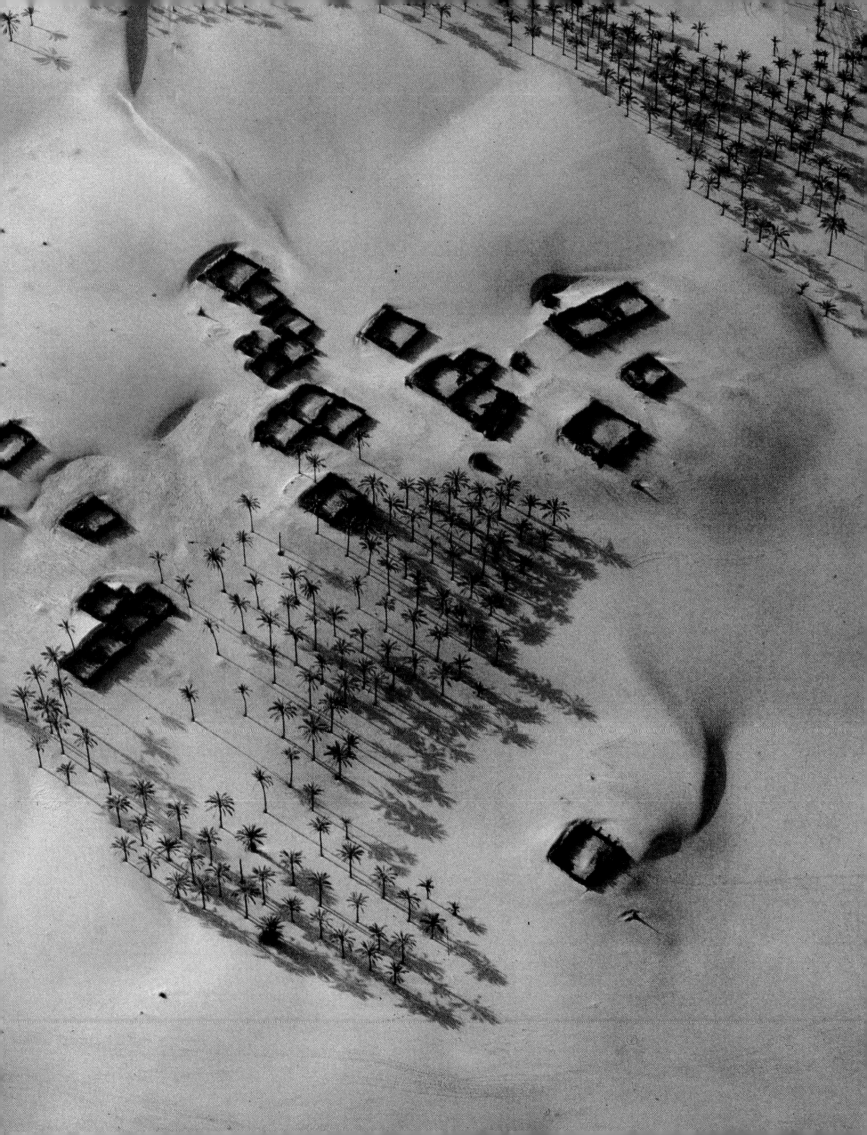

Exodus, Desert, Mount of God

Biblical Traditions of Sinai

Fig. 1: The sea engulfing the Egyptian pursuers. Passover Haggada, Amsterdam 1695.

MEMORIES   Sinai—the name stirs up memories. Unforgettable Old Testament stories come to life again. What they record of the early history of Israel occured very largely in the desert of Sinai and in the regions adjoining it to the west and to the east. After their shameful oppression, the early Israelite tribes left Egypt, the "house of bondage", in the direction of Sinai and were miraculously saved "by the sea" from a pursuing detachment of the Pharaoh's war chariots. They wandered about in the desert, hungry and thirsty, complaining because it contained only water and tasteless manna, and thinking back nostalgically to the flesh pots of Egypt. Then, on "Mount Sinai" they experienced a tremendous manifestation of the god JHWH[1], in whose name Moses had called for the exodus from Egypt. JHWH revealed Himself to them as their liberator and bound them to Himself by His Commandments; He became their God and they became His people. Thereupon the Israelites moved on into the Promised Land west and east of the Jordan. In the accounts of all these events, one incomparable figure occupies an outstanding place—Moses, who has gone down into history as his people's liberator from the house of bondage, their leader in the desert and the mediator of the covenant on Mount Sinai.

Geographically the Sinai region concerns the Bible only as the temporary place of passage of early Israelite nomadic tribes. For the faith, however, of both the Old Testament and the New Testament communities the concepts of "exodus", "journey through the desert" and "revelation at Sinai" have acquired a central significance. They lead us to one of the principal origins of biblical religious history.

The representatives of Old Testament scholarship generally agree in thinking that not all, but only part, of the subsequent twelve-tribe nation of Israelites participated in the Exodus, the journey through the desert and the revelation on Mount Sinai. There is some argument as to whether the events described should be assigned to different early Israelite groups or whether they represent stations on the road of one and the same group on its journey from Egypt to Palestine. There is much to suggest that the two concepts should be linked. Ever since scholars have again shown much greater confidence in the historical rôle of Moses than was formerly the case, this character is often linked with a "Moses group", composed of Israelite tribes who had been in Egyptian captivity, who really travelled with him from Egypt through the desert to the Mount of God and were thus involved in the whole series of events.[2] Because this group possessed in Moses a spiritually powerful and JHWH-inspired interpreter of these experiences, it was this group that became the most determined followers of JHWH and exercised the greatest influence when the tribes of Israel, following their seizure of land, united to form a larger entity in the name of JHWH. This does not necessarily mean that Moses' group was the only one that had sojourned in Egypt, in the desert and at the foot of the holy mountain. Indeed, with regard to the period spent in the desert, this seems unlikely. In the desert zones of Sinai and the Negev, more especially in the important area of the springs of Kadesh, an area evidently important at all times, there lived various other groups which were later also to become part of Israel as a whole. Between them and Moses' group there were various contacts which could have led to their exchange of stories of comparable experiences. The exceedingly complex movements of these tribes in the desert area and near the holy mountain can no longer be completely clarified in historical terms and cannot be even remotely outlined here. What is certain is that the subsequent amalgamation of all Israel in Palestine took place in the name of the God who had revealed His fundamental nature and His will during the Exodus, in the desert and on Mount Sinai.

THE EXODUS   How did early Israelite groups come to be in Egypt and in captivity there?[3] An answer to this question is provided by later Israelite tradition in the story of Joseph in Genesis 37–50, but this tradition proceeds from the historically inaccurate assumption that the entire twelve-tribe nation had been there and had emigrated from there. This tradition reflects the fact that—as we have just seen—the deliverance from Egypt by JHWH subsequently became the creed of all Israel. For the same reason the story of Joseph represents the immigration of the tribes of Abraham, Isaac and Jacob (Genesis 12–36) and the immigration of the tribes that came from Egypt and the Sinai desert as succeeding one another in time, and ascribes both immigrations to the same group. In reality, however, these were probably two independent land-seizure movements. Both these movements, admittedly, were only marginal features of a more comprehensive migration of nomadic peoples who, in the last third of the second pre-Christian millenium, pushed forward into the cultivated regions of the Fertile Crescent[4] and Egypt. The prolonged and complex land-seizure movements of the tribes which later formed Israel were part of this so-called Aramaic Migration. But while a northern branch succeeded in moving straight into the sparsely populated mountainous regions of Palestine and settling there, the southern branch first found itself in the Sinai peninsula, and this greatly delayed its ultimate seizure of land in Palestine. A few groups of this southern branch may well have remained in the desert and may have tried in vain for some time to advance northwards towards the mountains of Judah. Other groups crossed the Sinai desert and found themselves at the gates of Egypt, where they were admitted as sojourners with their flocks and tolerated for a time in the eastern Nile delta. It may well be that, following a phase of relatively untroubled sojourn, they experienced a phase of oppression because the construction of the "treasure cities of Pithom and Raamses" (Exodus 1:11) was just then beginning and cheap labour was welcome. The observation in Exodus 1:8 "Now there arose up a new king over Egypt, which knew not Joseph" records the memory of the clearly suggested vicissitudes to which nomadic groups who were temporarily in Egypt might find themselves subjected under certain circumstances. The story of Joseph is also historically accurate in quoting famine as the reason for the journey into Egypt; without pressing need, free nomads would scarcely seek the protection of the Pharaoh, especially as they had no hope of settling permanently in Egypt and enjoying more than the inferior legal status of sojourners.

The sojourn of early Israelite groups in the eastern Nile delta (called the "Land of Goshen" in the Old Testament) is not attested directly anywhere outside the Bible. However, contemporary Egyptian documents show that it was customary to admit Bedouin tribes from the Sinai peninsula—they are called "Shasu tribes" in the text—to state-authorized grazing grounds. About 1192 B.C. a frontier patrol on the eastern frontier of the Nile delta reported: "We have been able to let the Shasu tribes from Edom pass through Merneptah's fortress at Tkw as far as the Pools of Pithom belonging to Merneptah at Tkw, in order to keep them and their flocks... alive..."[5] Tkw may probably be connected with the biblical "Land of Goshen"; the place name Pithom is mentioned in Exodus 1:11 as being within the area occupied by the Israelites. The "fortress of Merneptah" guarded the frontier between Egypt and the Sinai territory to the east of the Nile delta. The formulation at the end of the Egyptian text quoted is strikingly reminiscent of Genesis 45:4–7 and 50:20, where Joseph says that God had sent him into Egypt to "save alive" his brethren. The Pharaoh Merneptah appears to have dealt kindly with the Shasu people mentioned in the frontier patrol report—unlike the way in which his predecessor, Ramesses II (1290–1224 B.C.), treated the Israelites—assuming that the observation in Exodus 1:11: "Therefore they did set over them taskmasters to afflict them with their burdens. And they built for Pharaoh treasure cities, Pithom and Raamses", falls within his reign. Egyptian sources testify that an extensive Pharaonic residence was being built or extended in the eastern delta at that time, an area in which "Pithom and Raamses" were situated. It is obvious that such a vast residence would include "treasure cities" (i.e. a vast complex of storehouses). There is therefore good reason to regard Ramesses II as the Pharaoh of the oppression; the Exodus probably took place under this Pharaoh or his successor, Merneptah. The dramatic background and history of that emigration is described in Exodus 1 to 15[6]. These chapters describe, firstly, the oppression of the Israelites, then Moses' flight to Midian, his recall and his return, his demands (supported by the plagues) that the Pharaoh should let his people go free, and finally, as the climax, the people's Exodus and deliverance "by the sea". The account was written down, not for its historical interest, but in honour of the irresistible power of JHWH, in whose name Moses was acting but who, in the final analysis, was the only true "actor". Nevertheless there can be no doubt as to the historical core of the tradition. As for Moses, he was, as the texts show clearly, at home both in Egypt and among the desert tribes of the land of Midian, within range of which the holy mountain must be sought. He bears an Egyptian name and may therefore be presumed to have been born and brought up in Egypt; on the other hand, having killed a taskmaster, he fled to Midian—surely no accidental choice—became the son-in-law of the Midianite priest and on the holy mountain was commanded by the god JHWH—who was presumably venerated also by the Midianites—to lead the Israelites out of Egypt. Moses, therefore, was as familiar with conditions in the desert as he was with those in Egypt, and was thus ideally equipped for his task.

As for the departure itself, different versions were subsequently in circulation and these have since become closely interwoven. According to one version, the Israelites fled and thereby triggered off the pursuit (Exodus 14:5a); according to another version the Pharaoh let them depart when the last plague had had its effect, but this he immediately regretted and tried to revoke (Exodus 14:5b). In any case, the operation, scarcely begun, ran into mortal danger when Moses' people suddenly found themselves trapped between the "sea" and a detachment of Egyptian chariots. Then came the totally unexpected deliverance, which opened a path to the threatened Israelites, while their pursuers lost their lives in the "sea".

This occurrence, too, was subsequently recounted in various ways. According to one version, an east wind dried up the "sea" in front of the Israelites and a divine

Fig. 2: Traditionally, the Exodus from Egypt proceeded from station to station into the south of the Sinai peninsula, where the Mount of God has been identified as Gebel Musa. Thence the route continued via Ezion-Geber and Elat to Kadesh-Barnea, the principal base of the early Israelite tribes prior to their seizure of land. In recent years a different route has been proposed, the so-called northern route. This considers Lake Sirbon (Sabkhet ei Bardawil) as the most likely location of the "Reed Sea", while the Mount of God is assumed to be the Seir Mountains or Gebel Halal. Other suggestions for the "Reed Sea" have been the area of Lake Manzala, Lake Timsah or the Bitter Lakes, where both routes originate.

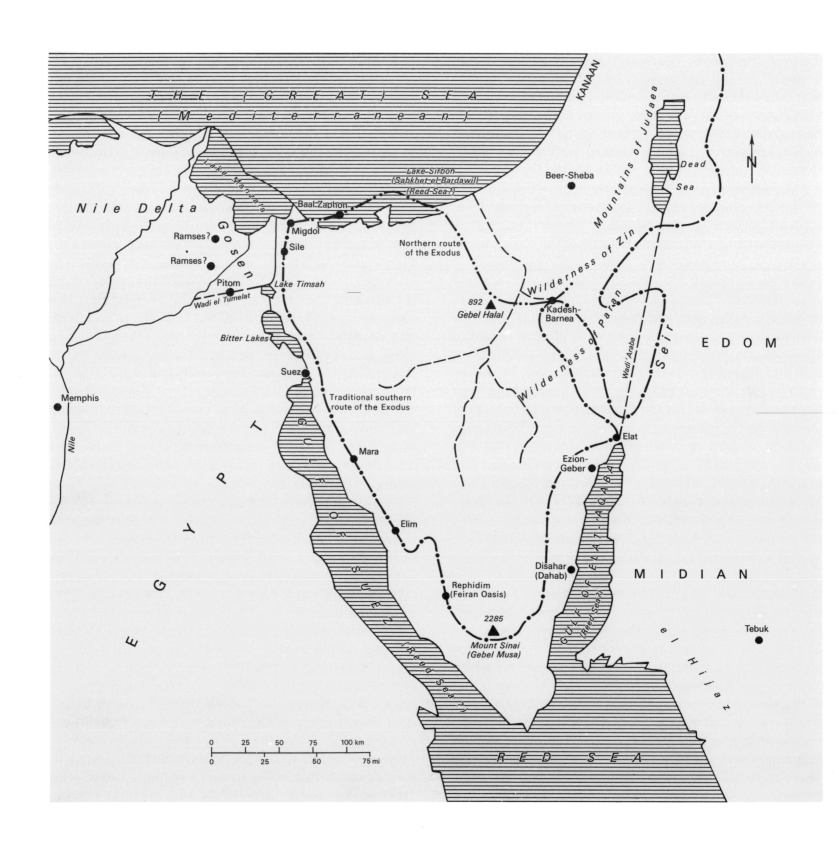

terror struck panic among the Egyptians, so that they drove headlong into the returning water and their dead upon the sea shore confirmed JHWH's miracle (Exodus 14:13f., 21, 24f., 27, 30f.). According to another version the wheels of the chariots were bogged down and sank into the mud (Exodus 14:25 a). Yet another version says that when Moses raised his rod, the sea divided, forming walls on either side to let the Israelites through, after which it returned and drowned the Egyptians (Exodus 14:15–18, 21–23, 26–29).

Just as these variants of the story cannot be fully reconciled, it is also impossible to identify definitively the geographical location of this miracle "by the sea".[7] Most of the texts in this connection refer only to the "sea", more rarely to the "Reed Sea". However, the "Reed Sea" in the Old Testament as a rule (though not necessarily) means the Red Sea or more particularly its easterly northern arm, the Gulf of 'Aqaba (= Gulf of Elat). However, the texts link the Exodus and the miracle of the sea so closely in space and time that the distance from the eastern delta to the northern end of the Gulf of 'Aqaba would seem to be rather too great. A more plausible identification would be the northern end of the Gulf of Suez which, as the westerly northern arm of the Red Sea, would in fact be covered by the name "Reed Sea". Among other proposals, the location at Lake Timsah, situated on the central sector of the present-day Suez Canal, has the advantage of greatest proximity to the Wadi el Tumelat, which extends westwards and constitutes an important part of the "Land of Goshen". In favour of the southern tip of Lake Manzala in the northeast of the Nile delta or of Lake Sirbon (now Lake Bardawil) on the northern coast of the Sinai desert is the direct connection which both have with the Mediterranean, which elsewhere in the Old Testament is simply called the "sea". However, the reference in Exodus 14:2–3 points clearly to Lake Sirbon.[8] According to the text, the Israelites were enjoined to "encamp before Pi-hahiroth, between Migdol and the sea, over against Baal Zephon". The lagoon is separated from the Mediterranean only by a narrow spit of land that might

easily have offered itself as a route which would avoid the military road to Palestine, which ran south of the lagoon. From Hellenistic-Roman times, Baal Zephon, situated at the western end of the spit, is known to have been a shrine to Zeus Kasios. A locality named Migdol in its proximity is attested to also in Egyptian sources and appears to have been the location of an Egyptian garrison, from which a detachment of chariots might easily have taken up the pursuit.

The choice of Lake Sirbon gains in probability through ancient authors of a later period, who reported the loss of entire armies in those shallow and treacherous waters. We need quote here only the graphic account given by the historian Strabo, who reports some strange occurrences in connection with a military conflict on the coast between Tyre and Ptolemais, and at the same time refers to similar occurrences "at Kasion adjoining Egypt"—which undoubtedly means the area of Lake Sirbon: "For just when the citizens of Ptolemais had won a splendid victory in battle against the general, Sarpedon, and had been left behind at that place, the flood-tide, like a huge wave, engulfed the fleeing men, sweeping some into the sea and killing them, while others were left lying dead in the hollows left by the retreating waters. The succeeding ebb-tide then caused the land to reappear, revealing the dead bodies of those lying there among the dead fish. Similar phenomena occur also at Kasion adjoining Egypt, in that the earth, seized by a single sudden spasm, moves simultaneously in two directions, so that the raised part thereof drives away the sea while the sunken part receives it, and through a reversal of the movement the scene then once more acquires its former appearance, whereby a certain transformation may sometimes appear and sometimes not, and whereby these processes may be linked to certain periods known to us, as is said to be the case also with the spates of the Nile, which are different but display an order unknown to us[9]." Whether the events "by the sea" occurred here or elsewhere, and whether the details follow one or the other pattern, there is one point on which all reports agree unanimously: the deliverance was the work of

JHWH alone. This conviction is expressed in its earliest and also its most impressive form in the brief, moving and memorable song of praise to JHWH the victor, in Exodus 15:21:

"Sing ye to the Lord, for he hath triumphed gloriously; the horse and his rider hath he thrown into the sea."

This song, possibly the very oldest passage in the Bible, still breathes the exultation of the people over their recent deliverance from mortal peril. It was only after that deliverance that the Exodus was truly crowned with success. The song was handed down from generation to generation. An indication of this is the later psalm in Exodus 15:1–18, which begins with exactly the same song of victory and then goes on to portray the deliverance by the sea in glowing colours. Since the psalm concludes with the foundation of the Temple of Solomon in Jerusalem it cannot have been written before the building of the Temple at the end of the 10th century B.C. and was probably written even later. Here is its vivid description of the miracle by the sea:

"I will sing unto the Lord, for he hath triumphed gloriously; the horse and his rider hath he thrown into the sea. The Lord is my strength and song, and he is become my salvation:
he is my God, and I will prepare him an habitation; my father's God, and I will exalt him.
The Lord is a man of war: the Lord is his name.
Pharaoh's chariots and his host hath he cast into the sea: his chosen captains also are drowned in the Red sea. The depths have covered them: they sank into the bottom as a stone.
Thy right hand, O Lord, is become glorious in power: thy right hand, O Lord, hath dashed in pieces the enemy.
And in the greatness of thine excellency thou hast overthrown them that rose up against thee:
thou sentest forth thy wrath, which consumed them as stubble.
And with the blast of thy nostrils the waters were gathered together,
the floods stood upright as an heap, and the depths were congealed in the heart of the sea.
The enemy said, I will pursue, I will overtake,
I will divide the spoil; my lust shall be satisfied upon them;
I will draw my sword, my hand shall destroy them.
Thou didst blow with thy wind, the sea covered them:
they sank as lead in the mighty waters.
Who is like unto thee, O Lord, among the gods?
Who is like thee, glorious in holiness,
Fearful in praises, doing wonders?
Thou stretchedst out thy right hand, the earth swallowed them."

It seems almost like a summary of these praises when the Prophet Hosea, in the 8th century B.C., reminds his people:

"I am the Lord thy God from the land of Egypt,
and thou shalt know no God but me: for there is no saviour beside me." (Hosea 13:4)

When Israel set about summing up in a terse creed the most important events of the early history of their salvation, its central theme was its deliverance from Egypt. Such a "historical creed" is spoken by the husbandman taking his gift of the firstfruits of his harvest to the altar (Deuteronomy 26:5–10). It is spoken by the father to his son as he explains to him the reasons and meaning of the Commandments (Deuteronomy 6:20f.). This bracketing of the events of the deliverance with the giving of the Commandments is of fundamental importance: the deliverance "by the sea" not only precedes in time the proclamation of the Commandments on the holy mountain, but also in the sense of God's plan, the fundamental divine deed. God first delivers and then imposes obligations. Thus, in the Old Testament, the Commandments are seen as helpful guidance for the right use of the God-given freedom. The classic demonstration of this is in the famous introduction to the Ten Commandments in Exodus 20:1–17, revealing as it does the true meaning of the Commandments:

Fig. 3: Exodus from Egypt—crossing of the "Reed Sea", drowning of Pharaoh's army. Earliest printed Haggada, Prague 1556.

"I am the Lord thy God, which have brought thee out of the land of Egypt, out of the house of bondage. Thou shalt have no other gods before me. Thou shalt not make unto thee any graven image... (etc.)."

Even at a later period quite specific instructions on probity in business are found to be justified by the authority of Him who delivered Israel from Egypt:

"Ye shall do no unrighteousness in judgement, in meteyard, in weight, or in measure. Just balances, just weights, a just ephah, and a just hin shall ye have: I am the Lord your God, which brought you out of the land of Egypt." (Leviticus 19:35–36).

THE DESERT   No less impressive than the Exodus, in the memory of the people of the Bible, is the early Israelites' sojourn in the desert. Accounts of this are in Exodus 15:22–18:27) and in Numbers (10:11–21:25). The reader of these texts will, of course, find it exceedingly difficult to follow, let alone trace, these complicated movements in detail. Evidently the desert traditions of different groups, originally operating independently, have later been interwoven. This has produced the impression that Israel as a whole had journeyed through the desert to the holy mountain and thence onwards through the desert south and east of the Dead Sea into the land east and west of the Jordan. In actual fact it was

probably only Moses' group that undertook such a prolonged trek. On the way, this group encountered other bands of Israelites who, in an earlier phase of the "Aramaic Migration", had not advanced as far as Egypt, but had remained in the desert area of the northern Sinai peninsula and the Negev. These other tribes were probably those which succeeded, not at once but gradually, in advancing in a northerly direction into the northern part of the Negev and towards the mountains of Judah, where they settled. Moses' group, on the other hand, had to make its way in a large arc around the Dead Sea to the cultivated land, possibly because earlier direct attempts in a northerly direction had failed.

In view of the complexity of this situation, it is not surprising that certain stories and motifs frequently recur in the desert tradition, or that the localities recorded cannot readily be arranged into a reasonably plausible route with a particular destination in view. Instead, the accounts are grouped around local centres with springs of water, which were of course of vital importance for nomadic herdsmen. They would meet there to do business, for joint religious observances, and to make and administer laws. Among those centres, the springs of Kadesh—also called Kadesh-Barnea—were of special importance. The Old Testament places this region of springs and wells in the "wilderness of Paran" or in the "wilderness of Zin". That is the area of the present-day springs of 'Ain Qadeis, 'Ain el Gedeirat, and 'Ain el Qusaima in a lateral valley which extends towards the east of the Wadi el 'Arish, 80 km (50 miles) south of Beer-Sheba. According to Genesis 14:7, Kadesh was also called En-misphat, the "well of the law", and according to Numbers 27:14, the "water of Meribah", the "water of legal dispute" flows there. This points to the paramount importance of the locality, and it has been assumed that the enactment of laws and the dispensing of justice practised by Moses—as referred to in Exodus 15:25 and Exodus 18—originally took place in that area. It was probably at Kadesh that the tribes who had remained in the desert made contact with Moses' group and, more importantly, with the god JHWH proclaimed by Moses. In that case the foundations for the subsequent unification of all Israel in Palestine in the name of JHWH would have been laid for many of the people by such earlier contacts at Kadesh. It is in the nature of narrative texts that a great deal must remain supposition. In any case, nomadic societies scarcely ever leave records, but instead their oral tradition is enriched during its transmission with the experiences of later generations, so that it is difficult to draw historical conclusions from such oral traditions.

More important than a historical reconstruction is the question of the importance that these experiences in the desert have acquired for the faith of the people of Israel and their understanding of themselves. Any attentive reader will soon notice that the desert stories were not merely strung together anyhow by later narrators but were closely linked by thematic motifs. One such recurrent element in the stories of their sojourn in the desert is the grumbling, the "murmuring of the people". This was caused by various difficulties such as lack of water or bitter, unpalatable water (Exodus 15:23; 17:3; Numbers 20:2) or lack of bread and meat (Exodus 16:2; Numbers 11:13). The murmuring soon increased to accusations:

"Who shall give us flesh to eat? for it was well with us in Egypt" (Numbers 11:18)

and to the thought:

"Were it not better for us to return into Egypt? And they said one to another, 'Let us make a captain, and let us return into Egypt'" (Numbers 14:3 f.).

With this half-desperate and half-defiant rebellion the people questioned not only Moses' authority but also JHWH's power to help:

"Why chide ye with me? wherefore do ye tempt the Lord?"
The departure from Egypt, celebrated in the song of praise to the victor "by the sea" as a glorious triumph (Exodus 15:21), was now felt to have been a disaster. Would it not have been better to be a bondsman in Egypt by full flesh pots than a free man in the desert by empty ones?
A contrast to the people's complaints is provided by the motif of the miraculous help invariably given by JHWH in difficult situations. Water flows from the rock, bitter water becomes palatable, manna and quails appease their hunger. This timely help given by JHWH stands, as it were, in contrast with their murmuring, and with His help JHWH tries to arouse the people's faith and thus overcome their tendency to complaint. With touching care JHWH tries to win over the people in the desert to Himself. Only when He sees that the people have learned nothing from their experience of His help does He inflict severe punishment upon them (Numbers 11:33; 14:28 f.).
At a later date there was a tendency in Israel, when referring to this divine help, to speak of God's leading, bearing or feeding them in the desert:

"Yet the Lord hath not given you an heart to perceive, and eyes to see, and ears to hear, unto this day. And I have led you forty years in the wilderness: your clothes are not waxen old upon you, and thy shoe is not waxen old upon thy foot... Keep therefore the words of this covenant, and do them..." (Deuteronomy 29:4 f., 9).

"Hear ye the word of the Lord, O house of Jacob, and all the families of the house of Israel: Thus saith the

Lord, What iniquity have your fathers found in me, that they are gone far from me, and have walked after vanity, and are become vain? Neither said they, Where is the Lord that brought us up out of the land of Egypt, that led us through the wilderness, through a land of deserts and of pits, through a land of drought, and of the shadow of death, through a land that no man passed through, and where no man dwelt?" (Jeremiah 2:4–6).

"I did know thee in the wilderness, in the land of great drought. According to their pasture, so were they filled; they were filled, and their heart was exalted; therefore have they forgotten me" (Hosea 13:5–6).

But terms of praise or encouragement may also be used:

"…To him which led his people through the wilderness: for his mercy endureth forever" (Psalm 136:16);
"The Lord your God which goeth before you, he shall fight for you, according to all that he did for you in Egypt before your eyes; And in the wilderness, where thou hast seen how that the Lord thy God bare thee, as a man does bear his son, in all the way that ye went…" (Deuteronomy 1:30–31).

THE MOUNT OF GOD   When we hear the name "Sinai" today we think of the peninsula of that name. In the Bible, both in the Old and the New Testament, the name means the mountain on which the god JHWH appeared to Moses, gave him His Commandments for Israel and concluded a covenant with the people. In the memory of the people of Israel this mountain has remained a place of very special and unparalleled theophany (manifestation or revelation of God). It was here that JHWH revealed His unique nature and His will which was binding on His people; it was really here that lie the roots of that sense of community which may be summed up in the so-called "formula of the Covenant": JHWH, the God of Israel—Israel JHWH's people.[10] So closely is JHWH's name, nature and will linked with Mount Sinai in the minds of the people of Israel that JHWH may quite simply be called in the Hebrew text "Him of Sinai" (Judges 5:5; Psalm 68:8; the words are lacking in the English version). The question of the site of the biblical mountain has no more been resolved than has that of the site of the miracle "by the sea". Even the name itself is not unambiguous. One strand of the tradition calls it Sinai, another Horeb; besides these two traditions reference is also made simply to "the Mount of God". It seems probable, although it is not certain, that these are only different names for one and the same mountain. Where is it to be found?[11]

To the god-fearing anchorites of the third century A.D. and to the pious pilgrims of the fourth century, who set forth to seek out the holy places of the Bible, Mount Sinai was to be sought in the great central massif of the southern Sinai peninsula, where St. Catherine's Monastery now clings to the foot of the mountains. The impressive granite peaks of Gebel Musa and Gebel Katherina, not far from the famous Feiran Oasis, were undoubtedly regarded as sacred mountains even earlier and as such were probably frequently visited by the Nabataeans.[12] It is doubtful, however, whether nomadic tribes made pilgrimages to these southern mountains as early as the time of Moses. However this may be, the Egyptians who mined turquoise a little further to the north, in the Wadi Maghara and at Serabit el Khadim, have left no traces further south. For this reason Gebel Serbal, south of Feiran—whose possible identity with the biblical Mount Sinai has also been considered—has no greater claim than, say, Gebel Musa. Both are a long way from any conceivable route from Egypt to Palestine. Besides, to get so far south, Moses' people would have had to pass through the turquoise-mining areas dominated by the Egyptians— and that, after what had happened by the "sea", would have been too great a risk.

The difficulty of the great geographical distance also speaks against the suggestion that the biblical Mount Sinai should be sought in the region east of the southern end of the "Gulf of 'Aqaba" (= Gulf of Elat), or to be more exact, in a mountain range south of Tebuk. Others have gone even further southwards into the Hejaz (el Hijaz) region, east of the Red Sea. These suggestions, admittedly, enjoy greater support from the biblical texts. A

Fig. 4: Mount Sinai, Mount Horeb and Saint Catherine's
Monastery (woodcut by Bernhard Walter von Walterweyl, 1587).

list of localities in Numbers 33 possibly represents stations along an ancient route of pilgrimage into the region concerned. More important is the fact that the biblical texts link the holy mountain with the Midianites; it was to them that Moses fled and it was there that he received his calling out of the midst of the burning bush on the Mount of God (Exodus 3:2–3). To the Greek geographers, the land of Midian was in fact east-southeast of the Gulf of 'Aqaba, in the northwestern part of present-day Saudi Arabia. This situation was accepted also by St. Paul (Galatians 4:25) and by the Jewish historian Josephus. It is further supported by the fact that, of all the proposed sites, this is the only one that still had active volcanoes in historical times[13] and the overpowering manifestation of God on Mount Sinai, as described in Exodus (19:16–19), appears to have been accompanied by a volcanic eruption:

"And it came to pass on the third day in the morning, that there were thunders and lightnings, and a thick cloud upon the mount, and the voice of the trumpet exceeding loud; so that all the people that was in the camp trembled. And Moses brought forth the people out of the camp to meet with God; and they stood at the nether part of the mount. And mount Sinai was altogether on a smoke, because the Lord descended upon it in fire: and the smoke thereof ascended as the smoke of a furnace, and the whole mount quaked greatly. And when the voice of the trumpet sounded long, and waxed louder and louder, Moses spake, and God answered him by a voice."

In this passage, admittedly, three different sets of ideas are interwoven. Only one single strand of the tradition reports features suggesting a volcanic eruption (smoke, fire, furnace, quaking). A second strand describes something more like the phenomena of a severe thunderstorm (thunder, lightning, cloud), whereas a third clearly has in mind a grand ceremonial or cultic occasion (the sound of trumpets, Moses addressing God). The importance of the volcanic features should not therefore be overestimated.

A third site can also claim strong support from biblical texts.[14] This proceeds from the observation that the traditional account of Mount Sinai (Exodus 19; Numbers 10) stands among stories of episodes that take place in the Kadesh area. Does this mean that the events and traditions of Mount Sinai originally had nothing to do with those of Kadesh-Barnea, but were inserted among them at a later date? Or does it, on the contrary, mean that both these events and traditions are closely linked and that Mount Sinai, the sacred mountain, is to be sought in the vicinity of Kadesh-Barnea? Having long inclined towards the former interpretation, scholars today tend more towards the latter. This second interpretation receives some strong support from two poetic passages which obviously link Mount Sinai closely with the Seir mountains. The verse—no doubt of very great antiquity—from Judges 5:4–5 reads:

"Lord, when thy wentest out of Seir,
when thou marchedst out of the field of Edom,
the earth trembled, and the heavens dropped,
the clouds also dropped water.
The mountains melted from before the Lord,
Him of Sinai,
from before the Lord God of Israel."

The passage in Deuteronomy 33:2, which may also be very old, emphasizes the close connection between Sinai and Seir. Moreover—and this deserves particular consideration—it places both of them clearly in the vicinity of the springs of Kadesh:

"The Lord came from Sinai,
and rose up from Seir unto them;
He shined forth from mount Paran,
and he came from Meriba-Kadesh:
from his right hand went a fiery law for them."

Seir is the central part of the land of Edom, a mountainous region on the eastern side of the Wadi 'Araba. Opposite it, on the western side of the wadi 'Araba, rises Mount Paran. Kadesh itself lies to the west of that mountain and, as we have already seen, is part of the "wilderness of Paran" in the Old Testament. The passages quoted therefore undoubtedly locate Mount Sinai closer to the springs of Kadesh-Barnea than is possible on the basis of earlier suggestions. A hypothesis placing the Mount of God in the general area of Kadesh, eastwards as far as the eastern marginal mountains of the Wadi 'Araba, should therefore be given preference to those other suggestions. This is true even if one may have to give up the idea of pin-pointing a specific peak within that area. The suggestion, for instance, that the biblical Mount Sinai should be identified with Gebel Halal, 40 km (25 miles) west of 'Ain el Gedeirat, is scarcely justified.

But does the association of Sinai with Midian and the volcanic aspects of the theophany not argue against the surroundings of Kadesh? Not necessarily. The Midianites were, after all, camel-owning nomads, genuine Bedouin, whose living space, or range of activity, cannot be confined to a strictly limited region. At times they roamed a long way to the northwest, and in the time of Judges they even fought against Israelite tribes in Palestine (Judges 6–8). As for the volcanic phenomena accompanying the Sinai revelation, they belong to the typical vocabulary of Old Testament accounts of any theophany; they need not necessarily be interpreted realistically. Besides, as we have seen, only one strand of the tradition invokes volcanic features, whilst another reports phenomena associated with a thunderstorm, and a third has clear links with a cultic or ceremonial occasion. These two strands of the tradition do not therefore necessarily point to northwestern Saudi Arabia but are quite compatible with a location nearer to Kadesh.

More important than the historic site of Mount Sinai is the event associated with it, which is the centre of interest of those who handed down the biblical tradition. The most significant features of this event, for the faith of Israel, may be placed under the following headings: the theophany, the giving of the Commandments, the conclusion of the Covenant.

The account of what happened on Mount Sinai—the original nucleus of the account stands in Exodus 19–20; 24; 32–34—begins with the description of a theophany. In an overpowering divine manifestation JHWH descends on to the mountain and draws near to His people. Israel can belive in JHWH's presence only because He Himself has descended from His remote and hidden existence and has come to His people. No human endeavour could have compelled Him to come. God Himself makes Israel a gift of His sanctifying presence. Yet Israel always remains aware of the fact that it is also a consuming presence; God remains the Holy One and does not give men the power to dispose over Him. That is why Moses must warn the people "lest they break through unto the Lord to gaze" (Exodus 19:21).

The theophany is followed by the giving of the Commandments. Again it is Moses who announces the "words of the Lord" to the people at JHWH's behest (Exodus 24:3). Precisely which of the Commandments were originally given on Mount Sinai can no longer be determined. In the course of its history Israel constantly added new commandments and laws—which became vital to its existence as historical circumstances changed—linking them with the tradition of the Sinai revelation, because it conceived them to be the manifestation of the will of JHWH, the God of Sinai. Thus the Sinai tradition grew into the extensive complex of texts that now extend from Exodus 19 to Numbers 10. In terms of contents, the range of the Commandments, as summarized in the Decalogue of Exodus 20, undoubtedly comes closest to the ancient manifestation of JHWH's will on Mount Sinai, even though the Decalogue, in its present form, cannot simply be attributed to Moses, either in its entirety or in part. The first two Commandments are quite certainly of great antiquity—those commanding the exclusive and non-representational veneration of JHWH. These two commandments were unparalleled at that time in the Ancient Orient:

"Thou shalt have no other gods before me.
Thou shalt not make unto thee any graven image…".

It may, however, be assumed that the Mount Sinai Commandments concerned not only man's relations with

JHWH but also human co-existence within the family, the tribe and tribal groups, like those enumerated in the second part of the Decalogue—the Commandment to honour one's parents and those forbidding murder, adultery, theft, and the bearing of false witness. The Commandments are "like a net cast over Israel"[15], a net in which the god who has descended towards His people now draws them closer to Himself. That net has never been felt by Israel to be an instrument of capture, but has invariably been praised as an aid to right living in the liberating proximity of God:

"...the commandment of the Lord is pure, enlightening the eyes" (Psalm 19:8),
"Thou art near, O Lord; and all thy commandments are truth" (Psalm 119:151).

In the Old Testament, especially in the later writings, the bond between God and the people, actually established on Mount Sinai through the theophany and the imparting of the Commandments, is called a covenant between JHWH and Israel.[16] This word "covenant" is in effect a key concept whenever Israel is made to reflect on how JHWH stands to the people of Israel and they to JHWH. In these reflections Moses has been seen increasingly clearly as the great mediator of the Covenant. The earliest tradition, in Exodus 24:11, merely reports that, following the theophany and their receiving of the Commandments, the representatives of the people feasted before God:

"...they saw God, and did eat and drink".

Perhaps this was a meal of the kind that was customary at that time upon the conclusion of an alliance. Perhaps, on the other hand, it was quite simply a thanksgiving in the presence of the God who had come to the people and drawn them closer to Himself.

The events of Mount Sinai had a tremendous and lasting effect in Israel. Whenever the belief that God was still present and powerful threatened to become lost, the events on the Mount of God were called to mind. The prophet Elijah, for instance, totally exhausted by his struggle against the people's worship of alien gods at the time of King Ahab (871–852 B.C.), journeyed to Mount Horeb, where JHWH appeared to him in a new theophany (I Kings 19). When King Josiah (639–609 B.C.) undertook his vast work of reform, by which he intended to bind the people of Judah more closely than before to JHWH alone, he based that movement of spiritual revival upon the undiminished force and the eternal validity of the Sinai covenant:

"The Lord our God made a covenant with us in Horeb. The Lord made not this covenant with our fathers, but with us, even us, who are all of us here alive this day" (Deuteronomy 5:2,3).

HOPES The spiritual stimulus of the tradition of the Exodus, the journey through the desert, and Sinai have not only been the foundation of Israel's present, but also provided the model and the creative energies for its future hopes. This may be shown by two instances. About the middle of the sixth pre-Christian century, the anonymous prophet whose words are collected in Isaiah 40–55, and who has therefore been called *Deutero-Isaiah*, awakened among the Judaeans who had been deported into Babylonian exile, hopes of deliverance from captivity and of being led home through the desert:

"Thus saith the Lord, which maketh a way in the sea, and a path in the mighty waters; Which bringeth forth the chariot and horse, the army and the power; they shall lie down together, they shall not rise: they are extinct, they are quenched as tow. Remember ye not the former things, neither consider the things of old. Behold, I will do a new thing; now it shall spring forth; shall ye not know it? I will even make a way in the wilderness, and rivers in the desert." (Isaiah 43:16–19).

In the book of the prophet Jeremiah the promise is made of a new covenant which will make the people more able and willing to give obedience to JHWH than did the ancient Sinai Covenant:

"Behold, the days come, saith the Lord, that I will make a new covenant with the house of Israel, and with the house of Juda: Not according to the covenant that I made with their fathers in the day that I took them by the hand to bring them out of the land of Egypt; which my covenant they brake, although I was an husband unto them, saith the Lord: But this shall be the covenant that I will make with the house of Israel; After those days, saith the Lord, I will put my law in their inward parts, and write it in their hearts; and will be their God, and they shall be my people." (Jeremiah 31:31–33)

Finally, the New Testament community interpreted the story of Christ and the history of its own origin in the light of the Old Testament, referring back to the Exodus, the journey through the desert and the Mount of God. Here, too, a few examples must suffice. Just as the Deutero-Isaiah had called for the desert road to be made "straight and plain" for JHWH to lead the banished people home, so John the Baptist now appealed to his listeners to make their evil way of life "straight and plain" again and thus to prepare for Christ's coming (Luke 3:1–18, quoting from Isaiah 40:3–5). In the coming of Christ, God's great work of salvation, which had been begun with the Exodus out of Egypt and the deliverance "by the sea", acquires an entirely new and universal aspect and significance that now applies to all nations.
To St. Paul the deliverance "by the sea" is a prefiguring of Christian baptism, the feeding in the desert with manna and water from the rock an anticipation of Christian Holy Communion. Through the sacraments, the Christian participates in God's salvation and constant help, made present and efficacious in unprecedented abundance by Christ's death on the Cross:

"Moreover, brethren, I would not that ye should be ignorant, how that all our fathers were under the cloud [in the desert] and all passed through the sea; And were all baptized unto Moses in the cloud and in the sea; And did all eat the same spiritual meat; And did all drink the same spiritual drink: for they drank of that spiritual Rock that followed them: and that Rock was Christ." (I Corinthians 10:1–4). Just as Moses had been the mediator of the Old Covenant, so Christ is now the mediator of the New Covenant promised in the Book of Jeremiah. According to St. Matthew (26:28) and St. Luke (22:20) this new covenant or testament is based upon Jesus' sacrifice and death, and it applies to the faithful in the sacrament of the Lord's Supper, being valid also for them; according to St. Luke:

"…this cup is the new testament in my blood, which is shed for you".

In an exhaustive exposition, the Epistle to the Hebrews, chapters 8 and 9, compares the new testament mediated by Christ with the old Sinai Covenant. With extensive quotations from Jeremiah 31:31–35, the author calls the new covenant promised there a "better covenant, which was established upon better promises" (Hebrews 8:6). Put into force by Christ's death (Hebrews 9:15), this new covenant now becomes a token that God will no longer judge, but save, even those who had broken the Old Covenant.

These examples must suffice. They show how important to the New Testament and to the early Christian communities were the events of Israel's early history, the events which took place in the region of the Sinai peninsula. This observation by no means exhausts the spiritual and historic impact of the Jewish and Christian traditions of Sinai. Since biblical times a great many people have acknowledged JHWH, the god of Sinai, who delivers and saves men, helps them through the desert, allies Himself with them and lays them under an obligation. Many, whether in the Jewish way, the Christian way, or some other way, will remain faithful to Him also in the future. All of these will feel reverence and affection for that wilderness of Sinai, the birthplace of unique memories and ardent hopes.

Martin A. Klopfenstein

Notes

The exposition in the preceding chapter takes account both of the findings of modern research into the early history of Israel and also of the religious content of the biblical texts which contain that history. The scope of the present picture volume has obviously necessitated considerable simplification.

The Bible quotations in this English translation are those of the Authorized Version, except for a line from Judges 5:5 and Deuteronomy 33:2, where the text of the Authorized Version is clearly a mistranslation.

[1] The usual pronunciation of the Hebrew name of God is Jahvé (with the stress on the final syllable). Jews generally avoid uttering the Holy Name and instead say Adonai, "Lord". This usage is followed by the Greek translation of the Old Testament, which uses "Kyrios", and by most of the English translations, which use "the Lord".

[2] See Georg Fohrer, Geschichte Israels, 1977, pp. 55–65 (further literature quoted on pp. 64f.).

[3] See especially Siegfried Herrmann, Israels Aufenthalt in Ägypten, 1970 (English translation: Israel in Egypt, 1973).

[4] The term "Fertile Crescent" refers to the cultivated regions of Palestine, Syria and Mesopotamia.

[5] Quoted from Kurt Galling, Textbuch zur Geschichte Israels, 2nd edit. 1968, p. 40.

[6] On Exodus 1–15 see Georg Fohrer, Überlieferung und Geschichte des Exodus, 1964.

[7] For a list of proposed sites see J. Philipp Hyatt, Exodus (New Century Bible), 1971, pp. 156–161.

[8] For the location on Lake Sirbon see the convincing arguments of Otto Eissfeldt, Baal Zaphon, Zeus Kasios und der Durchzug der Israeliten durchs Meer, 1932.

[9] Quoted from Eissfeldt (Note 8), pp. 62f. On p. 63 and pp. 61f. further ancient graphic accounts of the dangerous nature of the waters.

[10] See Rudolf Smend, Die Bundesformel, 1963.

[11] See the survey of proposed locations in Hyatt (note 7) pp. 203–207.

[12] On the Nabataeans see the chapter by Beno Rothenberg, p. 170.

[13] See Jean Koenig, Le site de al-Jaw dans l'ancien pays de Madian, 1971.

[14] See especially Herrmann, Geschichte Israels in alttestamentlicher Zeit, 1973, pp. 97–115 (English translation: A History of Israel in Old Testament Times, 1975).

[15] Gerhard von Rad, Theologie des Alten Testaments, Vol. I, 6th edit., 1969, p. 205 (English translation: Theology of the Old Testament, 1965).

[16] See Lothar Perlitt, Bundestheologie im Alten Testament, 1969.

9 Typical street scene in the business quarter of El 'Arish.
10 In a Bedouin tent on the north coast: neighbours meet for a chat. The women, however, always keep to themselves.
11 The great mosque at El 'Arish.
12 The grain market at El 'Arish; in the background a typical residential quarter of the town.
13 Each property is surrounded by a mud-brick wall. In the courtyard between the dwelling house proper and this wall most of the everyday life takes place; the wall ensures the women's isolation from the men of the neighbourhood.
14 On the way from the well, across the dunes, to the tent where they live. Water is carried in canisters on the camel's back.
15 Among the endless dunes on the north coast—a real feast of colour and form.
16 Barbed wire—a reminder of the Sinai wars—with springtime blossoms.
17 Scorpion *(Buthus quinquestriatus).*
18 Modern desert highway from the shore at El Bardawil to Bir Gafgafa.
19 Modern well near Abu Aweigila in the Wadi el 'Arish, built by the Israeli authorities for the Bedouin.
20 *Nectarinia osea,* sunbird of the Nectariniidae family (from: H. B. Tristram, Fauna and Flora of Palestine, London 1884).

◁14 15

16 17

Geography
Contrasting Landscapes

The Sinai peninsula, with an area of about 60,000 km² (23,000 sq miles), forms a transition between Asia and Africa. Its width is about 200 km (125 miles), while its maximum north-south dimension is about 380 km (235 miles). Much of it is surrounded by seas, which leave between them a relatively narrow land bridge to connect the two continents. Sinai is inhospitable to human existence and supports only a small and poor population, mostly nomads. Permanent settlements are few. As a result of the arid climate most of the area is a rock-strewn desert, and what is left is largely covered by dunes. The landscape is bare, devoid of plant life, without forest or lakes. The bedrock lies exposed, under constant attack by the elements. Islands of verdure are found only where water accumulates in consequence of exceptional circumstances. Otherwise only sparse vegetation can survive. No less important in shaping the landscape is the influence of the disturbance of the interior of the earth: Sinai lies between huge faults, branches of the system of rift valleys extending from Africa to Turkey. These faults produced the troughs occupied by the Gulf of Suez and the Gulf of Elat ('Aqaba).

The combined action of natural forces has produced in Sinai a variety of desert landscapes, differing in colour, shape and relief. Some travellers may find the scenery repellent, depressingly lifeless, often monotonous and gaunt. Others find it inspiring and are attracted by the vigour and contrasts of the landscape, by its vast empty spaces. To some, the few scattered patches of life and greenery seem like a miracle; others are depressed by the paucity of life in the desert.

In terms of the character and the nature of the land, Sinai can be divided into two distinct parts: the northern part comprises three-quarters of the total area and consists largely of flat plains or hilly country, with little colour or contrast. This region is composed of stratified chalky calcareous rocks and of alluvial plains and sands, which usually have some slight tinge of colour. Most of the area consists of wide, empty spaces with little relief, broken only occasionally by mountains and cliffs. The southern boundary of this part of the Sinai peninsula is formed by the huge precipice of the Tih plateau (Gebel el Tih), in places 500 m (over 1,600 ft) in height. This wall of rock extends across almost the whole peninsula and is difficult to traverse. It forms a very real barrier between two entirely different regions.

The southernmost quarter of Sinai, situated between the Gulfs of Elat and Suez, consists of steep, high mountains composed of massive and strongly coloured granites, which dominate the scene. These ranges are traversed by deep, narrow valleys and canyons. The strong colours, the high, steep mountains, and the varied shapes combine to produce a unique, bold, vigorous and majestic landscape. It is not surprising that this region attracted hermits and pilgrims in search of inspiration, seeking the place where the Lord gave his Commandments to Moses. It is here that the magnificence of nature is displayed at its best. In the open, empty expanses of the north one may feel lost, isolated from the rest of mankind. Among the mountains of southern Sinai one feels dwarfed, as if confronted by superhuman forces. Unique also are the coasts of southern Sinai, especially the coast of the Gulf of Elat ('Aqaba). Here the steep dark or reddish mountains combine with the exquisitely calm blue waters of the gulf to produce magnificent scenery. The palm trees in the oases add to the effect.

The different regions and natural divisions faithfully reflect the geological structure of Sinai: it is a block that was separated from the adjacent regions by the faults of the system of rift valleys, then tilted towards the north. The area close to the Mediterranean Sea is therefore low-lying, and there are no natural barriers to separate it from the neighbouring regions. Farther south the topography rises: the main land mass is delimited by faults and dominated by high precipices and steep slopes that separate the interior of Sinai from the adjacent regions. The uplifted Sinai slab was attacked by vigorous erosion; hence much of the original rock overlay has been exposed. The oldest rocks—mainly granites, gneisses and Precambrian schists—outcrop in the south. They build the spectacular rugged mountains of southern Sinai. Several peaks rise to more than 2,500 m (8,200 ft) above sea level. To the north, these rocks dip under a layer of variegated sandstones which now form a narrow belt across the peninsula, bordering the rugged southern Sinai region. This belt is known for its mineral deposits. The sandstones in turn disappear beneath a calcareous series of Cretaceous age that forms the impressive elevated Tih plateau extending from the vicinity of the Gulf of Suez to near that of Elat ('Aqaba). Originally the Cretaceous limestones and the underlying sandstones covered the entire peninsula, but they were eroded in the southern region. The Gebel el Tih represents the southernmost edge of the region where there are still outcrops of limestones. The Gebel Egma marks the edge of a still younger and stratigraphically higher group of strata, of early Tertiary age, which originally also covered the whole of the Sinai peninsula. These two calcareous rock series dip imperceptibly towards the north and underlie most of the northern two-thirds of Sinai. In most regions these beds are virtually tabular and horizontal. However, in northern Sinai they were upfolded and now form chains of hills and isolated mountain ranges.

To the west, the high Sinai block is bordered by a low-lying belt of foothills and plains. This is part of the faulted strip of land that comprises the Gulf of Suez rift valley. There is no corresponding area on the east side of the Sinai peninsula—there the high mountains fall abruptly to the Gulf of Elat ('Aqaba), usually leaving no coastal plain. However, the structure of the mountain range has pronounced fractures. The many linear valleys reflect such faults.

CLIMATE AND LIFE   Desert and wilderness are the most appropriate terms to describe Sinai. This implies aridity and scarcity of life. The high desert temperatures are very well known, but an equally important climatic factor is the difference between day and night temperatures. According to season and elevation, it may be cool, warm or unbearable hot at noon. The nights are invariably much colder. In winter the nights are bitterly cold, and even in summer it may be uncomfortably chilly in high areas. Thus, paradoxically, it is the cold nights that are the most difficult for the permanent inhabitants to endure, although it is usually of unbearable heat that we think when we speak of the desert.

The year is divided into two seasons: summer is dry, with very hot days. Winter, usually from November to April, is cooler, and is the season of occasional rains and in some parts even of snow. The humidity is greater in winter, and dew may be heavy at night. The sky is often overcast, and strong winds blow. This is also the time when there may be flowers in the desert, but not enough to be called a real spring.

As far as life in the Sinai is concerned, the most outstanding characteristic is lack of water. Annual precipitation is less than 100 mm (3.94 inches) in most parts of Sinai, which is totally inadequate to satisfy the needs of any widespread vegetation. There are no rivers, no lakes, no forests, no meadows—just bare rock, boulders and sand, with only a few plants adapted to these harsh conditions. Rain rarely falls, but when it does, it is torrential. It often happens that in no time the valleys are filled with huge masses of raging water. These flash-floods sweep along everything that lies in their way, until their energy is spent and the water is absorbed by the parched ground. Shortly afterwards, the scorching sun reappears, and the desert is again exposed to heat and wind. In general, winter is the rainy period, and only on rare occasions do storms come up in the Red Sea in May or even later in the summer. In most of the regions in the Sinai peninsula, rain and dew are the only forms of moisture; but on the higher-lying mountains in the south, snow is an almost annual visitor.

The little water there is is not entirely wasted, nor are destructive floods the only result of rain. Some rainwater and melted snow percolate into the ground to reappear as springs. Where the water-table lies close beneath the surface, it is marked by relatively dense vegetation. However, a continuous covering of green plants is found extremely rarely. Elsewhere water can be retrieved through wells. Small oases are formed, with limited vegetation and human activity. The courses of dried-up

43

streams are often indicated by rows of acacia and tamarisk trees, because the water is collected in the low-lying valleys, and occurs in sufficient quantities in the gravels close beneath the surface. The roots of trees and bushes can tap that moisture. This fact is known to the Bedouin, who dig shallow wells in *wadi* beds. Away from these river-valleys, at topographically higher elevations, water is less abundant or occurs at greater depths; thus only small shrubs and grasses can survive there for any length of time. They are usually thinly scattered on the ground. However, when rain moistens the desert soil, the seeds that are buried in it will germinate, and plants, some with magnificent flowers, will develop. This is the time when colourful blooms cover the otherwise barren desert for a short period. However, the plants must produce a new crop of seeds quickly, before the ground dries up again. The accelerated life-cycle may well have inspired the ancient traditions that the gods died, were resurrected and died again—analogously to the processes in nature. In the rocky parts of the desert, rainwater or meltwater may accumulate in small shady crevices or hollows. Here the water is trapped, unable to penetrate the compact rock. Protected from the heat of the sun, this water may remain for some months to quench the thirst of those who are familiar with the topography.

The desert has its own laws as far as life is concerned. Water, so vital to life, also causes great destruction. While the vegetation tends to thrive along the *wadis*, the dry water-courses, it is also there that the destructive floods occur. Thus, in the central parts of the *wadis*, where the water flows after a shower of rain, there are no plants and no trees. Any small plant that ventured into this area would be washed away. On the barren subsoil of the Sinai peninsula the blessing brought by water is far more apparent and lasting than the destruction caused by the floods. The inhospitable region only tolerates life where there is sufficient moisture. Such places stand out from the bare, desolate surroundings. This scanty vegetation supports little animal life. Reptiles, insects and birds are the creatures most commonly seen. But occasionally various rodents, foxes, ibexes and

other mammals are encountered. Man brought with him camels, goats, sheep and dogs. Camels are numerous and are the animals most typical of the desert. Their ability to drink huge draughts of water at one time allows them to go without for several days. They will eat any kind of plant they come across, including the dry, thorny vegetation of the desert. These characteristics, combined with its strength, make the camel the most useful companion of the Bedouin.

POPULATION AND SETTLEMENTS—THE BEDOUIN The desert supports a numerically small population—only a few tens of thousands live in the whole of Sinai. There is no part of the peninsula that is totally uninhabited, for the nomadic Bedouin wander far and wide, but the majority of the people are found around definite centres that have been inhabited since antiquity. The largest of these is the town of El 'Arish on the Mediterranean coast, with a population of about 30,000 (prior to 1967). Other important centres are found in the area of El Quiseima, in the Wadi Feiran and along the coasts of the Gulf of Suez. The shores of the Suez Canal have mostly been settled in more recent times. The chief occupations of the inhabitants are the raising of camels, goats and sheep, agriculture and, near the coast, fishing. Trade, often illegal (e. g. drug smuggling), is also an important source of income. Modern industrial developments, especially along the Gulf of Suez and the Canal, have provided many labour opportunities during the last century.

The inhabitants of the Sinai peninsula, though mostly described collectively as Bedouin, are in fact not true nomads as are the Bedouin of the Arabian peninsula. They may spend a large part of their lives roaming from pasture to pasture, but they are usually restricted to a definite territory and are tied to permanent settlements or homes close to sources of water, where they also engage in agriculture. This way of life is the result of the poverty of the land—a single occupation is usually inadequate to support a man and his family.

Agriculture is limited to places with permanent sources of water—as, for instance, around El 'Arish, near El

Quseima, in the Wadi Feiran, and around St. Catherine's Monastery. These springs provide water for palm groves and fruit orchards. In other places low dams constructed across major *wadis* can trap enough water for the irrigation of cornfields. However, in antiquity, especially before the Muslim invasion, the use of dams was much more extensive than it is today, especially in northern Sinai. Many abandoned dams of this period can still be seen.

Important as agriculture may be, it is inadequate as the only source of income; other occupations must also be pursued. Predominant among these is animal husbandry, which calls for a nomad existence, as no single locality can provide enough permanent grazing. Thus the Bedouin of the Sinai peninsula may spend one part of the year wandering around the country; many, however, must return at certain seasons to tend their palm trees and their orchards or to utilize the water trapped by the dams. In this way permanent habitations develop around the springs and wells. In some places stone houses or huts have been built, while elsewhere people still prefer tents. It is easy to recognize temporarily abandoned encampments, since the Bedouin—at any rate many of them—will leave some of their belongings hanging on the trees. Such property is never stolen.

The territorial ties of the Bedouin are an essential part of their social organization. They are divided into several tribes, each of which is restricted to one definite area. This territorial arrangement, however, may change after violent conflicts resulting from overpopulation. Memories of such wars between tribes, and of the peace treaties ending the disputes, are preserved in Bedouin folklore. Descendants of an indigenous population of Sinai cannot be distinguished with any certainty. The present Bedouin population seems to have immigrated from neighbouring countries during the Muslim rule and to have adapted to local conditions, probably by admixing with the older population. One exceptional group is the Gebalia tribe, which lives under the protection of St. Catherine's Monastery. The members of this tribe are the only local inhabitants allowed to work within the monastery. These people are the descendants of the serfs whom the Emperor Justinian took out from Dacia (present-day Rumania) to build the monastery. Members of this tribe maintained their Christian religion until the eighth century. (Cf. p. 208)

THE NORTHERN PART OF THE SINAI PENINSULA   The area north of Gebel el Tih gives the impression of having little to offer the traveller, nothing that could persuade him to stay there. On the contrary, the emptiness of the desert, the absence of colour and form encourage the traveller to hasten on his way. This is largely a misleading impression since, in fact, the region exhibits a good deal of variety. However, the changes are often so gradual as not to be easily perceived. To notice the differences in the landscape, it is necessary to travel a long way. Spectacular views are hidden, often far from the main roads, revealing themselves only to those willing to explore the region and make the effort to choose the inconvenient routes.

The natural frontier in the north is the Mediterranean coast. From time immemorial, north and north-west winds have blown inland the sand from the sea-shore, piling it up to form dunes, which now extend 20–50 km (12–30 miles) inland. The shifting sand forms hills of various shapes, consisting of myriad small grains of sand, like giant ripples or waves on the surface of the sea. In places the sand has buried whole villages. Less successful were its attempts to cover the rocky hills of Risan Aneiza and the slopes of Gebel el Maghara. The natural features proved to be stronger than the constructions of men's hands. Not even heavy downpours can breach the dunes. Only the vast Wadi el 'Arish is powerful enough to make its way as far as the Mediterranean Sea through the drifting sand dunes.

These vast quantities of sand are transported to the coast by the River Nile. Some of the sand is shifted by the wind, some transported by longshore currents and piled up to form a long spit or barrier, which cuts off the Sabkhet el Bardawil (Lake Sirbon of antiquity) from the open sea. In places this bar is more than 1 km in width.

Sea-water flows into the lagoon through a few narrow inlets, but in summer evaporation is so great, especially in the shallow parts of the lagoon, that the salts dissolved in the sea-water crystallize out and form glistening white patches along the southern shore of the lagoon.

The sea, however, is not only the inexhaustible source of sand and salt. It also contributes to the variety of the desert scenery. The sea is also the source of the rare winter rains. This rainwater seeps into the sand and re-emerges in lower areas, sometimes rising only close to the surface, but this is enough to support some vegetation. In fact, the Mediterranean coast is the richest in water in all Sinai. Oases of vegetation and groves of palm trees are scattered among the dunes, and they delight the eye of the traveller following the ancient coastal road from Gaza to Egypt. The most attractive features are the large palm groves near the mouth of the Wadi el 'Arish. It is these springs which, for thousands of years, have served as bases for the various armies that made use of the land bridge between Egypt and Palestine.

South of the sand dunes there is a region of bare rocks and boulders. Massive limestones build isolated mountain ranges (Gebel el Maghara, G. Yelleq, G. Halal, etc.). They rise several hundred metres above the surrounding extensive flat areas consisting of either soft chalky rocks or of strata of debris. This landscape has been shaped by erosion over millions of years. Geological processes originating deep in the interior of the earth upfolded the earth's crust in this area. The resulting elevations and folds of the harder limestones remained as mountains, while the much softer chalky limestones between them could not resist the forces of erosion and were washed away, leaving low-lying depressions. The hills and mountains are often dome-shaped, generally without prominent peaks. The strata, originally flat, are now precipitous and broken. They are a silent record of the powerful forces active in the geological past.

South of these mountains the area has less relief, and is largely flat or has slightly rounded, flat-topped hills. Much of the area is covered with extensive sheets of gravel. Everywhere here are water courses, characterized by strips of scanty vegetation. These plants, struggling for existence, add to the feeling of desolation. The plain rises imperceptibly towards the south, to become an elevated limestone plateau dissected into an intricate pattern by the lateral valleys of Wadi el 'Arish. This high plateau is bounded by steep cliffs on all sides except to the north. The Gebel Egma range crosses the plateau and makes communications and transport exceedingly difficult.

Monotonous flat or slightly undulating areas with little variety in colour or shape occupy most of this region which nature seems to have neglected. In many places, however, nature was more imaginative and gave free rein to her playful fancy. Walls of rock of various shapes, intricately dissected wastlands, *wadis* that make their way between picturesque rock walls, and strange fantastically shaped cliffs are scattered throughout the countryside. The perceptive eye will also notice that the appearance and mood of the desert changes according to the time of day and year. At dawn the desert is pure and clear. As the sun rises, the colours seem to fade and the air becomes hazy. Towards evening the appearance of the desert softens again, the colours become subtle and delicate, while the sky may assume a pinkish tinge in anticipation of a glowing sunset.

Flint is a widespread but minor component within the rock series that build the area. As the surrounding material is eroded away, pieces of flint are concentrated in the gravels and cover extensive areas known as "hammada", which, by their darker colour, stand out in contrast to the otherwise lighter-coloured terrain. During the early stages of human development, flint was much sought after as a raw material for the making of tools. Remains of early industries are still found here and there where a large supply of flint was available.

The roadways crossing this area have been used since earliest times to travel from the central part of the Nile delta to Palestine. They passed close to the few wells in this area, such as Bir el Themed, Bir Gafgafa and Bir Hasana. In the east, the roads converge on the Nitzana (Nessana) and the el Quseima areas, where many springs were discovered. The water enables a rich vegetation to grow and agriculture to flourish. The most abundant is the spring at the site of biblical Kadesh-Barnea, which served as the chief base for the tribes of Israel during their wanderings in the desert of Sinai under the leadership of Moses. Settlement of this area of springs continued for long periods, which has been confirmed by archaeological finds from many epochs. The modern highways follow the ancient routes through the desert.

Farther south runs the ancient road, the Darb el Hagg, which was used during the period of Muslim rule by pilgrims making their way to the holy city of Mecca. In the west the road has to climb the cliffs bordering the plateau of central Sinai. Of several passes used, the most famous in modern times is the strategic Mittla Pass. To the south of this pass is the Wadi Sudr, which has many springs and wells. To guard this passage, Saladin built the fortress of Qal'at el Gindi on the top of a picturesque hill. From there the road continued eastwards to the wells of Nakhl, where the Turkish rulers constructed another fortress to protect the pilgrims. In the east, the road rises to cross the steep, high cliffs of Ras el Naqb, then descends again to Elat.

The area to the south of this "pilgrims' way" is the most desolate part of Sinai. It is a barren stony plateau high above sea level, with no water, and very difficult to cross. Lack of water and the harsh climate make this area exceedingly inhospitable to man. This region is called Badiet el Tih, the "desert of wandering". Like many other names in the Sinai peninsula, this one can also be associated with biblical events. The name aptly describes the nature of this desolate region.

The area east of the northern section of the Suez Canal is part of the Sinai peninsula geographically, but is entirely unlike the rest of the peninsula. In fact it is part of the estuary of the Nile delta. Here there is dark soil containing freshwater snails—a material that was brought down by the Nile floods. Indeed, Herodotus refers to an arm of the river Nile extending as far as Pelusium, present-day Baluza. The course of this silted-up Pelusian arm can still be identified on aerial photographs. It

would appear that the land has sunk a little there, so that is now lies partly below sea level. The influence of the salty sea-water has turned this area into an infertile land, like the rest of Sinai.

SOUTHERN SINAI This part of the peninsula differs from that previously described in almost every respect. While stratified calcareous sedimentary rocks, soft and light in colour, outcrop in northern Sinai, southern Sinai is built of massive granites, gneisses, schists and similar rocks. These are crossed by numerous dykes, i. e. flows of magma which have forced their way up along fissures in the rocks. This mixture of rocks displays various shades of red, pink, black and purple, while the numerous dykes add streaks of dark green, black and red. Southern Sinai lies considerably above sea level and is bounded by steep scarps. For millions of years this mass of rock has been exposed to the eroding action of flowing water and dissected drastically into numerous mountains separated by deep gorges. This has resulted in magnificent scenery, displaying the rich colouring of the juxtaposition of the massive rocks. Sharp rugged peaks and steep rock walls dominate the scene and display a rich variety of shapes and colours. Table mountains and flat areas, so characteristic of northern Sinai, scarcely occur in the zone of sandstones to the south of the Tih plateau. The sandstones, too, create a rugged, sombre and dark-coloured landscape similar to that described above with granitic bed-rock. The rocky mountains are bare, with neither soil nor vegetation—there is literally nothing to cover the "skeleton" of the countryside. Only rarely do screes and boulders cover the slopes. The steep mountainsides and peaks, with their varied shapes and colours, have a character all their own, proud and sublime. It is among these rock walls that the awe-inspiring power of nature is felt and experienced as nowhere else in the Sinai peninsula.

The steep slopes all around look like forbidding fortifications built to protect the higher peaks against intruders. The bold and persevering climber, however, who overcomes these obstacles will be rewarded for his efforts. The higher he climbs, the more breathtaking and exciting are the panoramas and views that lie spread out before his eyes, especially the views from the highest points, such as Gebel Umm Shomer and Gebel Katherina. Up there, amidst the extreme stillness of nature, we imagine that we can hear the mountains, the hills and the valleys praising their Creator. In every direction rise bold mountains, a multitude of rock structures of curious shapes, one beyond the other, no two alike. According to the temperament and momentary mood of the spectator, they may look like the work of a master-mason, or like a host of bowed and petrified giants. Others may feel they are looking at a battlefield abandoned by giants who had been hurling stones at each other. Whatever the feeling, one senses something strong, dramatic, superhuman. No wonder that it is in these surroundings that so many have sought to find the mysterious and legendary Mount Sinai, where Moses spoke with God.

The nature of these massive and rocky mountains is indeed essentially lifeless, even hostile to life. Yet whatever life there is in this region depends entirely on this exceedingly inhospitable environment. This is the paradox of life in the desert. As always, water is the essential requirement for life. The impermeable rock does not absorb much of the water that flows down the slopes and through fissures in the rock to collect in pools in hidden places or, what is more important, in the alluvial infill of the valleys. The snow that falls on the high peaks melts slowly and feeds the subsoil, so that abundant supplies of water are found in the low-lying parts. The water-table in the layers of gravel may lie quite close to the surface, especially after rainfall; elsewhere it rises to form true rivers, which are later absorbed again by the ground. Elsewhere the precious water is tapped by wells and used for irrigation. In this way patches of green appear—islands of life scattered among the dead rock masses. Here and there are valleys covered with low bushes, elsewhere with clumps of acacias and tamarisk, while in the well-watered oases palm trees thrive. It is difficult to imagine any greater contrast than that be-

Fig. 5: Gebel Serbal (after W. A. Bartlett, 1848).

tween the masses of lifeless, rugged rocks and the luxuriant green oases.

Water is not only the prime supporter of life but also the main agent of destruction. The heavy downpours often cause wild torrents that rush between the walls of rock and sweep away everything before them. Nothing is spared—grasses, shrubs, trees, houses, people and animals are carried away by the masses of water. Only in such streams is there sufficient water to support a dense vegetation; but it is also here that the floods rage fiercest and take their heavy toll, in compliance with the curious and paradoxical logic of life in the desert.

The sandstone belt south of the Tih plateau has few natural springs. However, from the very dawn of history, it has attracted men on account of its mineral deposits. In very early times turquoise was the most sought-after and highly prized item of this mineral wealth; copper came somewhat later. At the beginning of the present century, attention was focused on the manganese ores in the Umm Bogma region. This raw material was of no use and no interest to the ancients, but is important today in the production of steel. Modern mining operations in this region exceed any undertaken in the past.

The most famous part of southern Sinai is the area along the road that runs from the Gulf of Suez to St. Catherine's Monastery. The variety and majesty of the scenery of southern Sinai is here revealed in its greatest perfection and grandeur. It is also here that the most luxuriant oases are found and it is in fact the most densely populated mountain region in southern Sinai.

On leaving the Gulf of Suez, the road to the monastery first runs through the region of the turquoise mines, then through the lower part of the Wadi Feiran, which winds its way between sombre, bare and rocky peaks. The Wadi supports only a scanty vegetation, which emphasizes the barren and lifeless nature of the desert. Then, all at once, the traveller finds himself among the flowering gardens and graceful palms of the renowned Feiran Oasis. It is not the vegetation itself, attractive as it undoubtedly is, that is the most amazing, almost incredible thing, but the fact that it is found in such an unlikely place, where it is least expected. Near the oasis towers Mount Serbal, rising about 1,500 m (nearly a mile) above the *wadi* bed. This formidable ridge, crowned with several peaks, towers above its surroundings. It is a veritable giant, which dwarfs the peaks around it.

Continuing into the interior of the mountain range of southern Sinai, the road reaches the Watia Pass. This cleft in a peculiar wall-like body of granite suggests the work of some giant who has cut a passage through the rock into the very heart of the country with one stroke of his sword. Beyond the pass, the landscape changes; the mountains become wilder and higher. The ascent of one of these peaks is the highlight of any journey to the Sinai peninsula. The higher the climber rises, the more impressive and sweeping do the prospects become. At the summit he can only stand and marvel at these sublime vistas. He begins to understand how it was possible for men to believe they were seeing on these mountain peaks one of the wonders of the world, and that they felt closer to God.

Fig. 6: The Valley of El Raha near Saint Catherine's Monastery (after W. A. Bartlett, 1848).

THE COASTS OF THE GULF OF ELAT-'AQABA   The Gulf of Elat-'Aqaba, with a maximum water depth of about 1,800 m (6,000 ft), is a deep scar on the earth's surface, produced by strong faulting that led to the formation of a rift valley system. Huge blocks of the earth's crust lie under the Gulf. The steep scarps along its coasts indicate the course of the main faults. Further faults cross the eastern part of the Sinai mountains, which became greatly fissured in consequence. Along many of these faults narrow crevices have been formed, now filled with huge blocks of limestone and sandstone, which once extended over the whole of Sinai; they can be recognized by their lighter colour, which contrasts with the surrounding dark Precambrian rocks. Later, the weakened rocks along the faults were easily eroded, which led to the formation of numerous linear *wadis,* practically parallel to the coast. Only three large *wadis*—Watir, Dahab and Kid—have cut their way through to the Gulf and drain all the valleys in the interior of the country. These three *wadis* have built large alluvial deltas which project into the Gulf, forming small coastal plains at the foot of the mountains.

In the past, this region was one of the least accessible parts of the Sinai peninsula. Very few trade routes ran through the rugged mountains in the south, since the trade to and from Elat was mostly by sea and had little impact on the areas bordering the Gulf. Only a few small settlements could subsist by trade. However, recent political and strategic changes have opened up this part of the country with the construction of an excellent road from Elat to Sherm el Sheikh. There is hardly room for a coastal strip between the water and the mountains, whose flanks mostly rise straight out of the sea. The road winds its way up in zigzags from the coast into the neighbouring mountains, often taking advantage of the linear valleys along the above-mentioned faults.

Only in the south is there a real coastal plain, from which rise isolated granitic hills. Much of the coastline of this area is fringed by cliffs formed by a raised coral reef. These are breached by several *wadis*, producing a number of secluded and charming bays. A special attraction are the mangrove trees that flourish in the shallow water. This is their most northerly habitat in the northern hemisphere. Off this part of the coast lies the island of Tiran, which guards the southern entrance to the Gulf. It rises more than 500 m (1,600 ft) above sea level and stands out as a striking mountain peak against the horizon.

It would be hard to find anything in nature more beautiful than the coast of the Gulf of Elat-'Aqaba. The combination of the blue sea with the red, black and pink of the mountains colours and tints that change, moreover, as the day advances—is incomparably lovely. The calm sea relieves the ruggedness of the mountains. Unspoiled by our noisy civilization, this region is still peaceful and secluded. It is also a land of sunshine, with only a few days of bad weather a year. In summer it is hot, it is true, but the cool sea is refreshing. On the other hand, there are few springs and oases. In the bigger oases, at Nuweiba and Dahab, the green of the palm groves that are a characteristic feature of any oasis is added to the blue of the sea and to the colours of the rocks. Small wonder that the region has become a haven for tourists seeking the sun, the sea, and above all seclusion, which is an assurance of relaxation from the hectic life of our times.

Most of the Gulf is fringed by coral reefs, which shelter an amazing variety of fish and other living creatures—a true paradise for the hobby-diver and underwater photographer. The wealth of colour and form hidden in the blue waters of the sea is in striking contrast to the barrenness of the neighbouring land.

On leaving Elat towards the south, the road first runs close to the sea. The traveller can admire the combination of wild mountains and blue waters. Scattered vegetation adds its modest contribution to the varied shapes and colours. At Nuweiba, however, the water which infiltrates the alluvial fan of the vast Wadi Watir supports a luxurian vegetation. This area at one time attracted the Bedouin and is now a haven for tourists seeking to escape from civilization.

The traveller who follows the road along the seaboard becomes acquainted with the grandeur of the southern Sinai mountains and the varied types of countryside there. In places the road crosses gentle hills and mountains traversed by numerous dykes. Elsewhere, as in the Wadi Kid, the mountains are dark and steep, as if trying to crush the roadway between them. Farther south the landscape is more open, with light-coloured granitic hills and alluvial plains. From the coast, the highest and most majestic mountains can only be seen in the distance.

There are several side-roads leading into the heart of southern Sinai. Along them lie many oases, and many a breathtaking view may be obtained in places. In the south, the wide *wadis* support a rich vegetation. Curiously shaped acacia trees abound. In places an extensive covering of grass and low shrubs appears after showers of rain, providing excellent grazing.

THE GULF OF SUEZ REGION   The Gulf of Suez also extends along a rift valley, but it is much shallower than the Gulf of Elat-'Aqaba. Much of it is flanked by coastal plains and foothills which form a separate geographical entity along the western foot of the elevated Sinai mainland. The depression of the Gulf tapers out in the region of the Bitter Lakes, but a shallow trench extends farther northwards and was used in the construction of the Suez Canal.

The strip of land along the Gulf of Suez combines a variety of landscapes and rocks. In a certain sense all the

Fig. 7: The island of Geziret el Fara'un (after W. A. Bartlett, 1848).

zones of the Sinai peninsula, from north to south, are represented there. However, they appear at lower elevations on account of the continuing faulting of the ground in this rift valley system. Hot water escapes to the surface from great depths along some of these fractures. The most famous are the Hammam Farra'un springs, where the almost boiling water flows directly into the sea. Near El Tor are the hot springs of Saidna Musa. Their water is pleasantly warm and is exploited for its healing properties.

Compared with other parts of Sinai, this region is relatively rich in natural springs, which support several settlements and are utilized for irrigating the fields. The springs of Ayun Musa in the northern part of the Gulf, and the springs and wells of the Wadi Gharandal and the Wadi Tayiba are famous.

Farther south lie the Wadi Sidri and the Wadi Feiran, where there is plenty of water, and near El Tor there is another group of wells, which for centuries have supplied with water the small town of El Tor and the palm groves in the environs.

Since the dawn of history, the coasts of the Gulf of Suez have seen various types of human activity. The road from Egypt to the turquoise mines used to cross this region. Miners and merchants passed along it with their loads of this blue-green mineral. Moreover, the Gulf of Suez was an important sea route from ancient Egypt to the east coast of Africa (the land called "Punt" in ancient Egyptian inscriptions), whence fabulous wealth was brought back. The Pharaohs of ancient Egypt dug the first canals connecting the Mediterranean with the Gulf of Suez, to facilitate communications with the Red Sea and the Indian Ocean. These canals were used by ships for many centuries—several thousand years before the modern canal was constructed. Besides these merchants, pilgrims also used to pass through the land along the Gulf of Suez. Christian hermits and pilgrims travelled to Feiran and into the heart of the Sinai mountains to seek the place where the Lord appeared to Moses. Muslim pilgrims sailing to Mecca stopped at the small town of El Tor, and on the return journey they had to spend some time in quarantine there.

In recent times great changes have taken place in this part of Sinai, perhaps more than anywhere else in the peninsula. The major events were the construction of the Suez Canal and the discovery of oil; no less important was the working of the manganese mines at Umm Bogma. All these developments carried modern technology into the peaceful desert. The construction of the canal also determined the present political status of Sinai: for centuries it was under Egyptian domination, though never considered part of Egypt proper. Under Ottoman Turkish rule, Sinai was cut off from Egypt. When Egypt broke away from the Turkish domination it laid claim to the Sinai peninsula, but only the construction of the Canal prompted the British to annex Sinai to Egypt and to establish the present international frontier.

Sinai owes the present-day activity on the land mainly to its oil. The first discoveries of oil were made as early as the beginning of this century, but exploitation was on a small scale. Near Abu Durba there is an abandoned borehole of that period. Its site is marked by a small oil well, where a trickle of petroleum forms a black patch on the light sand near the beach. However, in the 'fifties and 'sixties very rich oil fields were discovered on both sides of the Gulf and under the sea. Camps were built at Sudr and Abu Rudeis. Pumps, pipes, tankers and black

Fig. 8: Ayun Musa, south of Suez (after W. A. Bartlett, 1848).

patches of spilled oil became a part of the landscape. Of less significance is the shipping of manganese ores in the small port of Abu Zenima.

New opportunities of employment were provided for the local population. Contact with the most up-to-date technology of the oil industry has had its impact on the Bedouin. Motor vehicles proved to be in many ways superior to the camel, the traditional "ship of the desert". New gadgets found their way into the tents in the desert. Contact with all these technological and civilizing achievements revealed a vast resource of latent mechanical skill among the natives of the desert. However, it is impossible to erase thousands of years of life in the wilderness. Technology can infiltrate into the remotest spots, but old traditions are still very much alive. It would be a mistake to assume that transistor radios and cars could undo the spiritual heritage of whole peoples. Nevertheless, the modern trend toward industrialization has also had a great influence on the natural scenery. Roads and huge buildings disturb the harmony of the desert landscape. Pollution—a less acceptable aspect of technology—is also conspicuous. Piles of garbage, industrial waste and oil spills are unfortunately a rather common sight. The most serious effects of the modern technological era are the numerous oil slicks from ships sailing through the Gulf or tankers loading oil from the Sinai peninsula and at offshore oilfields. Today (1979) miles of beautiful beaches are covered with a thick layer of tar. In some places the patches of tar form one continuous black band, as if the Gulf was set in a black frame.

Zvi Garfunkel

21 The Wadi el 'Arish at the edge of the great desert of the Tih plateau traverses strata of limestone and flint. Ancient terraces testify to man's attempt to wrest food from the arid desert (aerial photograph).

22 Aerial photograph of the dry bed of the Wadi el 'Arish near Gebel Halal. Traces of ancient terraces are a reminder that agriculture was practised here in past ages.

23 Bedouin fields on the Tih plateau, near Gebel Halal.

24 A herd of goats on their way to a well.

25 At the entrance to the Wadi Sudr, through which the ancient desert road of Darb esh Shawi runs to the west coast, Saladin built, in the twelfth century, a big fortress—Qal'at el Gindi—against the attacks of the Crusaders from the east. The fortress is surrounded by a high wall and the gateway shows the typical stylistic features of the period.

26 Below the great mosque in the fortress courtyard is a large underground cistern with pointed Moorish arches.

27 Ornamental Arabic inscription over the gateway of Qal'at el Gindi.

28 Ras el Gindi, crowned by Saladin's fortress.

29 *Zilla spinosa,* a crucifer plant related to mustard.

30 Inflorescence of a species of acacia originally imported from Australia.

31 The wolf *(Canis lupus),* having been all but exterminated by the Bedouin, has become rare in Sinai. It is now protected.

32 Fluvial gravel plain (hammada) at the foot of Gebel Halal, a mountain recently identified by certain scholars as the mountain of the theophany.

33 Mountains above the Wadi Sudr, covered with fluvial gravel, totally waste and devoid of vegetation. In the background the majestic calcareous mountain Gebel Sinn Bishr.

34 Granite / gneiss and limestone mountains on the Red Sea south of Elat.

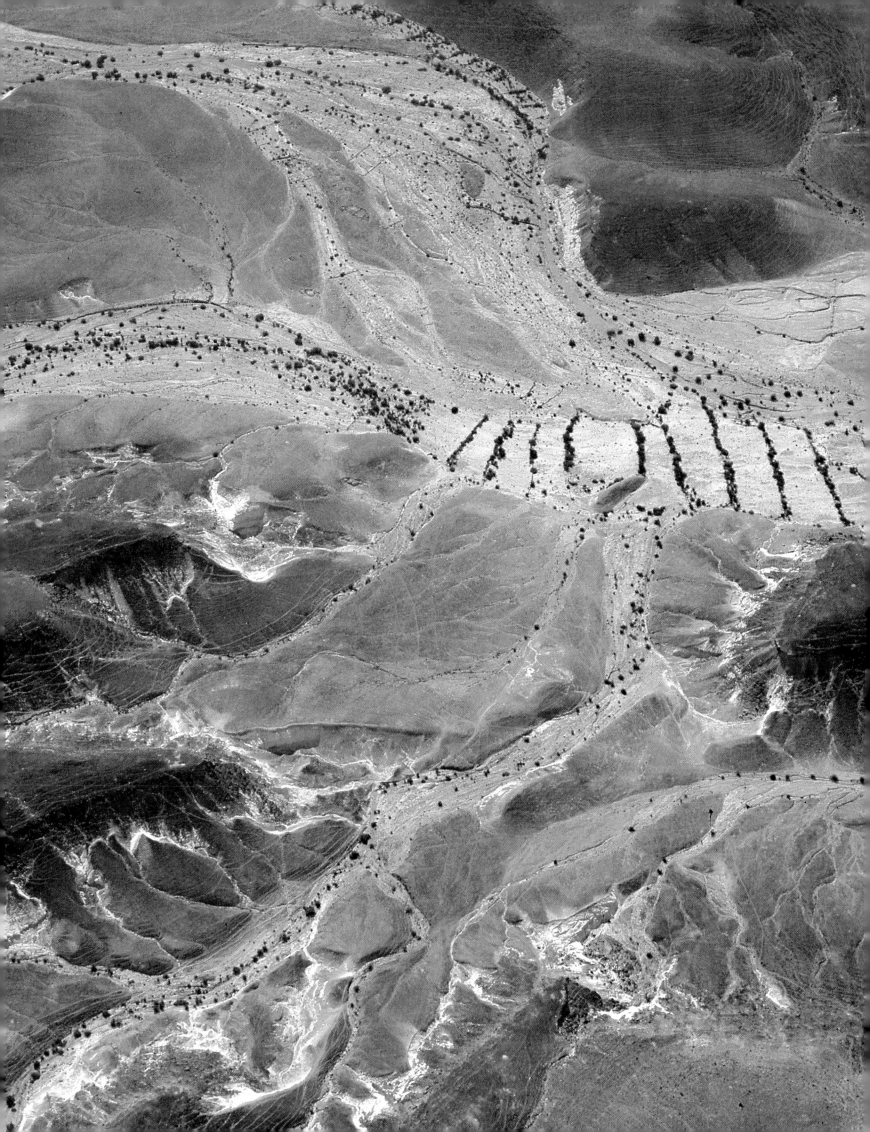

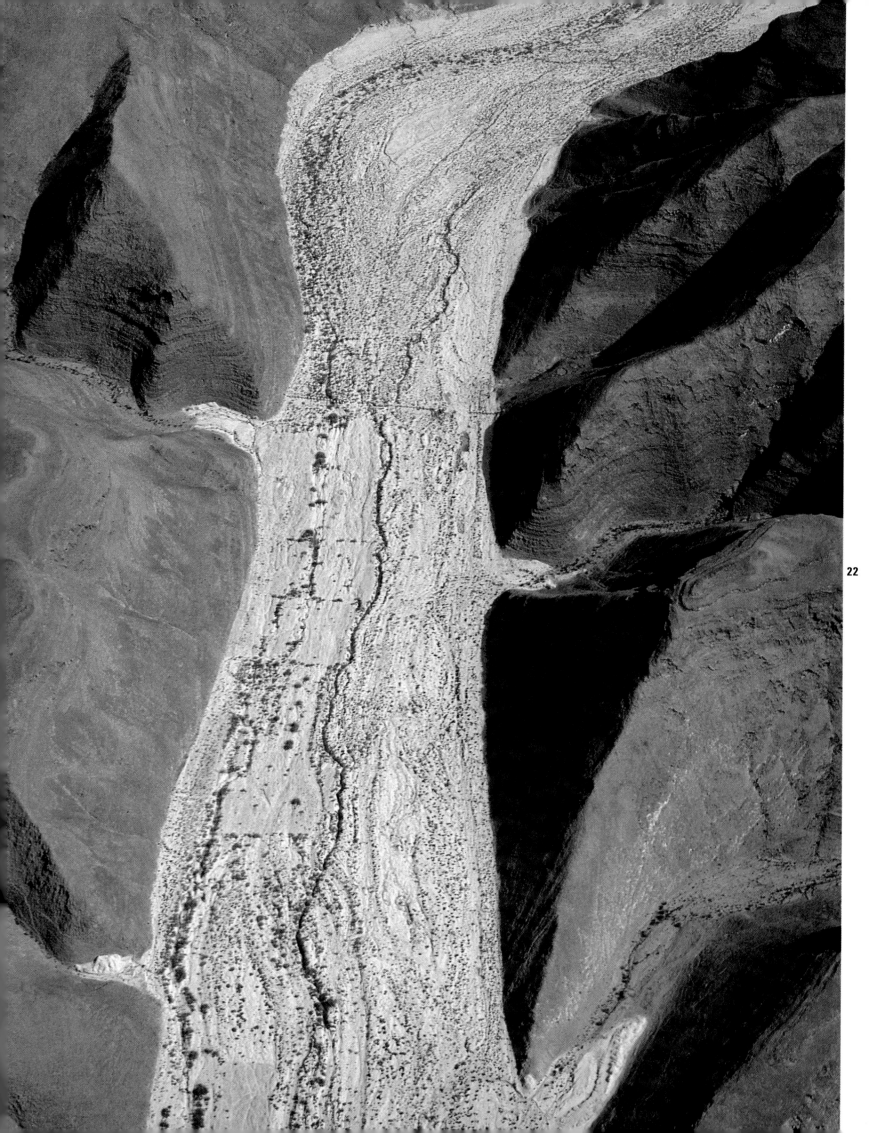

23   24

25 26

27

Geology
Dramatic Upheavals

The pronounced barrenness of the rock formations that build up the Sinai peninsula is due to the arid climate and reveals a great number of geological phenomena. The rock masses form one of the most important elements of the sights of Sinai. Even the geological layman will sooner or later be surprised at the diversity of the various rock formations he meets with on his journey through Sinai.

The geological investigation of Sinai began in the last century already; it was greatly intensified at the beginning of the present century, when many European scientists visited the area. Significant work was done by the British geologists of the Geological Survey of Egypt. Among the early explorers, the most important were Hume, Barron, Beadnell, Moon and Schürmann. They worked together with Egyptian geologists, who later became their successors (Sadek, Shata, Farag and many others). The search for oil in the area of the Suez Canal promoted geological research quite considerably. After 1968, remarkable work was accomplished by a research expedition of the Hebrew University of Jerusalem and by members of the Israel Geological Survey. These studies have greatly extended our knowledge of the geology of the Sinai peninsula.

The geological history of Sinai can be divided into three distinct epochs, during which the area developed in very different ways. During the first stage, in the late Precambrian (about 1,000[?]–550 million years ago), the Sinai peninsula was the scene of violent geological activity. At that time the area was probably part of a big mountain range, similar to the American Cordillera or the chain of the Japanese islands. During this period the disturbances in the interior of the earth caused an upfolding of rock masses and a considerable quantity of molten rock (magma) to well up to the surface from great depths. This intensive activity came to an end about 550–530 million years ago. The mountain chain was eroded until the area was reduced to a huge flat highland, or peneplain. From time to time the area subsided until it was below sea level, while at other times it rose slightly. During this second phase Sinai was covered by sediments, mainly sandstones and limestones. The third phase in the history of the area began about 45–30 million years ago, when the activity in the interior of the earth increased again and caused faults in the earth's crust. These fractures form a system of rift valleys. As a result, the Sinai peninsula was broken off from the neighbouring lands. It was then that the peninsula was extensively uplifted and deeply eroded, which gave it its present relief. Erosion was most extensive in the southern part of the peninsula, where the deepest and oldest bodies of rock became exposed.

THE PRECAMBRIAN AGE   Rocks of this age are exposed in southern Sinai, and also in adjacent areas. These were once a continuous mass, which was later broken by faults. The rocks of Precambrian age consist of two groups of different origin and age. The oldest and more extensive group comprises a variety of rocks which were formed deep down in the earth's crust, probably 5–10 kilometres (3–6 miles) beneath the surface. The second and younger group comprises rocks which were formed either on the earth's surface or at relatively shallow depths, probably only 1–2 kilometres (about 1 mile) down.

The former group comprises an intricate mixture of metamorphic and plutonic or igenous rocks of many kinds. The metamorphic rocks, mainly schists and gneisses, have lost their original appearance and have been reshaped as a result of heating and severe deformation. The plutonic rocks were formed by the solidification of large masses of magma which rose from a great depth and were injected into the deeper parts of the earth's crust. Some of the metamorphic rocks were originally sediments and volcanics which sank deep beneath the surface. As a result they became heated again and the original mineral grains which constituted them were metamorphosed into other minerals, just as clay changes into pottery when heated in a furnace. The process was greatly intensified by the deformation of the earth's crust, which distorted the rocks into intricate folds varying in size from a few centimetres to some kilometres. In most areas, various degrees of deformation and heating can be observed. The principal masses of metamorphic rocks in Sinai are found in the Wadi Feiran and to the north of it, some distance northeast of St. Catherine's Monastery (near the Wadi Saal), in the Wadi Kid on the way to Sherm el Sheikh, and south of Elat; however, small outcrops are fairly widespread. Greatly deformed metamorphic rocks are characteristic of all large mountain chains.

Another characteristic is the presence of large masses of plutonic rocks, which were formed by the cooling and soldification of magma intruded into the earth's crust. As the magma slowly cooled, deep beneath the surface, large crystals grew out of the liquid. The result is a rather homogeneous rock built of mineral grains up to several centimetres in diameter. Each grain is a crystal, but attractive crystal faces cannot develop, as the individual crystals interpenetrate each other. The masses of molten rock thrust upwards and forced their way into metamorphic rocks or into older masses of plutonic rocks which had already hardened. The plutonic rocks therefore occur as discrete bodies of varying rock types. They range from a few hundred metres in size to 10–20 km (6–12 miles) in extent. The most common type of rock, as in other mountain chains, is granite, which is usually grey, various shades of pink, or red in colour. The granite bodies that outcrop here compose more than 50% of southern Sinai and can be seen everywhere along the main roads that run through this region.

At a later period, after the formation of this deep-seated complex, the area was greatly uplifted and erosion set in. The overburden was worn away and the rocks that now outcrop in Sinai rose towards the surface. As a result the roots of the older mountain chain became exposed. This process led to the formation of the younger group of Precambrian rocks, either on the earth's surface or at a very shallow depth.

Lava continued to rise from the depths at intervals, though on a much smaller scale. Younger igneous rocks of several types were thus formed. Many veins were formed when magma filled the numerous cracks. As they cooled they produced dykes consisting of dark-coloured rocks—black, green, brown and red. The dykes are very striking in the light-coloured granites, but they also cut across other rocks. They are up to several metres thick and are practically parallel. As a rule they comprise less than 5% of the total volume of the rock, but in some places they may account for up to 30% or more. These dykes were not all formed at the same time, so that some of the earlier ones were cut across by younger ones. It seems that some of the streams of lava forming the dykes never reached the surface, while others were merely vents to volcano-like structures on the surface. The material of these dykes consists of lava which did not rise all the way to the surface. The lava that actually did reach the surface either built volcanic cones or erupted through fissures. The eruptions were fairly violent, and the lava was thrown into the air and dispersed in small blobs. Many of these eruptions were violent and disastrous, like those which occurred in 1902 on the island of Martinique in the Antilles (eruption of Pelée; 40000 people lost their lives then). The consequence was the formation of extensive volcanic rocks, sometimes several hundred metres thick. The largest outcrops are at Gebel Katherina, Gebel Ferani and near Elat. These are remnants of much more extensive outcrops which have largely been eroded. In places the lava mixed with sediments consisting of the debris of older granites, metamorphic rocks and dykes, and also of fragments of the surrounding volcanic rocks.

In some cases, however, the rising magmas produced extensive bodies of rock 1–2 km (about 1 mile) below the surface; some even intruded into the volcanics. The main type of rock was again granite, but the younger granite differs from the older ones in its mineral content and chemical composition. This younger granite is usually darker, sometimes even dark red. In comparison with the older granite, it is much more resistant to erosion. Indeed, it forms the highest peaks in southern Sinai, such as Gebel Serbal, Gebel Umm Shomer, Gebel Musa, Gebel Sahara and the wall of rock crossed by the Watia Pass road.

Concurrently with this later volcanic activity, the area was faulted, and rock masses were displaced or tilted. However, there was no folding of the type that affected the older metamorphic rocks. The period when the younger group of Precambrian rocks were formed was much less disturbed than the one when the deep-seated complexes originated. The diminishing influence of the disturbance of the interior of the earth heralded the quiescent period which was to follow.

This turbulent development was in no way restricted to the Sinai peninsula. It was shared also by the adjacent regions. Similar processes occurred in many other parts of the world, though at any given time they affected only a fraction of the earth's surface. Today, for instance, it is most apparent in the area of the Pacific Ocean. At the end of the Precambrian, the region of violent volcanic activity and deformation of the earth's crust shifted away from Sinai and the surrounding areas. These then became a part of the stable regions of the earth, similar to the situation in northern and eastern Europe today.

In many parts of the world, bodies of rock like the Precambrian ones of Sinai are traversed by veins and pockets of mineral ores, and these are sometimes rich enough to be of great economic value. In Sinai, however, the basement rocks are unprofitable, and mineral veins are decidedly rare and of poor quality. Only manganese and, above all, copper are occasionally found. Other metals are very rarely discovered. Yet in antiquity these mineral deposits were of great importance. The copper ores, recognizable by their typical greenish colour, were smelted to metallic copper. Moreover, below the earth's surface, pieces of green and blue turquoise were discovered. Copper and turquoise were highly esteemed in antiquity. Slag heaps and archaeological remains associated with them bear witness to these early metallurgical enterprises.

THE PERIOD OF GEOLOGICAL QUIESCENCE (PALAEOZOIC AND MESOZOIC) When Sinai and the surrounding areas became part of a relatively stable region, they were very greatly eroded and became a vast flat peneplain. Only a few resistant rock masses remained in the form of hills and low mountains. The topography probably resembled the flat areas in Africa or other major continents, extending over distances of many hundreds and even thousands of kilometres. The plain was covered with a layer of soil, formed as the result of the distruction, by the action of water and air, of the underlying rocks. However, as life did not at that time exist on land, the landscape must have been barren, different from the present extensive steppes, the grass-covered plains of Africa or Asia. During the following 500 million years, the only manifestations of the internal activity of the earth were slow vertical movements of the earth's crust. This behaviour is typical of the major continental masses, and the Sinai peninsula was no exception. Some areas subsided for a certain time, and were even flooded by the sea. Sediments accumulated in the subsiding areas. When the movement was reversed, the sea retreated, sedimentation ceased, and erosion set in. Some of the rocks previously deposited were washed away again. In course of time, the whole of Sinai was covered with continental or marine sediments. However, there was not a single area in Sinai where sedimentation was not interrupted for a certain time. The amount of elevation relative to sea level was of the order of from some hundreds of metres to 1–2 km (about 1 mile). Pronounced inclination of the slopes was never produced. As a result, the conditions of deposition changed gradually, from place to place, which is reflected in the sediments, for these, too, change gradually from place to place, and certain strata can be followed over distances of several hundred kilometres, even beyond the present boundaries of Sinai. For during that relatively quiet period, Sinai behaved in the same way as the adjacent parts of Africa and of the Arabian peninsula.

The pattern of uplifting and subsiding changed in the course of geological time—but when Sinai alone is considered, it can be said that its southern part was raised higher generally, and subsided less, than its northern part. In the south there was a high region which was extensively eroded and scarcely subsided at all, while the area near the Mediterranean coast subsided a great deal and for long periods was covered by the sea. As a result, the sediments in southern Sinai are not so thick as those in the north: they have been greatly eroded, and their original thickness, even before erosion, was less than that in the north.

The lower part of the sedimentary series of southern Sinai consists predominantly of variegated sandstones, which were deposited by rivers or shallow seas. They compose the sandstone zone which fringes the southern Sinai mountains. The grains of sand were produced by erosion of the land masses which existed in the south and south-west. The official scientific name for them is "Nubian" sandstones, but the name is hardly relevant when applied to the Sinai peninsula. Several units outcrop, separated by unconformities which indicate the periods of erosion. Their total thickness is less than 1 km (0.6 mile). The oldest series is of Cambrian age. It lies directly on the ancient weathered stratum that covered the peneplain above the Precambrian rocks. This series contains some turquoise-bearing beds. Another important series is of Carboniferous age. It contains siliceous carbonates of marine origin, in which are manganese ores in the Umm Bogma area. The age of other sandy series is less certain, but they may be Triassic. These series are overlain by sandstones of early Cretaceous age, with a major unconformity at the base, which marks a period of extensive uplifting and erosion at the end of the Jurassic and the beginning of the Cretaceous.

Rocks of the same age as those of the sandstone zone rarely outcrop in northern Sinai: they are known from a few wells drilled in the search for oil. They show that the geological history of northern Sinai was rather different from that of southern Sinai: in the north thick marine series (over 2 km, or 1.5 miles) of Triassic, Jurassic and Early Cretaceous age were deposited. The sediments are predominantly limestones, dolomites and lumachelle (shelly conglomerate); sandstones are uncommon. Some of these series have no corresponding series of the same age in the south, or else they merge towards the south into thinner, essentially continental, sandy deposits. These facts provide unequivocal proof of the development of the Sinai peninsula outlined above. However, it should be noted that nothing is known about the Palaeozoic history of northern Sinai; during that era the palaeographical trends may therefore well have been different.

The deposition of the early Cretaceous continental sandstones (containing fossil plants) in southern Sinai heralded a new phase of subsidence, perhaps the most important in the history of the area. Northern Sinai was inundated by the sea in the early Cretaceous, so that in the north the continental sandstones pass into a partly marine sequence with schists and limestones. However, the great transgression began in the Cenomanian period, and from then onwards the entire Sinai peninsula was covered by the sea until the end of the Eocene epoch. During certain periods—in the late Cretaceous and the Eocene—the sea spread southwards to a distance of over 1,000 km (600 miles). Enormously thick layers of sediments were deposited in this area. Sedimentation was rapid enough to keep pace with the subsidence of the earth's crust, in consequence of which the sea remained shallow.

In the Sinai peninsula it was predominantly limestone rocks that were deposited by marine organisms (shells and skeletons of organisms, or the secretion of lime by organisms). In fact fossil remains are quite abundant; remains of various shells and other marine creatures are often found. Even more frequent are the remains of microfossils, minute animals and plants that can be seen only under the microscope. However, much of the original material was changed by reaction with the sea water. These predominantly calcareous series form the Tih plateau, and also most of the bedrock of the area north of it. In places, these strata are more than 1,000 m (3,300 ft) thick. They are also preserved in fault steps along the Gulf of Suez and west of the Gulf of Elat-'Aqaba. This series is widely spread in the Middle East. A frequent and conspicuous, though minor, formation is flint. It occurs in the form of lenses or thin irregular beds,

65

but rarely forms thick beds. The concentration of silica, which is the main component of flint, requires unusual conditions of deposition in shallow seas. It is very probable that it was partly concentrated by organisms—but the original material (silicon dioxide) has since been transformed and can no longer be identified.

Material derived from the continent in the south and southwest is contained in a small part of the Cenomanian-Eocene series of the Sinai peninsula. However, the land was generally too far away. During this period a secondary movement occurred—mostly a downward displacement. As a result the coast of the continent gradually shifted northwards and reached the Sinai peninsula. The consequence was that some erosion debris from the continent was transported by sea currents far to the north. Usually this material consisted of very fine clays. However, periods of regression are suggested by the appearance of sandstone beds, which are quite common in southern Sinai, but form only a few relatively thin layers in central Sinai.

In most of the outcrops north of the Tih plateau the Cenomanian-Eocene sequence consists of two distinct parts: the lower part, of Cenomanian-Turonian age, consists mainly of hard limestones or dolomites, which form escarpments or steep slopes. The hanging wall is mainly chalky and less resistant to erosion. These beds usually form plains, low hills or "badlands". The highest part of this complex is of Eocene age, and again consists of hard limestones forming broken plateaux such as G. Egma and G. Raha.

During the period beginning with the Cambrian there was very little geological activity apart from the vertical displacements of the crust. Volcanic activity was insignificant. A layer of lava and a few dykes may be seen in the sediments of the Umm Bogma area (Carboniferous or Jurassic). A few lava flows occur among the early Cretaceous rocks of Gebel Areif el Naqa.

Folding and faulting, much less violent than in the Precambrian, affected mainly that part of Sinai lying north of the line from Gebel Areif el Naqa to Gebel Raha. The beds were thrown into large folds which extend in a north-east to east-north-east direction and are traversed by fractures. The anticlinical folds increased in size and formed hills in the late Cretaceous. On these the sediments are thinner than in the intervening downfolded synclines. Some anticlines occasionally rose above sea level and were eroded. Folding began again some time after the sea had retreated from this area near the end of the Eocene.

The sediments that cover Sinai contain few economically significant mineral deposits. Most famous are the turquoise deposits that lie at the base of the sandy series, exploited since antiquity. The manganese ores of Umm Bogma are restricted to the strata of the Carboniferous series. This ore has been mined since the beginning of the present century, and the reserves are now largely exhausted. The Carboniferous series also contain many coal seams, but they are too thin to be of economic interest. Recently a deposit of low-grade coal was discovered in Gebel el Maghara, and mining operations were begun in 1966. Its low calorific value and distance from populated areas considerably reduce the value of this deposit. A further material that is of economic significance is clay, used in the ceramic industry and also as a building material. Distance from industrial centres again decreases its value.

The turquoise deposits in the sandstones were produced by redeposition of the copper contained in the Precambrian rocks: the older copper minerals were dissolved and then precipitated again in shallow seas or lagoons. The copper minerals occur as thin seams interbedded with sandstones or shales, but also as irregular lenses along certain strata. The action of ground-water in the geological past has redistributed some of this material and formed veins. The average concentration is hopelessly small by modern ideas. However, the ancients picked out the copper-bearing fragments one by one and thus obtained both gem-quality turquoise and ores which contained enough metal to be smelted. What seem to us insignificant deposits were a source of wealth in antiquity and an important economic asset for the early inhabitants of Sinai. The best-known mines are situated in western Sinai, in Gebel Maghara and the Serabit el Khadim region. Copper minerals of varying quality are found everywhere in the sandstone belt that crosses the Sinai peninsula.

THE FAULTING PHASE   The third phase in the geological development of Sinai is characterized by the fracturing and breaking up of the old Arabian-African crustal block. The fault zones are visible as large scars on the surface of the earth. They are zones of very different topography. Frequently, long and narrow areas of depression, rift valleys, are formed. In our region the Red Sea is the largest fracture; it was produced when Arabia drifted away from Africa. The cleft left between the two blocks that were moving away from each other was partly filled by material that welled up from the depths of the earth, so that an area with a young crust was formed between the two blocks of the Precambrian basement. At the same time sediments also accumulated in the depression. In the north this fault zone bifurcates, on the one side into the Gulf of Elat-'Aqaba and the Dead Sea and on the other into the Gulf of Suez system. The two rift systems frame the Sinai peninsula. In the south, the Red Sea is connected with the Gulf of Aden and the so-called Carlsberg ridge. This deep-sea ridge on the floor of the Indian Ocean is the place where the lithospheric plates are moving apart. A new sea-floor is being formed in the area between these plates. Another branch of this same fracture system extends through East Africa, where it has given rise to the famous East African rift valley system.

The formation of the rift valleys between the Arabian and the African land masses seems to have begun 30–45 million years ago. In course of time the process gained momentum, and by about 20 million years ago the rift valleys were fully formed and deep enough to be flooded by the sea. The present distribution of land and sea was reached, and the Sinai peninsula became a separate geographical entity.

The various crustal blocks on each side of the fracture zone or rift valley system are moving relatively to each other. The detailed structure of any fracture zone or rift valley depends on the type and the speed of movement. The movement of the Arabian peninsula relative to Africa immediately to the south of the Sinai peninsula, amounted to 120–140 km (75–87 miles) and today moves at a rate of about 1 cm (0.4 inch) per year. The direction of the relative movement formed an obtuse angle with the fault-system that separated the basements; this again has led to the formation of the wide and deep Red Sea, its central part being underlain by newly formed crust. The amount of movement in the fault-system of the Gulf of Suez was much smaller—only about 20 km (12 miles)— so that a shallower and narrower rift was produced. The marginal faults of this rift gave rise to the foothills along the western edge of the Sinai peninsula. These foothills consist of numerous blocks which broke away from the higher-lying Sinai mainland. Similar blocks occur also west of the rift. These blocks are a few hundred metres to several kilometres wide, and up to a few dozen kilometres long. They are separated by normal faults, which run more or less parallel to the Gulf of Suez. Similar but smaller blocks lie beneath the central part of the rift, now mostly covered by the sea. This trough was filled with a thick series of sediments, which contain considerable petroleum deposits. The Gulf of Suez rift greatly resembles the Upper Rhine Trench both in size and in structure.

The structure of the rift that links the Gulf of Elat-'Aqaba with the Dead Sea is very different, because the movement of the Sinai peninsula relative to the Arabian peninsula was mainly parallel to the rift, the displacement amounting to about 100 km (60 miles)—i.e. the rift is essentially a strike-slip fault zone. Most of these faults occurred along fractures that lie deep down, but the eastern margin of southern Sinai was also affected. This area is crossed by some faults, with displacement of up to several kilometres. The amount of displacement can be calculated with the aid of various Precambrian rock complexes. Frequently the weakened rocks along such faults are more greatly eroded, determining the course of the linear *wadis* which are typical of this part of Sinai. On the other hand, there are no marginal blocks such as form the Gulf of Suez rift. The movement between the Sinai peninsula and Saudi Arabia was not merely a strike-slip fault, for a narrow cleft opens at an acute angle to the fracture that separates the two land masses. This cleft is filled by the Gulf of Elat-'Aqaba, which is some 1800 m (nearly 6,000 ft) deep.

Movements between two major crustal blocks never proceed smoothly, but erratically, spasmodically, or sporadically. The rock masses glide against each other and eventually break to give way to the tensions to which they are subjected. When such a sudden shock occurs, it is felt as an earthquake. The rift valleys of the Sinai peninsula are epicentres of such tremors. However, compared with other active fault zones, the activity of those around Sinai is very slight.

Such processes, leading to the dismembering of old crustal blocks, originate deep in the interior of the earth, where extensive disturbances affect vast areas. The Middle East and the Sinai peninsula are no exception. Two main effects are evident: vulcanism and general uplifting. In the Sinai peninsula vulcanism was very insignificant: a few dykes and lava flows occur, but are concentrated mainly in the west, where, in some regions, they lend some colour to the landscape. All such activity took place millions of years ago, and it would be a mistake to link them with the events described in the Bible, which might suggest volcanic eruptions (Exodus 19, 16–19; cf. the chapter entitled "Exodus, Desert, Mount of God", p. 27). The other effect, uplifting, is more marked and affects areas extending up to several hundred kilometres away from the rifts. The uplifting of the land seems to be still continuing in some parts. It is this process that was of fundamental importance in the shaping of the present-day landscape. As a result of this upward movement, southern Sinai was raised higher and was eroded more than the neighbouring areas.

As the rifts subsided the advancing sea filled them with sediments. The ooze at the bottom of the sea invariably contains remains of various organisms that lived on the sea-bottom or were suspended in the water. Under normal circumstances organic material disintegrates, but if buried fast enough may be converted into petroleum. This accumulates and is stored in porous rocks, which can be exploited economically. Such conditions obtained in the Gulf of Suez. First, the erosion of the neighbouring regions piled up vast amounts of sand in the Gulf. These grains of sand formed porous layers in which the oil squeezed out from neighbouring areas was concentrated. Secondly, communication with the sea was cut off at certain periods; as a result, evaporation was so intense that the salts normally dissolved in sea-water crystallized out. These formed thick layers of impermeable gypsum and salt, which prevented the oil from escaping. Thirdly, continual fracturing in the Gulf of Suez produced graben[1] and horsts[2]. Petroleum tends to accumulate in the porous beds of horsts, as it is displaced by the heavier ground-water, until its flow is halted by impermeable beds. Such horsts were the targets of drilling and prospecting; in many cases this paid off by the discovery of sizeable oilfields under the coasts of the Gulf and, as technology advanced, also under the floor of the Gulf.

Zvi Garfunkel

---

[1] trough, rift valley   [2] an upthrown area between two parallel faults

35 'Ain el Gedeirat, the most abundant spring in the Tih desert (on the Negev border), has been identified as the biblical spring of Kadesh-Barnea.

36 Water is life. Fruit, olives and vegetables are planted by the Bedouin in the Wadi el Gedeirat and irrigated with spring water.

37 In the middle of the Wadi el Gedeirat, by the spring of Kadesh-Barnea, stands a hill where the ruins of a Judaean fortress of the 8th century B.C. has been excavated during the past few years by Rudolf Cohen. In the foreground are Bedouin fields and plantations.

38 Aerial view of Kadesh-Barnea. In the centre of the picture—to the right of the stream—are the excavations of the Judaean fortress. A flowing stream, fed by the spring a little above the fortress, is an unusual feature in this desert landscape.

39 Greatly eroded Mesozoic chalk landscape—so-called ''badlands''—of Gebel Areif el Naqa, to the south of the Wadi el Gedeirat (Kadesh-Barnea).

40 Steppe landscape with *Artemisia monosperma,* a scene typical of the Tih plateau.

41 The huge limestone scarp of the Tih plateau, and beyond it a section of the broad sandstone belt which contains much of Sinai's natural wealth.

42 Lateral branches of the Wadi el 'Arish on the elevated southern point of the Tih plateau—a completely arid desert landscape carved out by the turbulent run-off after the occasional downpours of rain.

The Flora

Wild and Cultivated Plants

PHYTOGEOGRAPHIC SITUATION   The Sinai, a desert of the Saharan type, forms the land bridge between Asia and Africa. Its flora reflects the influence of four phytogeographical regions that meet and overlap here. The influences may be characterized as follows: most plant species growing in Sinai originate from the Saharo-Arabian region; in the warm lowlands near the Gulfs of Elat-'Aqaba and Suez, many Sudanese species thrive; Irano-Turanian species typical of the North African and Iranian (Persian) steppes inhabit the high mountains and plateaux, where the climate is moister than in the lowlands; the Mediterranean flora is not widespread, and its species are found in special situations only.

WEALTH OF SPECIES   According to the various authors, the estimated number in the Sinai varies between 820 and 900 species. An area the size of Sinai would support 200 species in the Sahara, 1,400 species in the British Isles, and 2,200 species in Israel—an interesting and instructive comparison. The number of species per unit of area is not the same for all parts of Sinai, and some regions support a richer flora than others. These are the high mountains of southern Sinai and the hills and mountains of northern Sinai, which have a gentler relief. These areas are characterized by many rock types which, by influencing the water regime, create favourable habitats. Higher rainfall, greater cloudiness and larger amounts of dew and mist result in a milder climate than that of the lowlands. Relatively poor in species are the boulder-strewn deserts (hammada), where the vegetation is concentrated in *wadis*, sand areas and salinas, or salt-springs.

ENDEMICS AND RELICTS   The number of endemics, which are restricted to a small area in Sinai, is 34 (4.2% of the total flora of the Sinai peninsula). There are also 23 endemic species that spread beyond the borders of Sinai, and are also found in the Negev, in Edom (Transjordan) and Egypt.
Most of the endemics are found in the highlands of southern Sinai; fewer of them inhabit the ranges of hills

of northern Sinai. Those areas that support a scanty flora are also poor in endemics. There is a group of species that generally inhabit damper regions than Sinai; in Sinai they are found mainly in rocky places. Many of them are believed to be relicts from periods when a more humid climate prevailed in the Middle East. *Juniperus phoenicea*, which flourishes in Gebel Halal, Gebel el Maghara and Gebel Yelleq in northern Sinai, where the mean annual rainfall reaches 100 mm (4 inches), is a well-known tree of the Mediterranean area. It also grows in Greece, where there is 500–600 cm (20–24 inches) of rainfall, as also in southern France and the Pyrenees, where the mean annual rainfall is 700–1000 mm (28–39 inches). How did the Phoenician juniper reach the Sinai desert and how did it manage to survive there? Prehistoric excavations in conjunction with radioactive carbon dating have shown that the juniper grew in Sinai 20,000 years ago. There is proof that during the last phase of the Ice Age the mean annual rainfall in Sinai, the Negev, the Sudan (i. e. the region, not the state) and northern Africa was higher than it is today.

As the climate of Sinai became more arid, only those trees with an adequate supply of water survived, while the others died out. The surviving species of trees are those which inhabit pockets of soil in outcrops of smooth rocks, or *wadis* with such rocks in their catchment area. These hard rocks do not absorb the water and the enormous downpours that run off them collect in these pockets. The water available to plant life in the pockets of soil and in the *wadis* after each shower may on occasion be as much as would elsewhere be the normal amount available to plants. Together with 500–1000-year-old junipers, a few specimens of Mediterranean woodland climbers—*Ephedra campylopoda* and *Rubia tenuifolia*—have been found. The smooth rocks support some 80 species with a scattered distribution between Sinai and their main areas. In these places, endemic species with a very small area of distribution have been found. *Origanum isthmicum* is endemic to 5 km² (2 square miles) of Gebel Halal; the closest relatives of this species occur in Europe. In the subalpine mountains of southern Sinai there are relict species which are also found in Lebanon. These include *Scrophularia libanotica*, *Campanula dulcis* and *Arenaria deflexa*. The smooth granite rock also supports endemics such as *Hypericum sinaicum*, *Silene schimperi*, *Micromeria serbaliana* and *Cotoneaster orbicularis*. The endemic *Primula boveana* is considered to be a relict of the Tertiary, when the cooler climate enabled it to reach Sinai. When the climate changed, this plant survived near small springs in the high mountains with a cool climate; its closest relatives occur in the high mountains of the Yemen, of East Africa, the Zagros range in Persia (Iran) and in the Himalayas.

FORMS OF LIFE The existence and survival of plants in the harsh conditions of the desert depends, among other things, on the morphology of their above-ground body, which is exposed to atmospheric influences. Many plants adjust their distribution in time and space to the amount of water available. Most of the annual species avoid confrontation with desert droughts by developing only in the relatively moist places in years when the rainfall is sufficient to enable them to complete their life cycle. The signal for the beginning of this activity is given when a sufficient amount of rainfall has been registered by the seeds or other parts of the plant. Such «rainfall gauges» contain germination inhibitors, such as the salts present in the fruits of *Zygophyllum dumosum*, which inhibit germination unless there is sufficient rainfall to leach out the salt. A low permeability of the seedcoat or of its fruits prevents germination after slight occasional showers. Another seed germination control is the inhibition of their dispersal unless there is sufficient rainfall. In some plants the seeds are enclosed in the tissues of the parent plant and dispersed only after sufficiently heavy showers have moistened the parent plant. This ensures an adequate supply of water for the survival of the young plants. Plants that open only after having received sufficient moisture used to be called "resurrection plants" by the pilgrims to the Holy Land. Examples are *Anastatica hierochuntica* (rose of Jericho) and *Asteriscus pygmaeus* (false rose of Jericho).

Even if the seeds were scattered in a year which proved to be too dry, so that the seedlings died before producing new seeds, there would always be some seeds left in the parent plant in readiness for another and more rainy season.

In addition to seeds with specific requirements for germination there are geophytes, such as various species of *Colchicum*, *Tulipa* or *Scilla*, which have bulbs or subterranean buds which function as a constant reservoir of nourishment. These bulbs may remain dormant for many years until enough rainwater penetrates the soil surrounding them.

Shrubs and trees, with their stems and leaves, are active all the year round. Many of them reduce their activity in the dry season and develop it in the wet season. The dwarf shrub *Zygophyllum dumosum* reduces its transpiration in summer to 1–5% of its winter transpiration by shedding leaflets and doubling the thickness of the epidermal layer of the remaining leaf-stalks, or petioles. Many of the dominant dwarf shrubs are stem or leaf succulents of the family of Chenodopodiaceae (goosefoot genus), whose fleshy tissues can store water in the wet season. In these plants the water is better protected against evaporation than it is in the soil. The *Acacia* trees, which are of Sudanese origin, shed their leaves in summer as they do in the East African savannas, but lose a great deal of water during a large part of the year.

A special kind of adaptation to desert conditions is exhibited by *Blepharis ciliaris*. The Bedouin call it "shok e dhab" which means the spine of the lizard *Uromastix aegyptius* (see p. 99) on account of the resemblance of its spiny stem to the tail of *Uromastix*. *Blepharis ciliaris* has an extraordinary mechanism of seed dispersal. When ripe, the seeds are not dispersed but remain in the tightly closed fruit. When rain falls it moistens the bracts and calyx-leaves covering the fruit and they open. As soon as the top of the fruit is exposed, the water begins to penetrate into a thin tissue less than 1 mm thick. About one hour after being wetted, the fruit explodes and two seeds are catapulted out to a maximum distance of 5 m (16 feet). When the seeds are wetted, the

Fig. 9: *Blepharis ciliaris* (after A. Raffeneau-Delile: Flore d'Egypte, 1813).

multicellular hairs of the seedcoat swell so that they drop the seed in such a way that the embryonic root comes to rest on the wet soil. The wet hairs become mucilaginous and grains of sand adhere to the seed. The sand makes the seed unattractive for herbivores, protects it against rapid desiccation, and acts as additional weight, thus helping the root to penetrate the soil. The sticky mucilage may also cause some of the seeds to adhere to birds' feet so that dispersal over long distances is guaranteed. There are therefore two sophisticated "water gauges" that prevent dispersal of the seeds of *Blepharis ciliaris* before sufficient rain has watered the ground to ensure that the seedlings can germinate and take root. The bracts and sepals prevent the opening mechanism of the fruit from operating after slight showers that last less than ten minutes. This opening mechanism on the upper side of the fruit has to be wetted for about an hour, so that a slight shower cannot release it. When the seeds have been dispersed and have found suitable conditions for germination they may start this process within 2 hours if the temperature is above 20° C (68° F). The fruits of this plant are the most interesting botanical souvenirs provided by the Sinai desert. The plant is found in the warmer parts of Sinai.

DISTRIBUTION OF THE VEGETATION The distribution of the vegetation is chiefly dependent on soil conditions. Fine-grained soils, which hold relatively large quantities of rainwater close beneath the surface, lose water by direct evaporation. Small amounts of salts in the rainwater accumulate in the course of time, forming a salty layer. In such places plants can develop only in leached depressions and *wadis*. In coarse-grained soils and fissured rocks, water penetrates deeper and no such accumulation of salts occurs.

In northern Sinai the sandy soils, which absorb all the rainwater, support a vegetation dominated by dwarf shrubs: *Artemisia monosperma, Convolvulus lanatus* and *Cornulaca monocantha*. In the sandy areas of southern Sinai, *Hammada salicornica* and *Haloxylon persicum* predominate.

Fine-grained soils, such as the drifting sands covered with gravels—which form the huge boulder-strewn plains (hammada) of central Sinai—produce vegetation only in the *wadis*. Here the dominant dwarf shrubs are: *Anabasis articulata, Salsola tetrandra, Artemisia herba-alba, Hammada scoparia* and *Zilla spinosa*.

Fissured hard rocks such as limestone, dolomite, granite and metamorphic rocks in the hills of northern Sinai support dwarf shrubs even on their slopes and not only in *wadis*. The dominant species are *Artemisia herba-alba, Zygophyllum dumosum, Anabasis articulata, Reaumuria negevensis, R. hirtella* and *Gymnocarpos decander*.

Salty soils occur in Sinai mainly along the coastal areas, where underground water rises to the surface of the soil and evaporates, leaving a residue of salt. Only a few species can thrive on the permanently salty and wet soils; they are: *Arthrocnemum macrostachyum, Halocnemum strobilaceum, Artiplex farinosa, Limonium axillare, Nitraria retusa* and *Zygophyllum album*.

Trees are found in three kinds of habitat—in *wadis*, on rocks and on saline soils. Large *wadis* can supply enough water for the deep-rooting *Acacia* trees even if rain does not fall every year in their catchment area. *Acacia raddiana*, the most common tree in southern Sinai, can live in the *wadis*, so the Bedouin say, even if there is no rainfall for ten years. It blooms in summer—the season when it blooms in its homeland, the East African savannas. Together with the various species of *Acacia* in the *wadis*, the following Sudanese species are found: *Capparis decidua, Moringa peregrina, Calotropis procera* and *Leptadenia pyrotechnica*.

Various species of *Tamarix* can grow near salty soils, in *wadis* where the ground-water is not too far down or too saline. Fresh water springs or other places with plenty of ground-water may be distinguished from afar by the date palm plantations (*Phoenix dactylifera*).

In northern Sinai, smooth outcrops of limestone or dolomite support, of Mediterranean species, the *Juniperus phoenicea*, and of the Irano-Turanian species, the *Pistacia atlantica*. In southern Sinai, outcrops of red granite support such trees as *Pistacia khinjuk, Ficus pseudosy-*

81

comorus, *Crataegus sinaicus* and bear shrubs such as *Rhamnus disperma* and *Cotoneaster orbicularis.*
Whereas the occurrence of perennial species is constant and may be found in well-defined places every year, the occurrence of annuals varies with the fluctuations in the amount of rainfall. A heavy shower may produce an upsurge of annuals. The dimensions of a cloud which has discharged such life-bringing rain can be determined exactly by the distribution of the annual species. The incidence of years when annual species flourish is more frequent in the high mountains and in the sandy areas of Sinai than in other regions.

RESPONSE TO RAIN   In the desert, rainy days are the most important pre-requisite for a long-lasting plant life. These are rare, however, in the real desert. Some places, mainly in southern and central Sinai, experience such rainfall only once in several years. When sufficient water has penetrated the soil, new life begins to stir and within a short time the desert is in full bloom. The year 1967 was a dry one in the region of Sherm el Sheikh. Apart from deep-rooted *Acacia* trees and some shrubs there was no plant life to be seen. On account of its desolate appearance some visitors to the area nicknamed it "the plains of the Moon". The following winter was comparatively rainy and in the spring of 1968 the "plains of the Moon" were completely covered with the fragrant yellow-flowering Compositae—*Pulicaria undulata*. The Bedouin use the green plant to make a hot drink which is very pleasant to the taste—it is the best substitute for tea that the Sinai has to offer the desert-dweller. The year 1968 produced such masses of *Pulicaria undulata* that it supplied the Bedouin's needs for many years. By 1969 the *Pulicaria* plants were dead.
In 1971 some small clouds, 1–5 km (0.3–3 miles) in diameter appeared, bringing heavy showers of rain, and the desert bloomed once more, but only in scattered patches. It would therefore have been possible to map the outlines of the life-bringing clouds. Between these patches of flowering plants the "plains of the Moon" were as devoid of vegetation as before. The heavy rain

Fig. 10: *Convolvulus hystrix* (after A. Raffeneau-Delile: Flore d'Egypte, 1813).

also caused the seeds of trees and shrubs to germinate. Only those seedlings survived which developed near rocks from which the water could drain off.

PLANTS USEFUL TO THE BEDOUIN   The Bedouin make use of many of the plants that grow wild in Sinai. The leaves of *Malva parviflora, Malva nicaensis, Sisymbrium irio* and *S. erysimoides, Atriplex halimus* and *A. leucoclada* are cooked like spinach. The roots of three species of *Scorzonera* are eaten raw or roasted. Tubers of *Erodium hirtum* are tasty and supply the nomads with some water during the dry season. The fragrant leaves of the following plants are used in the preparation of hot drinks as a substitute or flavouring for tea: *Teucrium polium, Teucrium pilosum, Artemisia herba-alba, Pulicaria undulata* and *Cotula cinerea.*
The following herbs supply flavouring for their food: *Majorana syriaca, Thymus decussatus, Thymus bovei* and *Origanum isthmicum.* Sweet fruits, which are eaten raw, are those of *Ochradenus baccatus, Nitraria retusa, Rhamnus disperma, Ficus pseudosycomorus, Crataegus sinaicus, Capparis aegyptiaca* and *C. cartilaginea.* The seeds of the last two species of capers mentioned taste exceedingly hot and the traveller is advised to be cautious. Poisonous plants that have become notorious in some criminal cases during the past few years are species of *Hyoscyamus* especially *H. boveanus* and *H. muticus* (henbane). These plants contain large amounts of the alkaloids atropine, hyoscyemine and hyoscine (scopolamine). Tourists promised a cheap "drug trip" have suffered injuries to their health as a result, and some of them were robbed into the bargain.
Various plants with strong fibres are used for making ropes and string. Among them are the date palms, both cultivated and wild, also *Colutea istria, Thymelaea hirsuta, Juncus maritimus* and *Scirpus holoschoenus.* Rope is produced in the same way as it was made thousands of years ago, as has been shown by archaeological excavations in Israel and Egypt.—Some species of *Phagnalon* supply the Bedouin with a wool-like material. This they use to light fires, using a flint and steel to strike the spark.

MANGROVE FORESTS   In estuaries and coastal plains in tropical latitudes the mangrove forests form a type of vegetation of their own. In the southern part of the Gulf of Elat-'Aqaba, mangrove forests of *Avicennia marina* occur. The water absorbed by the trees from the muddy sea-bottom has a reduced amount of salinity because the root-tissues prevent the penetration of most of the salts. The salt that does succeed in penetrating the plant is excreted again through special glands in the leaves. The lack of oxygen caused by the fact that the mangroves have their roots in the muddy silt is compensated for by the pneumatophores (respiratory or air-roots), which grow from the sea-floor to far above the surface of the water. Air enters the plant's aeration system through lenticles on the bark of these roots.

ANIMAL HUSBANDRY   The Bedouin breed mainly goats, which supply them with milk, meat, skins and goat hair. The desert breed of goat has a marked degree of resistance to high temperatures and drought conditions. Compared with the goats of the more humid areas of Israel or other Mediterranean countries it gives high yields of milk per feeding unit. The goats graze mainly on areas of permanent vegetation, as the fodder yield is relatively predictable. Certain areas where dwarf shrubs, such as the Chenopodiaceae of Gebel Egma, grow all the year round supply fodder for large herds of goats.

FRUIT TREES   On account of the great annual fluctuation in the amount of water available to plants, fruit trees can only be cultivated in places with a constant supply of water. Such places are the salty soils, where the fresh or brackish water, though deep down, is in constant supply. Date palms are cultivated in the oases of the Wadi Feiran and the Wadi Kid, along the shores of the Gulfs of Elat-'Aqaba and Suez, and along the Mediterranean shoreline. Those Bedouin who own date palms but also roam with their herds over the hills, descend to the date plantations of the coastal plains to pollinate the numerous female trees with the pollen of the few male trees growing in the area. In the neighbourhood of El'Arish date palms are the characteristic feature of the landscape. Freshwater springs supply the water necessary for the trees growing in the smaller plantations of southern Sinai. Near St. Catherine's Monastery, and even in remote valleys, there are small plantations of peaches, almonds, plums, apples, quinces, grapes, olives, figs and carobs. Seasonal vegetables are cultivated in small plots between the trees. Many of the various kinds of trees were introduced into Sinai by the monks of St. Catherine's Monastery hundreds of years ago. A similar diversity of cultivation is met with in northern Sinai, where the abundant water of the springs of 'Ain el Gedeirat is used for the successful irrigation of olive groves, interspersed with beds of seasonal vegetables.

VEGETABLES AND MELONS   The intensive cultivation of vegetables is typical for the coastal area north of El'Arish. Here, ground-water is found at depths of 2–3 m (6–10 ft) and the farmers uncover the loess soil buried by the sand to grow tomatoes and cucumbers on it. They use the advanced agrotechnique of covering the plants with polyethylene sheeting in the cold season and as a result are able to market considerable quantities of vegetables at high prices.

A considerable area of the Mediterranean coastal sands is planted with water-melons in years when at least 30 mm (just over 1 inch) of rain has fallen

WHEAT AND BARLEY   Extensive *wadis* in central and northern Sinai are still today culivated by farmers using the same system of irrigation as was practised by their forefathers. For this purpose a series of dams are constructed diagonally across the watercourse. The water percolates into the ploughed soil and winter crops of wheat and barley are sown after a heavy fall of rain. This method is used even in places with an annual rainfall of only 50 mm (2 inches). When the floods are late in coming and a sufficient amount of ground-water can be expected to remain in the soil during the summer, crops of millet and sunflowers are planted.

Avinoam Danin

Fig. 11: *Helianthemum kahiricum*
(after A. Raffeneau-Delile: Flore d'Egypte, 1813).

43 The mining temple of Serabit el Khadim yielded many representations of the Egyptian goddess Hathor, known in Sinai as the "Lady of the Turquoise Land": here she is also the goddess of mining. She is represented as a cow, with cow's ears or with cow's horns.

44 The goddess Hathor in the shape of a cow, wearing her customary neck ornaments and a *menat*, a ritual object. Discovered at Serabit el Khadim by Beno Rothenberg in 1957.

45 A stela of the XIX—XX Dynasty at Serabit el Khadim. It shows a king offering two small vases to a deity (on the right-hand side of the relief, now missing). Behind him stands a female figure wearing some of the emblems of the goddess Hathor: sun disc, uraeus and a sistrum (rattle) in each hand.

46 The ruins of the temple of Serabit el Khadim.

47 The ancient road to the temple of Serabit el Khadim, high up on a rounded mountain top, climbs up the steep cliff. At one point on this road—called Rud el 'Air (Valley of Donkeys)—numerous hieroglyphic inscriptions and drawings of the Middle and New Kingdoms have been cut into the rock faces.

48 One of the many pictorial representations of ships in the Rud el 'Air. This is a New Kingdom passenger vessel with cabin, rudder, and sails which are furled and tied with ropes.

49 The thistle *Echinops glaberrimus* thrives even in the driest regions of the Sinai desert.

50 Gebel Serbal, seen from the Wadi Feiran. This is one of the most impressive landscapes in southern Sinai. Gebel Serbal has been regarded by some Sinai scholars as the Mount of God, where the Lord spoke to Moses.

51 Evening sun on the Wadi Maghara, the location of the turquoise mines.

44

45

49

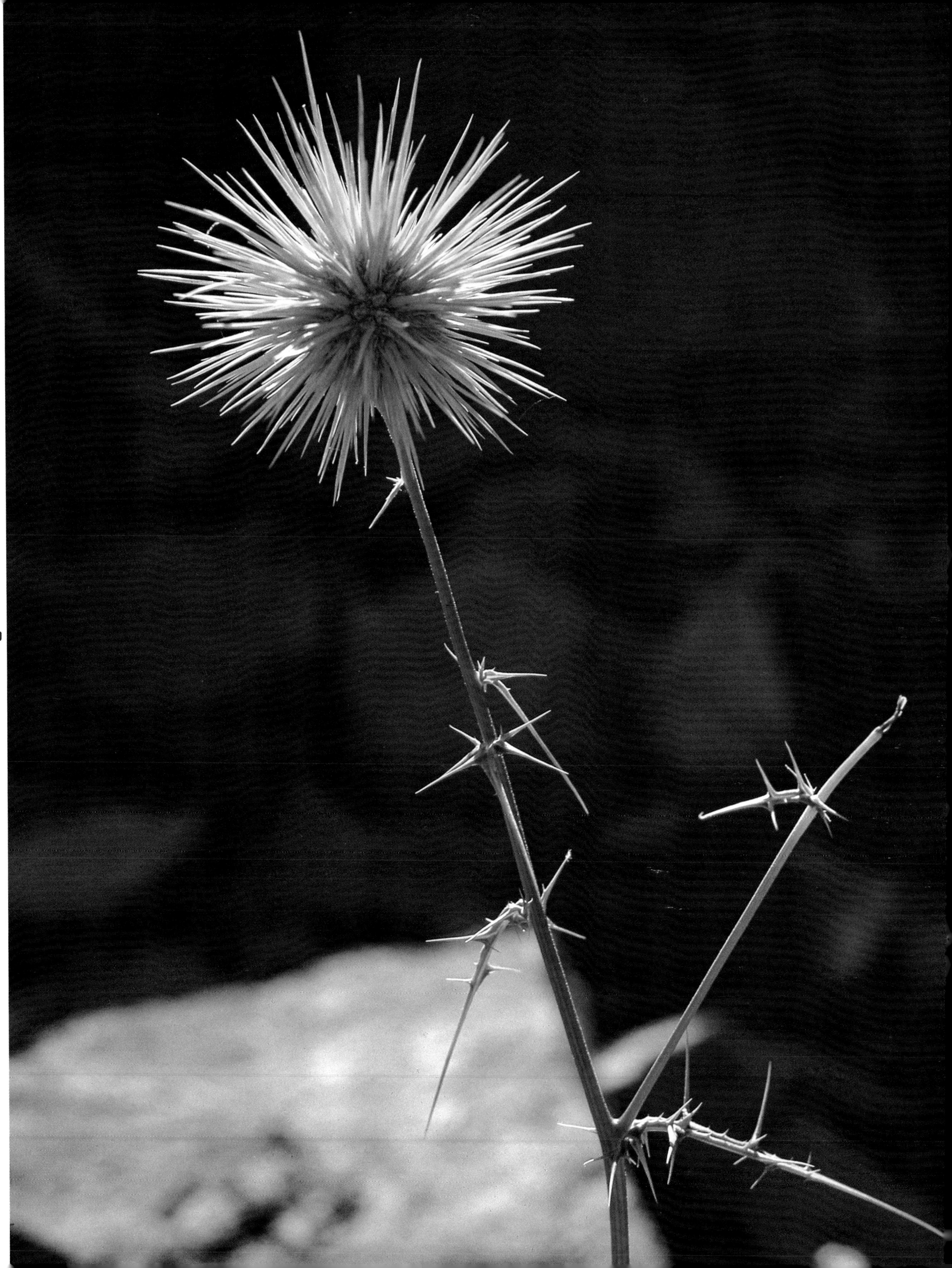

The Fauna
Meeting Point of Two Continents

The Middle East—the striking meeting-point of continents—is an area where several zoogeographical zones overlap, a living monument to a fascinating animal history. However, it is the Sinai peninsula which, in the course of history as well as during the whole of the Quaternary period, was the only land bridge between Africa and Asia.

Anyone crossing the gorges and *wadi* streams of Sinai, or exploring the neighbourhood of St. Catherine's Monastery, will be amazed to find himself surrounded by brilliant sunbirds, beautiful Tristram's grackles, chattering bulbuls and, here and there on a steep rock face, a group of rock hyraxes—all species that are typical of the tropics. In fact, their original habitat was Africa. Yet it is the circumstance that other kinds of animals, such as the rock partridge and the rock pigeon, foxes and wolves, and in particular the dormouse, all of which originally came from the northern Palaearctic region, now live in peaceful harmony side by side with the African elements that makes the animal scene so incredible and so difficult to explain.

In order better to understand the exceptional features of the Sinai fauna, it may be advisable to consider more in detail the history of the area. Towards the end of the Miocene period, some 12 million years ago, dynamic geological movements caused a world-wide change in the topography. One result was that the ancient connection between the Tethys Sea and the Pacific Ocean across central and northern Asia was broken. A global desiccation process followed and the southern part of the Middle East became an arid zone. This phenomenon affected virtually the same latitutes all round the globe, creating the "Northern Desert Belt" or, in the Old World, the "Southern Palaearctic Desert Belt".

Whereas there had been a lively exchange of the fauna between Africa and the Middle East before the Miocene crisis, the exchange of terrestrial animals or freshwater creatures between Europe and Asia was no longer possible after the Miocene. The Tethys Sea lay between them, separating the two regions. During that period, Sinai and the rest of the Middle East were integral parts of tropical Africa. However, following upon the regression of the Tethys Sea as a result of subsequent geological changes, the gateway to the north was suddenly wide open. At the same time, however, the developing desert belt was steadily erecting barriers between Africa and the Levant. Thus, animals associated with freshwater habitats were the first to be isolated from their relatives in the tropics. In the case of the terrestrial fauna, the desert belt did not become an effective barrier until somewhat later. This isolation of the fauna eventually resulted in endemism. Indeed, typical forms of the sunbird *(Cinnyris osaea)*, Tristram's grackle *(Onychognathus tristrami)* and the rock hyrax *(Procaria syriaca)* developed in Sinai and other parts of the Levant. The xerotropic forms, better able to resist aridity, kept up their links with tropical Africa until a considerably later period. Leopards, caracal lynxes *(Lynx caracal)* and honey badgers *(Mellivora ratel)* are only a few instances of animals which still have close relatives in Africa south of the Sahara.

The rapid desiccation process, intensified with time, forced the fauna that was left within the desert zone to undergo rapid adaptation to the arid environment. On the other hand, it was now possible for species whose original home was in the northern regions to immigrate unhindered to the Levant and North Africa, partly replacing the older African animals, but sometimes successfully coexisting with them in the same habitats. Thus the fauna from the north and from the south met and mingled in the remote desert of Sinai to form a new and bizarre union.

GAME ANIMALS AND OSTRICHES   Visitors to Sinai should not expect to find large numbers of game animals. Not only does the extreme barrenness of the land and its aridity preclude the existence of a wide range of large species, but the introduction of the rifle and the shotgun to this region a few generations ago has caused a drastic reduction in game animals. But even before then, sophisticated methods of trapping had kept populations at a low level. Ostriches, for example, still roamed the plains of northern Sinai in the last century. Until fairly recently their skins were sold in the markets of Damascus and Beer-Sheba and ostrich-eggs are still often found in the plains and dunes of Sinai.

ARTIODACTYLS The only representatives of artiodactyls (even-toed ungulates) are gazelles and ibexes, now confined to certain places in remote areas. The Dorcas gazelle *(Gazella dorcas)*, like most antelopes, is an animal of the open plains. Its general distribution is wide and covers the arid regions of Syria, Israel, Sinai, Arabia, North Africa, Sudan and Ethiopia. The Dorcas gazelle has a very graceful body and is characterized, like many other desert animals, by conspicuously large ears, presumably to enhance their sense of hearing. Its ground-colour is a pale fawn, and this, together with the white stripe running down each side of the forehead and the bridge of the nose makes it almost invisible when it is standing still. For an Asiatic gazelle it is on the small side, with a height of 60 cm (24 inches) and a length of 1.20 m (4 ft). The horns are relatively long and lyre-shaped. They thrive quite astonishingly in extremely arid areas, presumbably having no need for a regular intake of water. The Dorcas gazelle can survive even the hardest conditions on a diet consisting of practically nothing but acacia leaves, especially during the long hot summer months.

Little is known about its reproductive behaviour. Like most other gazelles, however, it is essentially a gregarious animal with more or less territorial males. The individual territories are marked out by scent, first by urination and then by defaecation at fixed places. Apart from man—its main chief enemy—the only predator of gazelles in Sinai is the wolf and, to a lesser extent, the striped hyaena. However, the merely sporadic distribution of the Dorcas gazelle at the present time can hardly support even small packs of predators.

The Nubian ibex *(Capra ibex nubiana)*, together with the hyrax, dominates the rocky regions and steep precipices of the scarcely accessible mountains of southern Sinai. Its numbers have been declining steadily and alarmingly during this century, owing to incessant hunting, so that its survival was for a time in very real danger. In recent years, however, the protection and preservation of the ibex by the authorities has already yielded positive results and at the present moment (1979) their number is again gradually increasing.

No other animal is so perfectly adapted to the menacing rocky country; it is almost as if it were an integral part of it. There is no experience comparable to watching a herd of Nubian ibexes moving along a scarcely visible track clinging to an almost vertical precipice—a picture of supreme agility, pride and apparent invulnerability. The herd is often led by a long-bearded old male with imposing horns curved like an oriental scimitar, followed by the females and the young animals, with smaller horns, trotting slowly in single file along the dangerous mountain tracks. The recurved horns of an adult male may attain a length of 80 cm (32 inches) with a distance of 50 cm (20 inches) between the tips.

The Nubian ibex has always been the best-known animal in the Arabian desert. It was glorified and sometimes even worshipped. From prehistoric times onwards, it was repeatedly drawn and carved on the desert rocks. It can hardly have been of any economic importance, but a great deal of symbolism, superstition and ritual has always attached to it.

Ibexes require a daily drink. During the long dry season they therefore keep within range of springs. During the winter, when pools are more plentiful, they may roam over greater distances. Apart from man, who has always threatened its survival, its only natural enemy that was equally well adapted to its inaccessible and forbidding terrain was the leopard. Unfortunately, the last leopard was killed in 1942 near Gebel Serbal in southern Sinai. Its stuffed body is preserved for posterity in the Cairo Museum. Leopards are, however, occasionally seen in the Jordan Valley, and in gorges around the Dead Sea.

FOXES The red fox *(Vulpes vulpes)* is by no means the most common predator. This handsome animal is frequently seen near Bedouin and army camps, or sniffing around garbage heaps, where it seeks out practically any kind of discarded food. Otherwise, all kinds of rodents, rabbits and birds may fall easy prey to it. Foxes may occasionally be seen during daytime, fascinating people with their rufous bushy tail, its tip conspicuously white, and with their thick, soft, wolly, reddish coats. Their long ears, big eyes and long pointed muzzle give them a knowing look. While the red fox is found in almost any kind of terrain, a close relative, Rüppell's sand-fox *(Vulpes ruppelli)* is almost entirely confined to sandy regions. More shy and less common, Rüppell's sand-fox rarely ventures near human civilization and avoids the proximity of man. This fox has more elegant and delicate body proportions, still longer ears and a bushier coat—an aesthetic contribution to the otherwise bare landscape of the shifting dunes.

No one will dispute that the fennec *(Fennecus zerda)*, another relative of the red fox, is one of the most beautiful of all living mammals. One of these rare animals, with still larger ears and an even more graceful body, a longer and bushier tail, and even finer and softer coat, was recently caught in western Sinai. It is a typical representative of the Sahara, rarely found or observed, so that its habits are largely unknown. Insects and rodents probably constitute its main diet, and these are never in short supply in Sinai.

HYAENAS AND WOLVES The striped hyaena *(Hyaena hyaena)* is undoubtedly a most impressive carnivore; together with the wolf *(Canis lupus)* it is the largest predator in Sinai. As a typical scavenger, the hyaena, although it may occasionally kill its prey itself, has strongly developed carnassial teeth, capable of crushing the hardest bones to extract the marrow. Its enormous strength, its rather disgusting habits, its curious gait (its forelegs are longer than its hindlegs), but especially its horrible unearthly cry, like demoniac laughter, were probably the main reason for the wealth of Arab legends attaching to this animal. It is a target of aversion, superstition and hatred. Yet there is no evidence of its ever having attacked livestock or human beings. On the other hand, the lo-

cal Bedouin often report that herds have been attacked by wolves. Being more dependent on animals for food, the wolf is the shepherd's enemy. Unlike the striped hyaena, which often leads a solitary life, the wolf is more gregarious and is often seen in packs. In much the same way as the hunting dogs and the spotted hyaenas of East Africa, wolves are capable of skilfully co-ordinating their attacks on livestock.

RODENTS Of all the mammals living in the desert, the rodents are certainly the most successful and flourishing group. Capable of exploiting all possible biological and ecological factors, they occupy virtually every possible habitat. Of all the desert rodents, the most fascinating are undeniably the jerboas. The most common is the lesser jerboa *(Jaculus jaculus)*. It measures 35 cm (14 inches) from the tip of its snout to the tip of its tail. With its greatly developed three-toed hind feet, it can jump several metres at a single bound with ease, its long tail, ending in a tuft, acting as a counterweight and aid to balance. Its tiny forepaws are used to pick up and hold its food, mainly seeds. Very common in the plains of Sinai, jerboas are often trapped in the headlights of moving cars and run over. Being nocturnal animals, they spend the day sleeping in burrows, the openings of which are closed and camouflaged with a plug of earth.

BIRDS The birdlife of Sinai is amazingly rich and has always attracted ornithologists, who observe and study the biology of the various species. In a short list of the most significant birds, the first will naturally be the vulture *(Gyps fulvus)*. This huge bird may fly over 100 km (60 miles) a day at a great height, in order to find sufficient evil-smelling carrion. Tristram's grackle *(Onychognathus tristrami)* and the brown-necked raven *(Corvus ruficollis)* are the predominant forms of life in the deep gorges near St. Catherine's Monastery. It is impossible not to become aware of the aggressive behaviour of the wheatear *(Oenanthe spp.)*. Its contrasting black-and-white colouring, which is very conspicuous when the bird is in flight, makes it absolutely invisible when it is

Fig. 12: The rock hyrax, *Procavia syriaca* (after H. B. Tristram: Fauna and Flora of Palestine, 1884).

standing still. With a display of impressive behaviour, the male tries to keep away everything and everybody from its well-defined and jealously guarded territory. The beautiful scarlet and pink colouring of the Sinai rosefinch *(Carpodacus sinoicus)* and the uniformly pale-pink colour of the trumpeter bullfinch *(Rhodopechys githaginea)* brighten even the most desolate rocky regions of Sinai. Both these finches may be seen regularly at sunset flying, sometimes over quite long distances, for their daily drink at a spring. Along the Gulf of Elat-'Aqaba, the reef heron *(Egretta gullaris)* nests in small colonies on the mangrove trees. It feeds on sea fish. In the same region, but especially on the small island of Tiran, colonies of osprey *(Pandion haliaetus)* have found refuge and protection. Everywhere else this magnificent bird has been brought to the verge of extinction. It is a most impressive sight to watch one of these big birds of prey fishing in such an experienced way, with faultless perfection and agility.

Yet it is the stirring beauty of the migration of birds in Sinai that surpasses all else. Sinai is a corridor for the passage of an incredible multitude of Palaearctic migrants en route for Africa in autumn and returning to the north again in spring. In northern Sinai a host of migrating water fowl may be observed immediately after their flight over the Mediterranean. This is also the region where, before the Second World War, the famous quails *(Coturnix coturnix)* were netted by the million and shipped back to Europe to be served to diners in high-class restaurants. It is this bird which, according to the Bible, was sent to feed the tribes of Israel thousands of years ago when they were crossing the desert of Sinai on their way to the Promised Land.

During the migratory period, the sky is sometimes full of birds of prey and storks on their way to Africa, while the *wadi* streams are alive with small European passerines, the sparrow-like songsters. This scene is in marked contrast to the otherwise peaceful and dormant landscape. It seems as if the desert has momentarily wakened to new life, only to relapse again into its usual dreamy state until the next period of migration.

Fig. 13: *Coturnix coturnix,* the biblical quail of Sinai (after W. A. Bartlett, 1848).

REPTILES   No less than six species of venomous snakes are found in Sinai. Most common are two species of sand viper: the smaller one *(Cerastes vipera)* is found above all in the northern and western parts of the peninsula, while the larger one *(Cerastes cerastes)* lives in the eastern part. Both are well adapted to life in the dry, shifting dunes, and both are capable of "side-winding"—an exceptional form of progression for a snake. It advances by throwing its body into loops, one after the other, sideways from the longitudinal axis of the body, with great speed and agility, leaving a broken trail in the sand. When discovered, both species can hide in the sand by means of a powerful wave-like motion along their sides, allowing them to sink rapidly beneath the surface of the sand, leaving only their eyes and the tips of their snouts visible. This kind of burrowing is vital in a terrain without protection or places to hide. In this way the snakes become practically invisible and can lie in wait patiently for their prey (rodents, lizards, insects). The bite of these two species of snake is poisonous, but not necessarily fatal.

The Palestinian horned viper *(Pseudocerastes)* is a relative of the two sand vipers, but lives in a much wilder or even rocky terrain. Like the two species of sand viper, the much longer horned viper is capable of producing threatening noises by rubbing its body-scales against

Fig. 14: From top to bottom: *Zootoca tristrami, Trapelus sinaiticus, Seps monodactylus* (after H. B. Tristram: Fauna and Flora of Palestine, 1884).

99

each other. The carpet viper *(Echis colorata)*, which is mentioned in the Bible, is an agile and rather colourful snake, always on the alert, often active in broad daylight and therefore more often seen—generally in rocky tracts. Its bite is fatal. Another poisonous snake, but one of much smaller size, is the burrowing black mole viper *(Atractaspis engaddensis)*. It belongs to a group of snakes that is typical of tropical Africa, with a short head and no neck. It is rarely observed or encountered.

There is only one poisonous snake belonging to the cobra group in Sinai, namely the desert cobra *(Walterinesia aegyptia)* which attains a length of 1.5 m (5 ft). It has no hood and does not spit its poison at its victim as do some of the more famous African and Indian species. It is nevertheless very dangerous, but fortunately it is rare. It is a nocturnal creature and feeds on rodents and lizards, which it searches out in their own burrows.

The two largest lizards of the Middle East are both found in Sinai. Both inhabit open plains and sandy regions, and as a rule they both hide in spacious burrows, which have the appearance of caves or dens. One of them, the desert monitor *(Varanus griseus)*, may attain a length of 1.2 m (4 ft), half of it accounted for by the tail, which it uses as a powerful and effective whip when cornered. The other giant lizard is the Egyptian spring-tailed agama *(Uromastix aegyptius)* which may grow to a length of 90 cm (3 ft). It has an impressively thick and relatively short tail, armoured with hard spiny scales arranged in rings. These spiked whorls provide the non-aggressive, sluggish lizard with its principal means of defence. A few blows from this heavy spiked club, wielded violently from side to side, will discourage most enemies. We cannot leave the reptiles without having mentioned

Fig. 15: Camel caravan in the Wadi Useit (after W. A. Bartlett, 1848).

one of the most beautifully patterned desert lizards. This is yet another kind of spiny-tailed agama *(Uromastix acanthinurus)*; a much smaller, fatter and flat African lizard (40 cm, or 16 inches in length). Its whole body is adorned with pink and red stripes—striking colours, unusual for a creature of the desert. Its habitat is exclusively the metamorphic massif of southern Sinai and the Red Sea coast, so that this colouring provides perfect camouflage among the brightly coloured rocks.

With this exotic lizard we may conclude our brief survey of the Sinai fauna. Although many of the above-mentioned species may not be seen at first glance, with comparatively little effort a magnificent world of dynamic desert life will open up to the observant eye: a dramatic meeting between Palaearctic and African forms of life in a harmonious ecosystem, offering a wealth of material for study and enjoyment to both the naturalist and the aesthete.

Eitan Tchernov

52 Bedouin girl in the Wadi Sidri.

53 The Wadi Mukattab ("Wadi of Inscriptions") links the ancient main road in the Wadi Feiran with the turquoise mining region in the Wadi Maghara. On the rock faces of the Wadi Mukattab there are thousands of rock carvings and inscriptions in a variety of languages and scripts. The picture shows a rock with Nabataean inscriptions and representations of warriors mounted on horses, donkeys and camels.

54 Greek was the everyday colloquial language in the Levant until the late Byzantine period. Christian pilgrims passing along this road usually immortalized themselves in Greek.

55 Visitors leave their "inscriptions" in the Wadi Mukattab to this day. This one reads: "Israel's defence army, Israel, 1956". It was cut into the rock in Hebrew during the Sinai campaign of 1956.

56 A Latin votive inscription dedicated to Tsar Nicholas I by Russian pilgrims in the 19th century.

57 First photograph of an Egyptian rock carving from the time of the Old Kingdom, discovered in 1868 by the Englishman E. H. Palmer. The picture contains three representations of the Third Dynasty Pharaoh Sechemchet (2600–2595 B.C.). On the left, the royal figure is striking a kneeling Asiatic with a club; above, the Pharaoh's name is inscribed within a *serekh* frame, on which stands the god Horus in the form of a falcon. The central figure wears the royal crown of Lower Egypt, the one on the right that of Upper Egypt. The fourth figure, a little lower towards the right, is identified by a hieroglyphic inscription: "The prince, commander of the expedition".

58 A picture typical of southern Sinai: an old acacia *(Acacia raddiana)* upon which a folded Bedouin tent has been hung. It is an unwritten Bedouin law that property left behind in this way is not stolen.

59 The native species of mullein *(Verbascum sinaiticum)* is frequently found in Sinai.

◁53 54

55 56

ΙΩΑΣΑΦ
ΡΟΔΙΟΣ

עתר נחשון ישראל
1956
68

Nicolaum

Badiet el Tih, the Desert of Wandering

Archaeology of Central Sinai

PREHISTORIC REMAINS MAKE HISTORY   There is probably no place where human existence and its history over thousands of years can be traced more conclusively as a function of natural conditions than the Sinai peninsula. Man cannot live without water; without cultivable soil and a minimum of irrigation there is no food for permanent settlers; and where the earth's crust is deeply furrowed by geological events and by rain and floodwater, considerable obstacles are even placed in the way of locomotion. But these are precisely the conditions prevailing in many parts of the Sinai peninsula as soon as one leaves the narrow, relatively fertile, Mediterranean coastal strip, the northern edge of the Sinai peninsula, in order to move southwards. This land bridge between Africa and Asia, densely inhabited since earliest times, has always had its own history—either as a part of Egypt or as a stage of the political and historical events of the settlement of the Levant. Leaving the coast, one first reaches high, shifting sand dunes and then, slowly rising towards the south, the plateau of northern and central Sinai, the "great and terrible wilderness" (Deuteronomy 8: 15), whose seemingly endless vastness is dominated by the huge dry river system of the Wadi el 'Arish. Viewed from the north towards the south, the Wadi el 'Arish represents a greatly ramified tree, whose far-reaching and increasingly thin branches and branchlets originate high up at the southern end of the Tih plateau, the Badiet el Tih, and reach out far towards the west and the east, while the mighty stem runs into the Mediterranean at El 'Arish.

But the emptiness of this virtually treeless plateau is deceptive: the vast flat regions at the centre of the plateau, covered with *loess* and *hammada*, may indeed be exceedingly poor in ancient remains, and to this day there is little human life to be found there, but now and again an unexpected "water hole" is encountered, a cistern dug into the *wadi* floor or a well hewn out of the white limestone. Around these there are slight traces of seasonal camps—and frequently also archaeological surprises. Amidst the refuse of Bedouin homes and the dung-pats and droppings of camels and goats, some ancient masonry may be found, a few prehistoric flint implements, some ancient potsherds and occasionally even a stone-built hearth still showing traces of charcoal or ash. It is these occasional remains that write history in the desert.

THE "GREAT AND TERRIBLE WILDERNESS" WAS NEVERTHELESS INHABITED   From the vast arid plain at the northern end of the Tih plateau rise a number of dome-shaped mountain formations. Gebel Halal, about 50 km (30 miles) south of El 'Arish, seems an insignificant elevation from afar—yet when one suddenly finds oneself in front of that ridge that rises to roughly 900 m (3,000 ft) it is a majestic sight. This mountain, regarded by the supporters of the new "northern theory" of the Exodus from Egypt as the mountain of the theophany, was first briefly investigated by the author in 1957.[1] Erosion has hollowed out a large crater in the mountain formation and there, but also in the more immediate neighbourhood of the mountain, we found 16 cisterns of varying types and undoubtedly varying antiquity, as well as numerous remains of human habitation and graves. At the very entrance to the crater there is a large settlement of Early Bronze Age IV and on the slopes within the crater, between remains of masonry, we found a large number of flint tools from various phases of the Upper Palaeolithic and of the Neolithic, potsherds from Early Bronze Age IV, as well as fragments of hand-made Early Iron Age cooking-pots. Between them were Nabataean and Romano-Byzantine fragments and the typical "Ghaza pottery" of the Bedouin.

Extensive terraced—now fallow—fields around Gebel Halal date mainly from Romano-Byzantine times, but from time to time the Bedouin have rebuilt the ancient terraces with shrubs and soil and have cultivated the fields again. Nowadays the boundaries of the fields are marked by barbed wire at chest height—a strange sight in this desolate wilderness and distinctly unpleasant in the dark.

Gebel el Maghara, west of Gebel Halal and considerably larger, has been extensively investigated by O. Bar-Joseph during the past few years.[2] These researches

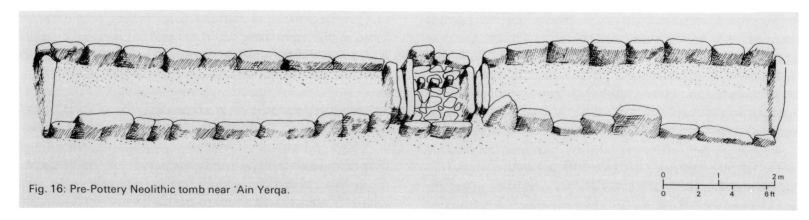

Fig. 16: Pre-Pottery Neolithic tomb near 'Ain Yerqa.

have produced important data demonstrating the direct dependence of the possibility of human settlement on environmental conditions, as well as contributing to the further understanding of the relations of the early inhabitants of Sinai with North Africa in the west, and with the Levant and the Arabian Peninsula in the north and east. Whenever the climate was more humid, as during the Palaeolithic and Epi-Palaeolithic Ages, from approximately 35,000 B.C. until about 7,000 B.C., and then again in the Pre-Pottery Neolithic Age, from 7,000 to 5,500 B.C., human settlements existed in the valleys, on the slopes and in the craters of Gebel el Maghara—but during the dry periods the region was absolutely devoid of people.

Upper and Epi-Palaeolithic stations and remains of settlements of the Pre-Pottery Neolithic Age were also discovered by our expedition in many parts of northern, central and southern Sinai—both in the west, in the immediate neighbourhood of the Suez Canal and on the well-watered edge of the Tih plateau, and in the east, on the boundary of the Negev and beyond that boundary deep into the Negev.

Particularly large and important concentrations of settlements of the Pre-Pottery Neolithic B Age were found by the author around the flint deposits at the southern end of the Tih plateau. As in later periods, good flint was an article of trade and everyday use, much in demand, and it attracted settlers from a long way off, who then developed flint industries locally.

In the neighbourhood of sources of water, especially on the high mountains at the western edge of the Badiet el Tih there are, in addition to centres of settlement, also central burial grounds, frequently extending over many square miles. In these burial grounds there are various types of tombs from different periods and the author succeeded in identifying the burial-type of the Pre-Pottery Neolithic Age. These Neolithic tombs are stone structures approximately 50–80 m (165–260 ft) long and about 1.5 m (5 ft) wide. Excavations by our expedition have proved that these are narrow burial chambers built alongside one another, whose "walls" are stone slabs placed on edge and covered with large flat stones. This creates the impression of long and straight walls.

Above 'Ain Yerqa, at the southern end of the Tih, the author's expedition disovered numerous "wall tombs" and one of them, 75 m (246 ft) long, was partially excavated. In it, decomposed human bones were found. At the foot of the burial ground hill, a number of irregular stone walls and typical flint implements indicate a Pre-Pottery Neolithic settlement area, and there, slightly apart, was a "wall" structure only 12 m (39 ft) in length. This we excavated and it was revealed to be a Neolithic cultic structure (Fig. 16).

Between two chambers approximately 5 to 6 m (16 to 20 ft) long and approximately 1 m wide, constructed of stone slabs placed on edge, was a small, almost square chamber, 1.4 x 1.2 m (4.5 x 4 ft), constructed of long massive stone slabs, with its floor carefully laid with small stone slabs. Into this floor, three small square-cut "stelae" were fitted and around them, as around the entire cultic chamber, there were clear traces of fire. Here, as well as in the lateral chambers, a large number of particularly beautifully worked flint implements were found. This is clearly a Neolithic cultic site, so far unparalleled elsewhere, possibly the shrine of a cult of the dead.

Aerial photographs of the east of the Arabian peninsula, published in 1973,[3] reveal graves which are absolutely identical in type with the graves of the great central burial grounds in Sinai. The long "wall tombs", which there, too, stand among the other types, testify to the direction and scale of the distribution of the Pre-Pottery Neolithic and to the close links between Neolithic Sinai and the great desert of the Arabian Peninsula. The earliest Stone Age remains are as a rule no more than "stations" i.e. the meagre remains of hearths with flint tools and flakes. The remains of bones and ostrich-egg shells indicate that hunting was the main occupation of the Upper Palaeolithic inhabitants. Later, during the Neolithic Age, low irregular, roughly circular, stone enclosures were erected, some of which may still be found in quite a good state of preservation.

The Upper Palaeolithic settlers probably came from the north-east of the Levant, but during the Epi-Palaeolithic Age there were also links with North Africa and the Nile Valley. During the Pre-Pottery Neolithic, Sinai, together with the Negev and the north of the Arabian Peninsula, were part of the cultural sphere of the Levant.

It is still rather difficult, at the present stage of research, to fit the early Stone Age developments in northern Sinai into a coherent picture of population movements, invasions and retreats, trade and barter, hunting, livestock raising and the beginnings of farming, in other words to link up the region with the early history of Egypt, the Levant and the Arabian Peninsula. It is certain , however, that at that early period northern and central Sinai was not merely a transit area, a bridge between Asia and Africa, but that it had its own indigenous inhabitants, who developed flint industries there and built their own

cultic buildings. Moreover, northern and central Sinai had, since the earliest days, been a much-frequented hunting area for tribes from adjacent regions.

From the middle of the 5th millenium B.C. there existed in northern and central Sinai two major cultural periods with an indigenous population, the remains of whose numerous settlements have been found at many water holes of the Tih plateau and above all along its well-watered edges—the Elat Culture (Elatian) and the Timna Culture (Timnian).

ELATIAN The earliest Copper Age settlements, those of the Elatian, about 4,500–3,500 B.C., were concentrated principally in central Sinai. Large clusters of small Elatian settlements—possibly family groupings—have been found both on the eastern side of the Tih plateau and on its well-watered western edge (with a perceptible "gap" in the totally arid centre of the Tih), emerging again around the outcropping flint deposits at the southern end of Gebel Egma. These deposits of good-quality flint, outcropping in thin tabular layers from the limestone of Gebel Egma, had been mined, as mentioned earlier, at various prehistoric periods; during the Elatian period, however, they were the destination of quite extensive population movements. The Elatian settlements along the way from northern Sinai to the flint deposits of Gebel Egma clearly indicate a much-travelled "flint route". Below Naqb Biyar, along the serpentine path leading down the steep Egma scarp into the large Wadi Zeleqa, extensive Elatian settlements and flint workshops have also been found; from there they extend a long way down towards the south.

The architecture of the Elatian period is primitive: in most cases it consists of strings or clusters of "semi-detached" near-circular enclosures, a kind of courtyard for man and beast, often with small chambers adjoining outside. The Elatian period, roughly from the middle of the 5th millenium B.C., marks the beginning of the Early Chalcolithic Age in Sinai and can be attested right through to its late phase. Its flint industry, of a type found only in Sinai—large crude implements of "Levallois"

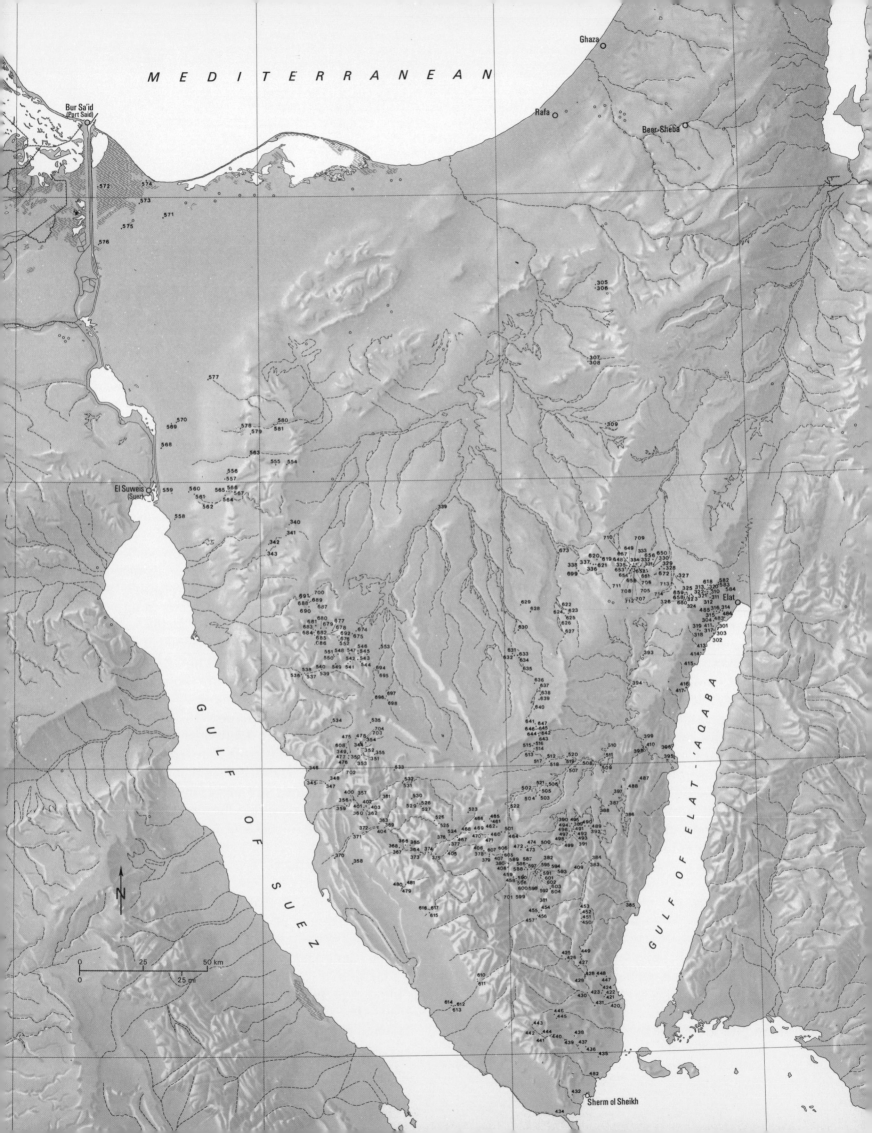

◁ Map of the archaeological survey of the Sinai peninsula 1967/78 by Professor Dr. B. Rothenberg's expedition. The map shows the scatter of ancient settlements, the vacuum at the centre of the waterless Tih desert, as well as the concentration of settlements in the regions of turquoise and copper ore deposits and of traditional biblical sites near sources of water, grazing areas and ancient desert roads.

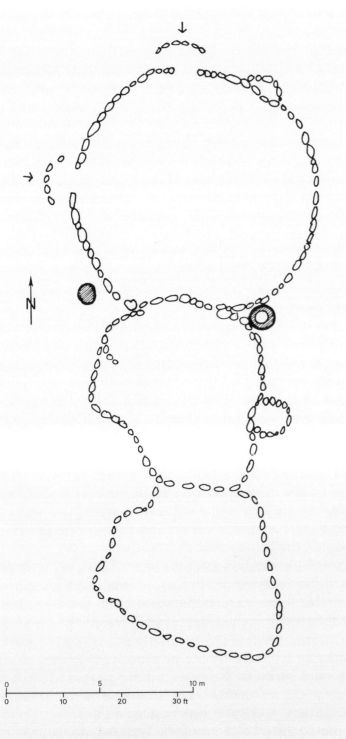

Fig. 17: Site N. 680 of the Elatian period.

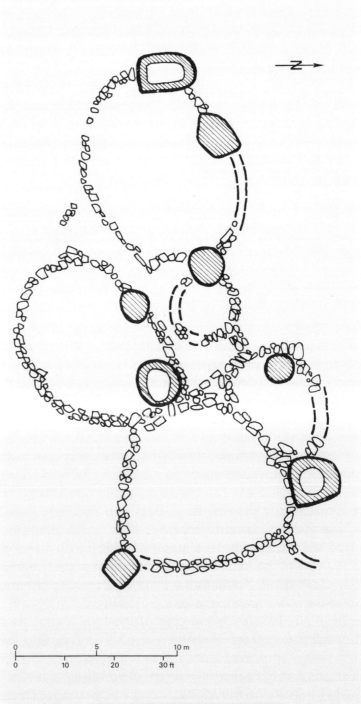

Fig. 18: Site N. 635 of the Elatian period.

tradition and tabular scrapers—testifies to connections both with Egypt's "Peasant Neolithic" and, especially with the appearance of axes, with the Ghassulian Late Chalcolithic of Palestine. We assume that the settlers of the Elatian period originally immigrated from the Arabian Peninsula.

The "Elatians" were semi-nomads, shepherds and flint workers, though occasionally they also cultivated flat *wadi* floors, where enough moisture was stored up from the winter floods. Sickle blades and flint hoes, found at a few Elatian sites on the Tih plateau, testify to crop farming.

TIMNIAN   During the period from about 3,500 B.C. until the middle of the 3rd millenium B.C. the Sinai peninsula was densely populated, and these settlers developed their own native culture. Named after the site first discovered, in the Timna Valley in the southern 'Araba, north of the Gulf of Elat-'Aqaba, it is characterized by its specific flint industry, pottery, architecture and metallurgy.

Admittedly, during the early period of Timnian—its Phase I—the flint industry still displays perceptible survivals of the preceding Elatian period, characterized by large and often rather crude stone implements and by marked links with southern Palestine; subsequently, the fully developed Timnian flint industry reveals clearly the influence of Egyptian and Nubian stone-working techniques with predominantly small and finely worked implements.

A considerable part of the pottery that has been found at Timnian settlements, together with locally manufactured vessels, also shows a marked kinship with the work of Egyptian potters of the Pre-dynastic and Proto-dynastic periods, while other groups of vessels, hitherto regarded by archaeologists as local products, have proved to be made of the typical clay of the Nile Valley. It is characteristic of the Timnian culture of Sinai that the clay vessels imported from Egypt were not large jars for the transport of foodstuffs, but small vessels for everyday use in kitchen and household, i. e. the belongings of local native settlers, who maintained lively trade and communications even over great distances and whose cultural characteristics can be traced from Nubia and Egypt into Sinai and which are probably also found, up to a point, further north and east. It is therefore entirely natural that archaeological finds in late Pre-dynastic and early Proto-dynastic Egypt suggest intensive contacts with the turquoise and copper mining practised by the Sinai population during the Timnian period, although there were also some connections with southern Palestine.

During the earliest phase of the Timnian culture (Timnian I) a settlement consisted of a circular or oval enclosure of undressed stone, sometimes with additional small stone structures built against it. Within these courtyard-type enclosures stood huts or tents, and it was there that the hearths were built. It is probable that the herds of goats and sheep were driven into such corral-like enclosures overnight.

In a territory such as Sinai, any cultural period extending over a thousand years was bound to witness not only substantial internal developments but also fundamental innovations, adopted from neighbouring cultural regions—especially if lively trade relations existed between them—and also, now and again, from new immigrants who brought with them different customs and practices. During the late phase (Timnian II) the structures became rectangular, with smaller structures built against the external wall. This new architecture would seem to reflect Egyptian influences such as can be traced also in the Canaanite building method of the Early Bronze Age II in southern Palestine.

The semi-nomadic way of life of the Timnian settlers did not differ greatly from that of the preceding Elatian settlers. They, too, were shepherds and cultivated grain; but by then small copper implements were being used and occasional traces are encountered of coppersmiths' work. As is shown by the numerous settlements of the Timnian period in the copper mining areas of southern Sinai and by Timnian traces in the turquoise areas, the "Timnians" were also experienced miners.

A particularly large group of Timnian settlements has been found on the eastern side of the Tih plateau, especi-

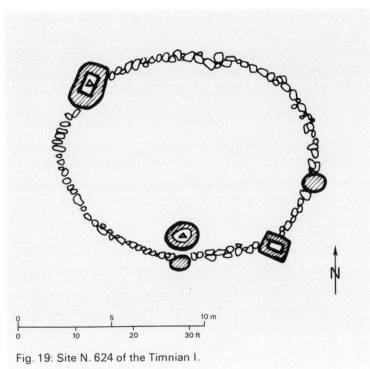

Fig. 19: Site N. 624 of the Timnian I.

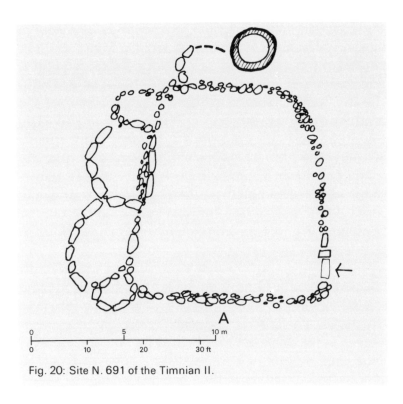

Fig. 20: Site N. 691 of the Timnian II.

ally in the area west of the Elat mountains and towards Bir el Themed, as well as along the east coast down to the far south of the peninsula. On the western side of the Tih plateau there was a further concentration of settlements, especially on the watershed between the big *wadi* system of the Wadi el 'Arish and the huge *wadis* descending towards the west coast, which are carved hundreds of feet deep into the Tih plateau and whose floors invariably contain rich sources of water. Occasionally, as for instance in the huge Wadi el Shallala, there are not only regular springs but also natural pools hollowed out of the white limestone base of the *wadi* by the turbulent rush of rain floods.

The fact that a number of typical Timnian I settlements have been found in the mountains of the Mittla and Giddi Passes and also directly on the edge of the Suez Canal, on the way from Egypt into Sinai and on the isthmus between the Gulf of Suez and the Small Bitter Lake, is of decisive importance for an understanding of the Timnian culture and of its relations with Lower Egypt. We

may take it as established that these settlements represent the link between the Timnian culture of Sinai and the contemporary population of Lower Egypt.

Viewed in a wider historical framework, Lower Egypt and the Sinai region as far east as the 'Araba, during the Timnian period, formed a homogeneous cultural zone whose inhabitants were probably identical with the nomads of Lower Egypt and the East in the early Egyptian sources, whose resistance to the "unification of the kingdom" by the rulers of Upper Egypt was for a long time a main theme of Egyptian history. During the Naqada II period of Egypt—this was the Timnian period in Sinai—there was already considerable tension between the advancing peoples from the south, the tribes of Lower Egypt (Maadi) and the Timnian settlers in Sinai. Subsequently, at the time of the early kings of the First Dynasty, there was continuous fighting as well as campaigns by the ruling dynasties against the hostile «nomads of the East», as represented, for instance, on the palette of King Narmer (see below).

The discovery of the Timnian settlements in Sinai and of their exceedingly close relations with the Maadi Culture inhabitants of Lower Egypt provides, for the first time, archaeological evidence that the repeatedly found "heroic" representation of the Egyptian kings as "the conquerors of the Asiatics" corresponds to reality. The continuous war-like clashes with the much more numerous and better armed troops of dynastic Egypt not only resulted in the "subjection of the Asiatics" but also slowly yet surely decimated the local inhabitants of Sinai. Towards the end of the Timnian period, at the time of Narmer, there were in consequence only a few Timnian II settlements left in Sinai.

"DESERT KITES"   During the early Timnian period there existed, in various parts of the Levant, mysterious stone structures, which have repeatedly been the subject of lively discussion in archaeological literature. Basically, these consist of two exceedingly long stone walls, 1–2 m (3–7 ft) high, forming in plan an open triangle at whose apex stands a tower-like building or a kind of enclosure. The first groups of these stone structures, resembling a pair of open arms, were discovered by F.L. Maitland in the Syrian desert in 1927 and on account of their shape called "desert kites". In 1959 the author found a similar pair of "kites" in the southern 'Araba, in the vicinity of the Timna Valley, and nearly thirty further "desert kites" have been recorded in central and southern Sinai by various researchers in recent years.

The "desert kites" served as traps for gazelles. Entire herds of gazelles, on their way to their water holes, were driven into that walled triangle and there killed. Such "kites" were still being used by the Bedouin for gazelle hunting until quite recently, but it had generally been assumed—without any archeological evidence at that time—that their origins went back to early prehistoric times.

The "desert kites" roused particular interest a few years ago because of an original idea proposed by Y. Yadin[4]: the famous palette of King Narmer, an almost legendary figure at the beginning of Egypt's First Dynasty, shows

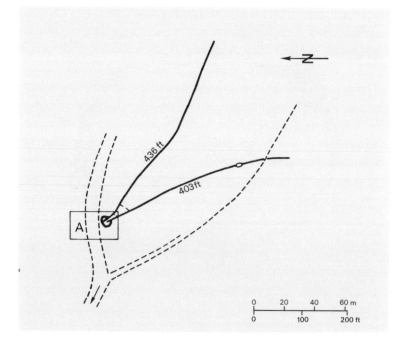

Fig. 21: "Desert kite" west of Ras el Naqb, near Elat.

a trapezoid sign as the symbol identifying a naked bearded man thrown to the ground, representing the enemies of Egypt. Yadin saw this representation as the earliest documentation of the conquest of those Asian territories east of Egypt in which the "desert kites" were found. Y. Yadin therefore proposes that the Narmer palette should be seen as the earliest record of a military campaign by King Narmer into Egypt's neighbouring regions to the east and thence further into Mesopotamia. Yadin's theory presupposes that the "desert kites" were widespread in these parts at least as early as the Egyptian First Dynasty, i.e. during the Timnian I period in Sinai and the Early Bronze Age I of Palestine.

The author's explorations in Sinai and in the 'Araba did, in fact, lead to the discovery in both regions of remains of settlements from that period, and similar settlements of that period have also been found in southern Israel.[5] The "desert kites" in the 'Araba and in Sinai are an integral part of the Timnian settlement complex. Within one of the "kite" walls our expedition discovered, a number of years ago, Timnian pottery, and throughout the vicinity numerous flint implements and sherds of that period were found. The "desert kites" should, therefore, be assigned, with a very high degree of probability, to the early phase of the Timnian culture, and it would seem that at the time, i.e. at the time of Narmer, a campaign was conducted into the areas of the "desert kites"—i.e. into Sinai, the southern 'Araba, Jordan and the Syrian desert. It is possible that this campaign by Narmer served mainly the subjection of those areas which had belonged to the cultural and settlement zone of Lower Egypt ever since the beginning of the Timnian period in Sinai, about 3500 B.C.

THE EARLIEST "CITY" IN SINAI—SITE N. 688   The ancient road from Egypt to the south of the Sinai peninsula did not run along the difficult and almost waterless western coast, but followed the above-mentioned great western watershed between the widely ramified lateral branches of the Wadi el 'Arish and the great *wadis* which are cut into the western edge of the Tih plateau. In contrast to the coast of the Gulf of Suez, which reveals scarcely any remains of settlements, or only temporary encampments of the early periods, the watershed had repeatedly been settled since earliest times.

Within a large group of lesser settlements of the Timnian period on the upper course of the Wadi el Fogeya, west of the majestic Gebel Bodhiya, lies site N. 688, which was discovered by our expedition in 1973 and probably represents one of the most important archaeological discoveries of Sinai's prehistory. Site N. 688 is a field of ruins of exceptional size for Sinai, immediately above a spring in the sandy valley floor of the Wadi Umm Gidla, a lateral branch of the great Wadi el Fogeya. It has an almost circular ground-plan, with a diameter of about 120 m (400 ft) and consists of living-quarters and enclosures closely ranged alongside each other and largely constructed of big stone slabs placed on edge. As in all Timnian settlements, we find enclosures which were erected around huts or tents. Most of the living-quarters are rectangular, while the larger enclosures often have a roughly circular shape. At the centre of many of the living-quarters, our expedition found columns constructed of round-trimmed flat stones. In this region, which lacks timber of any kind, these columns must have served as "posts" for tents or huts.

Settlement N. 688 had a simple but impressive ground-plan. Around a large semi-circular open area, reminiscent of the market or church squares at the town centres of medieval European cities, a number of buildings were erected, until the whole grouping developed into an almost circular area with streets in all directions being left clear. A rectangular building on the northern side of the open area shows a number of large stela-like stones, which lead us to assume that this was a cultic centre. It is possible that groups of unusual stone circles, built of gigantic stone slabs set around chambers cut into the rock floor, discovered on the eastern edge of the "city", also had a purely cultic function.

Many archaeological finds made at this settlement, including numerous typical Proto-dynastic potsherds and flint implements imported from Egypt, but also a great many Timnian artefacts. These finds and the architecture allow settlement N. 688 to be identified as belonging to the early phase of the Proto-dynastic period (Late Naqada II), corresponding in Sinai to Timnian I and in Palestine to the Late Chalcolithic Age or the Early Bronze Age I. It is still rather difficult to offer a sound explanation of the function of this large Egyptian settlement of the Timnian period in that location in Sinai, but it is evident that the process of urbanization, which was in full swing at that time in many parts of the ancient world, had also reached the Sinai peninsula.

The unusual buildings on the northern edge of the settlement—presumably stables, with troughs for horses or other pack animals—make it seem probable that this was a military post, possibly from the time of Narmer's operation for the subjugation of the eastern territories. If, on the other hand, this was a civilian settlement, then it reflects an unusual social pattern for the desert, one that led to the emergence of a very considerable sedentary community for such an inhospitable region—a large village or a small "city".

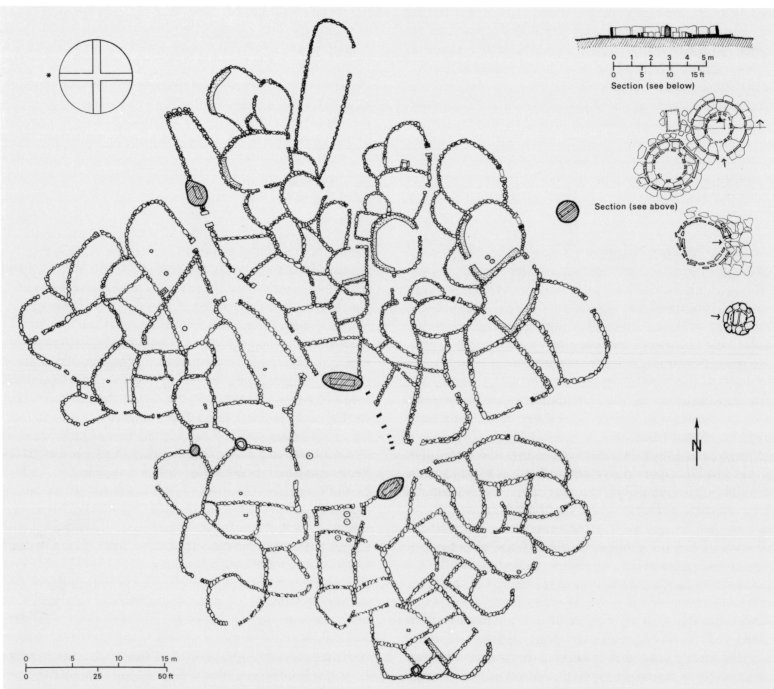

Fig. 22: Plan of the Proto-dynastic Egyptian settlement N. 688 by the spring of the Wadi el Fogeya. The four structures on the eastern side of the settlement may have been cultic shrines.

⊕ The hieroglyphic determinative for "city" shows the same diagrammatic plan as the settlements of the N. 688 type.

This "city" must have been of considerable economic and social importance. It was probably also the administrative centre for the early Egyptian settlement of central Sinai and a most important station on the caravan route from Egypt to the ore deposits of southern Sinai. Fragments of crucibles, copper melting slag and lumps of copper found at site N.688 certainly testify to such contacts with the south.

The careful layout of the "urban" settlement, N.688, is reminiscent of the hieroglyphic determinative for city ⊕ , representing a circular settlement quartered by two roads intersecting at right angles. Many archaeologists believe that this sign actually represents the diagrammatic ground-plan of an early Egyptian city, although no city built on this plan has so far been found in Egypt. Settlement N.688 may well be the first archaeological evidence of the origin of the hieroglyphic determinative for city, as well as testifying to the close relations existing between the Timnian culture in Sinai and Proto-dynastic Egypt.

NAWAMIS TOMBS IN CENTRAL AND SOUTHERN SINAI As early as the 19th century, European explorers described several groups of mysterious circular stone buildings in southern Sinai, called *nawamis*, meaning "mosquitoes", by the Bedouin. Bedouin legend regards these as houses erected by the Children of Israel at the time of their wandering in the wilderness for protection against the plague of mosquitoes. From the distance, a group of *nawamis* looks like a well-built and well-maintained settlement—but in fact they are burial places. These are meticulously constructed of stone slabs; they have an external diameter, on average, of 4 m (13 ft), an internal diameter of 2 m (6,5 ft) and a height of about 2 m (6,5 ft). The roof, which has often survived, usually consists of a massive stone slab, and the door, invariably facing west, is so small that it probably has only symbolical and ritual significance. Archaeological excavations, some of them conducted in the 19th century and others more recently, and again during the past few years, have yielded not only human skulls and bones but also numerous grave goods. The manner of burial often—though not always—suggests secondary burial, i.e. a method customary among Bedouin semi-nomads and nomads, whereby the dead are first buried in a temporary grave and their bones subsequently put to permanent rest in a traditional tribal burial ground.

Grave goods included bracelets and beads made of the shell of *Lambis truncata sabae*, a snail native to the Red Sea, beads of cornelian, copper pins and twisted copper wire, such as are familiar from Pre-dynastic and Proto-dynastic Egypt. Only a few flint tools were found, such as tabular scrapers and transversal arrow-heads, and even fewer (and not readily datable) fragments of pottery.

A particularly well-preserved group of *nawamis* was discovered by the author's expedition in 1970 near 'Ain Hudera, in the western part of southern Sinai, and provisionally dated to the period between the Late Chalcolithic and the Early Bronze Age I.[6] This group of *nawamis* was subsequently excavated by a team from the Hebrew University of Jerusalem and our tentative dating was confirmed. But in the absence of absolute dating evidence, the team of Jerusalem archaeologists also had to conclude their excavation report with the words: "The *nawamis* continue to present a mystery with regard to their function, builders and precise date."[7]

The discoveries made by our expedition on the Tih plateau and more particularly at site N.688 have now thrown new light on the *nawamis* enigma. In addition to the above-mentioned group of cultic stone circles on the edge of the "city" N.688, dated to the second half of Timnian I, stands a well-built *namusiyeh* (singular of *nawamis*) with its roof still intact, with a diameter of 3 m (10 ft), a height of 1.20 m (4 ft), and with a small door facing west. Artefacts found in that tomb were similar to the customary grave goods of the *nawamis*—and equally difficult to date. But in the wall, next to the door, was a round-hewn flat column element which had been picked up by the builders of the *nawamis* in the neighbouring "city" and re-utilized in their edifice. This provided us with two new points of reference for the origin of the

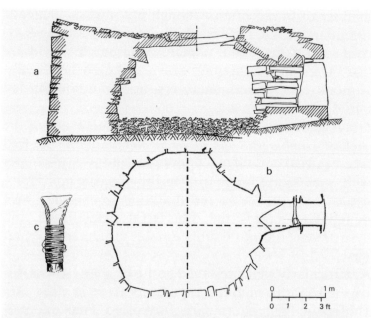

Fig. 23: a and b *Nawamis* tomb near 'Ain Hudera in longitudinal section (a) and in ground-plan (b) (after O. Bar-Joseph). c fitting of a transversal arrow-head (after Flinders Petrie).

nawamis builders and on their dating. It was now clear that, on the one hand, the *namusiyeh* of site N.688 must be later than the Proto-dynastic "city" itself and that, on the other, the finds in the *nawamis* do not permit of a later dating than Egypt's First Dynasty. We must therefore assign the *nawamis* to a later phase of Timnian I, i.e. the end of the 4th millenium B.C.

The *namusiyeh* on the outskirts of N.688 is the northern-most recorded find of a tomb of that type. Two more *nawamis* were found by us farther south on the Tih plateau, in the great central burial ground of the Wadi Shallala (N.676). The careful manner in which the *nawamis* were built as an "eternal house" for the dead, the Egyptian character of the grave goods, and the dominant geographical position of the tombs along the ancient caravan route from Egypt to southern Sinai, make it seem almost certain that we are dealing here with a Proto-dynastic wave of settlement from Lower Egypt. The geographical distribution of the *nawamis* suggests that these new settlers were shepherds and hunters, but

also displayed considerable active interest in Sinai's natural wealth—flint, turquoise and copper. Settlements in the mining districts, with artefacts identical with those in the *nawamis*, make it highly probable that the mineral deposits of southern Sinai were the immediate reason for this Proto-dynastic expansion into southern Sinai territory.

AMORITE SHEPHERD-WARRIORS ON ROUTE TOWARDS EGYPT During the fourth and final phase of the Early Bronze Age, towards 2200 B.C., there appeared, in many places on the vast Tih plateau, nomadic intruders who were evidently advancing with their herds in several waves from the north-east, and who settled for a short period wherever they found water. Frequently they moved into abandoned settlements of earlier periods—in which case we now find "mixed" remains, such as dwellings with flint tools and Timnian pottery fragments together with sherds showing the unmistakable decorations of Early Bronze Age IV—but often they also built their own primitive circular, oval or rectangular enclosures to protect their huts and herds.

The first traces of this historically significant nomadic invasion of the Sinai region were discovered by the author in 1956 in the area of Ruweiset el Akheider, east of the Mittla Pass, at the crossing of the Suez—Elat and the Bir Hasana—El 'Arish roads, and subsequently also along the desert road from Suez to El Qusaima and, with a relatively high density, in the oasis region of El Qusaima–'Ain el Gedeirat–'Ain Qadeis, including Gebel Halal.[8] These discoveries were interpreted by the American archaeologist and biblical historian W. F. Albright[9] as a major contribution to the understanding of the patriarchal period, since in his view these remains in Sinai represent established stopping points of donkey caravans between Mesopotamia and Egypt at the time of the Patriarch Abraham. In this connection, Albright quotes Genesis 20:1: "And Abraham journeyed from thence toward the south country, and dwelled between Kades [Kadesh-Barnea] and Shur [the Egyptian frontier on the present Suez Canal]." According to Albright, Abraham journeyed from his native city of Ur in Mesopotamia to the "south country", i.e. into the Negev and central Sinai, and was there an important figure in the caravan trade of his days.

This picture of stations along a great trade route of the Early Bronze Age IV, at the end of the 3rd millenium B.C., has, however, fundamentally changed as a result of intensive Sinai explorations during the past few years. Remains of settlements and resting points of the Early Bronze Age IV have been found not only at numerous locations in northern and central Sinai, on mountains and in *wadis*, near springs and water holes, but also in now totally arid parts of the vast Tih plateau, far away from any road, so that these remains of settlements can in no way be interpreted as traces of a major trade route. The area of distribution of the occupation wave of Early Bronze Age IV comprises the border region of the Negev all the way down to the Red Sea and thence towards the west into the deserts of the Tih plateau, past Ruweiset el Akheider in the direction of Egypt and then again on the western side of Sinai through the great Wadi Sudr to the Gulf of Suez, as well as the *wadi* systems of the Wadi Gharandal and the Wadi el Shallala. Considerable remains of that period were, astonishingly, found also on the Mittla and Giddi Passes, as far as the banks of the Suez Canal between Port Taufiq and the Small Bitter Lake—and across the Suez Canal to Gebel Atika in Lower Egypt. The majority of these sites, dated by pottery as belonging to the Early Bronze Age IV, were no more than rather simple enclosures, round huts or corrals for herds of sheep or goats.

The settlement of Sinai during the Early Bronze Age IV had the character of a purely temporary occupation of the land by nomadic groups, to whom Sinai was purely a transit country on their way to Egypt. Only thus can the fact be explained that nowhere in the areas of turquoise or copper mining in southern Sinai are even the slightest traces of that occupation to be found, even though archaeological finds at settlements of that period in the Levant and especially also in the Negev indicate clearly that metal production and metal working were of considerable importance to them. Settlements and graves of that period have produced considerable quantities of copper and bronze weapons, as well as stocks of copper ingots.

The new and fascinating historical picture which may now be outlined identifies these repeated intrusional waves by armed groups of shepherds with the semi-nomadic Amorites,[10] whose migratory movements had assumed, by the end of the third millenium B.C., the scale of a major warlike migration.

At the beginning of that operation, the Amorites, in the far northeast, caused the final collapse of Sumerian rule in Mesopotamia; then one nomadic wave of Amorites after another overran the territories of present-day Syria, Palestine and Transjordan, occupied the abandoned Early Bronze Age cities and villages in those regions, and also occupied vast and hitherto uninhabited tracts of land. From there the intruders advanced farther to the south; wherever there was water or pasturage in the Negev the Amorites settled for a certain period. However, the waves of intruders moved farther towards the west—across the great land bridge of central Sinai—and penetrated into Egypt. About 2155 B.C. the Egyptian Old Kindom collapsed and the First Intermediate Period (about 2155–2040 B.C.) witnessed a massive nomadic infiltration of the area of Lower Egypt, an infiltration that was not checked until the beginning of the Middle Kingdom. This dramatic picture of the Amorite migration and land-seizure as one of the most extensive and fateful events in the history of the ancient world has been substantially enriched by archaeological discoveries in the Sinai peninsula.

ON THE EASTERN BORDER OF THE SINAI PENINSULA—THE NEGEV AND KADESH-BARNEA   When reference is here made to prehistoric frontiers one should not visualize rigid, let alone marked, boundaries, or even frontier fortifications such as we know from Roman days. Mostly they were natural borders, determined topographically or climatically, even though such natural borders were occasionally guarded by fortified frontier settlements, as

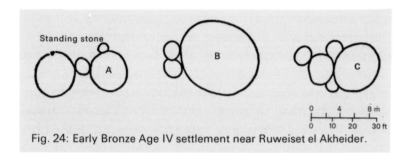

Standing stone

A

B

C

0 4 8 m

0 10 20 30 ft

Fig. 24: Early Bronze Age IV settlement near Ruweiset el Akheider.

for instance the ancient Egyptian frontier posts on the desert border with the Sinai peninsula.

The eastern border of Sinai is described in the Bible as part of the "south border of the Promised Land": "And their south border was from the shore of the Salt Sea, from the bay that looketh southward: And it went out to the south side to Maaleh-acrabbim and passed along to Zin, and ascended on the south side unto Kadesh-barnea... From thence it passed towards Azmon, and went out unto the river of Egypt; and the goings out of that coast were at the sea" (Joshua 15 :2–4). According to that account, the southern border of the land promised to the tribe of Judah ran from the southern tip of the Dead Sea through the vast Wadi Zin and along the Ramon Crater to the eastern spurs of the great Tih plateau, south of 'Ain el Qusaima–'Ain el Gedeirat–'Ain Qadeis (biblical Kadesh-Barnea) and thence in a northwesterly direction to the Wadi el 'Arish ("the River of Egypt") and along it to the Mediterranean coast (the "Great Sea").

In early prehistoric times, when only nomads without permanent settlements were wandering through the semi-arid zones of the Levant, there were no real political frontiers, and migrating groups moved through the Negev, the 'Araba and Sinai, leaving behind everywhere the scanty remains of their temporary occupation. However, towards the end of the Late Bronze Age and at the beginning of the Early Iron Age, an entirely new picture emerged: newly immigrated tribes were settling down, building houses, dams, terraces and small fortresses, ploughing fields and digging wells. They also produced their own pottery—rather primitive hand-made vessels for everyday use, called "Negev pottery".

At that time the mountains of the Negev were densely settled and a new frontier emerged between the almost uninhabited Sinai desert and the Negev. This frontier, too, is basically a natural boundary, resulting from the fact that the new arrivals settled wherever there was both cultivable soil and at least 50 mm (2 inches) of rainfall and a topography suitable for the retention of run-off rainwater (i.e. narrow lateral branches of the wadis, surrounded by bare hills). The area of El Qusaima–'Ain el Gedeirat–'Ain Qadeis is at the western end of the newly settled Negev mountains, a fertile oasis, densely settled at that period, on the edge of the arid Sinai desert.

But who were these first sedentary inhabitants of the Negev mountains and of the spring area of Kadesh-Barnea, which is so important in biblical history? The question is of considerable importance both for an understanding of the geographical and historical situation in the Negev and northern Sinai in the Late Bronze and Early Iron Ages and for the interpretation of the biblical account of the Exodus from Egypt and the occupation of Canaan by the tribes of Israel.

After many years of archaeological field-work in the Negev and intensive examination of biblical and historical sources, the author has come to the following conclusion: The above-quoted description of the frontier (Joshua 15) represents the borders of the land of Canaan in the Late Bronze Age as being the "south border of the Promised Land", but it does not describe the territory actually occupied and inhabited by the tribe of Judah. In 1953–1956, when the American archaeologist Nelson Glueck and the present author discovered the first Early Iron Age settlements in the Negev mountains, these were identified by Bible archaeologists as Israelite settlements and attributed to King Solomon. But the archaeological finds and, above all, the biblical sources, present a totally different picture: even prior to the Exodus of Israelite tribes from Egypt, the Negev mountains were inhabited by the Amalekites, the traditional arch-enemies of Israel. The Amalekites were ancient desert tribes who had settled in the Negev as early as the period of the Patriarchs and who, at the time of Abraham, about the middle of the 2nd millenium B.C., were living in Kadesh-Barnea —known as the "country of the Amalekites" (Genesis 14:7). The "Negev pottery", typical of the settlements and fortresses of the Amalekites in the Negev, is archaeologically attested by our expedition's excavations in the Timna Valley from the 14th until the mid-12th century B.C., though no doubt it appeared at an earlier date and continued beyond the later date as an established desert tradition. This pottery, which was found only in the Negev, in the 'Araba and in the northwest of the Arabian peninsula but nowhere in Sinai or Palestine, is archaeologically attested only for the period during which, according to our biblical sources, Amalekites were living in the Negev, i.e. until the 7th century B.C. The men who were sent out from the Sinai border ("the Wilderness of Paran") to "search the land of Canaan" reported (Numbers 13:29): "The Amalekites dwell in the land of the south"—in the Hebrew text this area is specifically called "the land of the Negev". Very much later, at the time of the Kings of Israel, the Amalekites were still in the Negev and there were repeated hostile clashes: "And Saul smote the Amalekites from Havilah until thou comest to Shur, that is over against Egypt" (I. Samuel 15:7) and again: "And David and his men went up, and invaded the Geshurites, and the Gezrites, and the Amalekites: for those nations were of old the inhabitants of the land, as thou goest to Shur, even unto the land of Egypt" (I. Samuel 27:8). As late as the 8th century B.C. Amalekites were still settled on the eastern border of Sinai: "And some of them, even of the sons of Simeon, 500 men, went to mount Seir [the Negev mountains, B.R.] ... And they smote the rest of the Amalekites that were escaped [in the original: "survivors"], and dwelt there until this day" (I. Chronicles 4:42–43). The archaeological finds in the Kadesh-Barnea area[11] fit the biblical accounts fairly well. Everywhere there are settlements with the typical pottery of the Amalekites, and on the high rocky bank of the Wadi el 'Ain, above 'Ain el Gedeirat, the main spring of Kadesh-Barnea, stands a casemate fortress in which Negev pottery has been found. Another casemate fortress stands in the vicinity of a large settlement, not far from 'Ain Qadeis, and at least one further fortress of the same type was discovered by the author near El Qusaima in 1957. In all three fortresses Amalekite pottery predominates, and these fortresses are parts of "settlement units" consisting of living-quarters, terraced fields surrounded by a dyke, and a fortress—a pattern typical of Amalekite settlements.

In striking contrast to the irregularly constructed casemate fortresses near 'Ain el Gedeirat is an eight-tower fortress not far from the spring in the valley of El Gedeirat. That fortress, the ground-plan of which was first published by Woolley/Lawrence[12] ("Lawrence of Arabia") as "Tell 'Ain el Guderat", has been systematically excavated in recent years by Rudolf Cohen, who found three fortifications built on top of each other, dating from the 10th to the 7th century B.C. Although it is not yet possible to give an accurate account of the history of these fortifications, it is nevertheless clear that both the architecture and the archaeological finds belong to a culture different from that of the native Amalekite settlements and fortresses. It may be assumed that "Tell 'Ain el Guderat" is a fortress built by the Judaeans after their victory over the Amalekite forces in the Negev, in order to secure the spring and as a frontier post against the Bedouin of the Sinai desert.

It is highly significant that nowhere in the Sinai territory proper have any traces of Amalekite or Judaean settlement ever been found and that the ancient road—known as "Darb el Ghaza"—which ran from the Mediterranean to the Red Sea and by-passed the Negev mountains in the west, had always been the natural and political frontier between Sinai and Palestine.

CENTRAL BURIAL GROUNDS AS A MIRROR OF HISTORY The true nomad who, by tribal law and desert custom, must not build himself a solid house and therefore spends his life in a tent, has a solid "house" of stone built for him after his death. The contrast between the temporary and invariably provisional dwelling that can usually be loaded upon a camel and the tomb intended

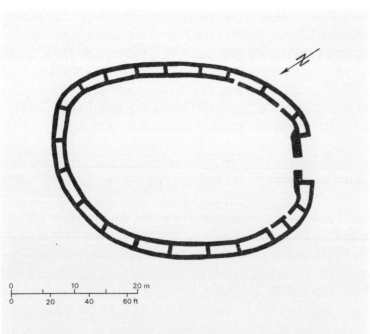

Fig. 25: Plan of an Amalekite fortress of the Early Iron Age near 'Ain Qadeis.

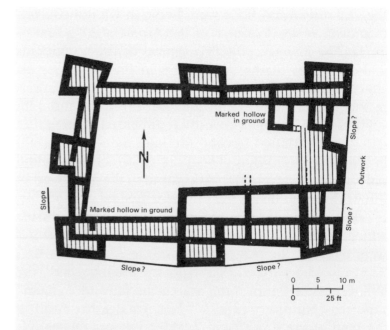

Fig. 26: The Israelite fort of the 8th century B.C. at 'Ain el Gedeirat (after Woolley and Lawrence).

"for eternity" is striking and perhaps more than any other aspect of Bedouin life, characterizes the ancient traditions of nomadic existence. Of particular interest are the large central burial grounds which, in Sinai—as in the neighbouring desert regions of the Arabian peninsula and the Negev—often extend over many square miles. In northern Sinai we found such huge burial grounds, with several hundred monumental tombs on high mountains, often indeed spread over entire mountain ranges, as well as on *wadi* banks in the neighbourhood of springs, and also on the summits of ancient passes. In southern Sinai, central burial grounds were frequently found also in the small valleys in remote *wadis*. What all these burial grounds—which often differ considerably in detail—have in common is their vast size, the huge number of their grave structures, and the often incredibly long period they were in use. There is at least one such central burial ground which has served as a traditional place of burial, from the Epi-Palaeolithic Age (about 15,000 B.C.) right down to modern times.

In spite of considerable difficulty in the dating of the graves, the central burial grounds may be seen as mirrors of the history of human life in the Sinai peninsula, reflecting also the great historical difference between the Tih plateau in the north and centre, on the one hand, and the high mountain group of the south, on the other. One of the most impressive central burial grounds, in which grave types of all the periods of settlement in Sinai are represented, from the Neolithic Age onwards, is situated above the huge Wadi el Shallala, on the western edge of the Tih (N. 676). Upon a flat mountain top some 1,000 m (1,100 yards) in length and 200 m (220 yards) in width, stand numerous tombs of different types in irregular confusion. At the centre there is a slight hill which dominates the entire neighbourhood and can be seen from a long way off. Here the author's expedition experienced a great surprise: eight roughly hewn stelae, 2–3 m (6,5–10 ft) long, with rounded or domed tops were lying in a row along the edge of the hill; the longest one, a little over 3 m (10 ft), was in the middle. Today the stelae are lying in a line on the ground, but in ancient times, when they were standing upright, they must have presented an impressive picture. At the foot of the hill of the stelae are two very extensive enclosures of large stone slabs set on edge, and within them a large number of flint implements and potsherds were found. This is quite certainly a ritual site, very probably associated with some kind of cult of the dead. We assume that this stelae shrine was erected in the Elatian period, i.e. in the 4th millenium B.C.

The tombs of the Shallala burial ground may be divided into five main types, each of which belongs to a different cultural period. They represent all the types of tomb so far found in the Sinai region:

1. *"Wall tombs"*—already mentioned in connection with 'Ain Yerqa—were built of two parallel rows of stone slabs set on edge, about 80 cm (30 inches) apart and covered or filled in with large stones. At both ends of the long "wall" towered a huge upright "headstone". This type of tomb can be clearly dated to the period of the Pre-Pottery Neolithic Phase B. While the "wall tombs" at the Shallala burial ground had a length of as much as 24 m (79 ft), "wall tombs" up to a length of 75 m (246 ft) were found at the central burial ground of 'Ain Yerqa. One of these 'Ain Yerqa "wall tombs" was partially excavated by us and traces of decomposed human bones were recovered.

Neolithic "wall tombs" exist in many places in the Sinai, but mostly where there are also remains of Neolithic settlements. Thus, an extensive burial ground consisting exclusively of "wall tombs" is situated approximately 30 km (18 miles) west of the Gulf of Elat-'Aqaba, near Khashm el Tarif (N. 672). "Wall tombs", in addition to tombs of other types, are also found further to the west, near Themed (N. 336), as well as in all the other central burial grounds on the western edge of the Tih plateau, as at 'Ain Yerqa (N. 695), on Gebel Abu Zurub (N. 549) and at the southern end of Gebel Egma (N. 642–643). Although Pre-Pottery Neolithic settlements have also been found in the area of the flint, turquoise and copper ore deposits in southern Sinai, the Neolithic "wall

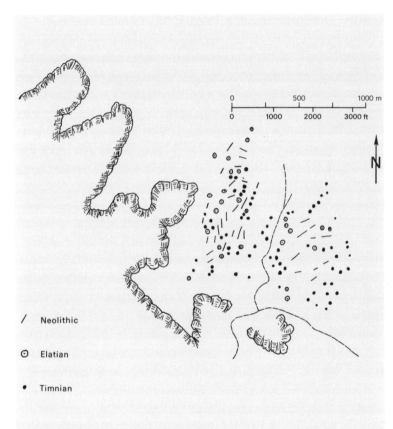

/ Neolithic

⊙ Elatian

• Timnian

Fig. 27: The central burial ground of Abu Zurub on Gebel el Tih.

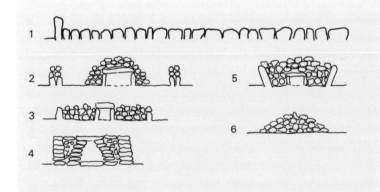

Fig. 28: Diagrammatic representation of types of tombs in Sinai central burial grounds.

1. Pre-Pottery Neolithic
2. "Empty" tomb ("E")
3. "Full" tomb ("F")
4. *Nawamis* tomb
5. Early Bronze Age IV (circular tomb)
6. Stone pile tomb (cairn)

tombs" are encountered exclusively at the central burial grounds or occasionally as individual tombs beside settlements of Pre-Pottery Neolithic B on the Tih plateau.

2. *Empty ("E") and full ("F") circular tombs* are two main types of tomb which are found together almost everywhere in the Sinai. Basically they consist of a coffin-like cist, which is the grave proper, and a stone fence surrounding it. In the empty ("E") type the space between the cist and the fence is empty; this type of tomb is, as a rule, much larger than the full ("F") type, where the space between cist and fence was filled with small stones. "E" and "F" tombs are the most frequent type of tomb in Sinai; according to the availability of suitable stones, they were built either of slabs set on edge or of loose stones set upon each other. The "F" tombs, in spite of the infill of small stones, which frequently also cover the burial cist, are low flat structures.

For a long time the dating of "E" and "F" tombs proved a considerable problem. Flint tools or pottery fragments found on the surface of the central burial grounds were not very typical and no datable grave goods were found during excavation. The author's expedition excavated a number of "E" and "F" tombs at the burial ground of 'Ain Yerqa, near the Neolithic shrine, but nothing was found apart from decomposed bones. Only one "E" tomb contained a most interesting collection of grave goods: 39 exceptionally large and finely worked flint scrapers were found arranged in a tower shape next to a skeleton; for these there exist comparable and datable Chalcolithic finds from southern Palestine. The discovery of a group of "E" tombs in the area of Serabit el Khadim, which unquestionably belonged to an Elatian settlement (N. 533), confirmed our dating of the "E" type tombs as belonging to the Elatian period.

The "F" tombs found in Sinai in their thousands, not only on the Tih plateau but also in the area of the high granite mountains of the south and in the broad flat *wadis* of the southern tip of Sinai, belong to the period of the Timnian settlement of Sinai. Both types, "E" and "F", were so-called crouched burials, i.e. the skeletons were buried in a squatting position.

3. *Nawamis tombs.* As mentioned above, two *nawamis* tombs were found by the author in the Shallala burial ground. They have a diameter of 3 m (10 ft) and a height of 1.2 m (4 ft) and had been carefully constructed of flat stone slabs; they have a small "door" 32 × 63 cm (12.5 × 25 inches) on their western side. Inside the grave chamber, approximately 60 cm (24 inches) high was a skeleton lying on its side in a crouched position[13] and next to it were snail-shell beads, flint flakes and a few pottery fragments. The burial chamber had been filled with earth after interment; only then had it been roofed over with large stone slabs. The *nawamis* of the Wadi el Shallala have been dated by these artefacts as belonging to the Timnian I period and a clear link with early Proto-dynastic Egypt has again been attested.

4. *Circular tombs.* A circle of large stones set on edge surrounding a cist made of boulders, the whole covered by a huge mound of stones in such a way that the stones of the outer ring are forced obliquely outwards by the enormous weight of the stone infill—this is the typical Early Bronze Age IV tomb in Sinai, well known from the many burial grounds of that period in the Negev.[14] A few tombs of this type are in the burial ground of the Wadi el Shallala and others were discovered by the author further north in the Wadi Sudr, on the Mittla Pass, and also in the neighbourhood of Gebel el Maghara and Gebel Halal, and near Themed. In Sinai this type of tomb has been found exclusively on the Tih plateau and does not occur in southern Sinai.

5. *Stone pile tombs (cairns).* Throughout Sinai, at the side of tracks, near wells and water holes, in natural caves and rock niches, on hills, and also on the steep slopes of *wadis*, and frequently also just anywhere in the wide flat *hammada* country, simple stone pile tombs are found—totally forgotten, anonymous and timeless. As a rule, when such a tomb is excavated, only bones are found and rarely any grave goods, such as simple ornaments or the remains of clothing. Such individual stone pile tombs, called "tumuli" by the archaeologists, are commonly found also in ancient settlements, often built upon the remains of older masonry and of stones from

such walls. Most of them have a burial cist at their centre and often the outer facing stones are very carefully set. There is no doubt that this type of tomb was built during various periods.

In summing up, it may be said that the differential distribution of the various of types tombs clearly reflects the history of the Sinai peninsula. Whenever northern and central Sinai was only a transit country, as during the Early Bronze Age IV, we encounter the appropriate type of tomb along the route from the eastern border of Sinai across to the frontier of Egypt, but not in southern Sinai. "E" and "F" tombs of the Elatian and Timnian periods, on the other hand, are scattered over the whole of Sinai and the density of their distribution is a reliable criterion of the number of inhabitants and of the duration of these cultures in Sinai.

Unfortunately very little archaeological information exists about the Arabian Peninsula and not much more about such "insignificant" remains as prehistoric burial grounds in Egypt itself. That is why, in our search for the origins of these Sinai cultures, we have to focus attention on the similarity between the scanty archaeological finds. Now and again, however, one is helped by an unexpected stroke of luck. In 1968 a Danish expedition under the leadership of T. G. Bibby conducted an archaeological survey in the east of the Arabian Peninsula and in 1973[15] published maps and plans, and above all

exceedingly good aerial photographs, of extensive burial grounds in the neighbourhood of Yabrin, south of Qatar. If we compare these aerial photographs with our own aerial photographs of the burial grounds of Wadi el Shallala or Gebel Abu Zurub, we find at Yabrin three types of tomb which we know well from Sinai—Pre-Pottery Neolithic wall tombs, Elatian "E" tombs and stone pile tombs. Moreover, a kind of archaeological stratigraphy emerges: one of the "E" tombs is built on top of the end of a wall tomb, and some stone pile tombs stand on top of "E" tombs; in other words, we have here the same chronological sequence as in Sinai. However, the significance of these aerial photographs lies not only in the fact that they attest the huge zone of distribution of the Pre-Pottery Neolithic B and the Elatian cultures, but that they confirm our assumptions, made on the grounds of the comparison of artefacts, of the areas of origin of these cultures. It is now clear that the Pre-Pottery Neolithic, as well as the Elatian culture of the Chalcolithic Age, were established over large areas of the Levant and the Arabian Peninsula and that Sinai merely represented a marginal or transit region of this vast area of distribution. It is also exceedingly interesting that the aerial photographs of the Arabian Peninsula fail to show a single "F" tomb anywhere — a type of tomb whose origin we believe to be most closely related to Egypt.

Beno Rothenberg

Notes

1. B. Rothenberg, God's Wilderness, 1961.
2. O. Bar-Joseph, J. L. Phillips, Prehistoric Investigations in Gebel Maghara, Northern Sinai, Qedem, 7, Jerusalem, 1977.
3. T. G. Bibby, Preliminary Survey in East Arabia, 1968, Copenhagen, 1973.
4. Y. Yadin, The Earliest Record of Egypt's Military Penetration into Asia? Israel Exploration Journal, 5, 1955, p. 1–16.
5. R. Gophna, Egyptian Immigration into Southern Canaan during the First Dynasty, Tel Aviv, 3, 1976, p. 31–37.
6. B. Rothenberg, Sinai Explorations 1967–1972, Museum Haaretz Yearbook, Tel Aviv, 14, 1972, p. 37; Id., Sinai Explorations III, M. H. Yearbook, 15/16, 1972/73.
7. O. Bar-Joseph, Anna Belfer, Avner Goren, Patricia Smith, The Nawamis near 'Ein Hudera, Israel Exploration Journal, 27, Jersualem, 1977, p. 86.

8. B. Rothenberg, God's Wilderness, 1961.
9. W. F. Albright, Archaeology, Historical Analogy and Early Biblical Tradition, 1966, Chap. II.
10. K. M. Kenyon, Archaeology in the Holy Land, 1960, p. 115; Id. Amorites and Canaanites, 1966, pp. 7, 34; Y. Aharoni, The Land of the Bible, 1966, p. 125/126.
11. B. Rothenberg, God's Wilderness, 1961.
12. On "Tell Ain el Guderat" see C. L. Woolley/T. E. Lawrence, The Wilderness of Zin, Annual, Palestine Exploration Fund, 1914–15 (1935 edit., pp. 81–84).
13. As the roof had been slid aside by illegal excavators the skeleton was in an advanced state of decomposition and in disorder. It is not therefore impossible that this, too, was a case of secondary burial.
14. B. Rothenberg, God's Wilderness, 1961.
15. T. G. Bibby, Preliminary Survey in East Arabia 1968, Copenhagen, 1973.

60 Countless dykes of lava have intruded into the granite rock of southern Sinai—often an impressive sight.

61 Oasis in the Wadi Nasib in the evening light. A few palms and vegetable beds are sufficient for the few Bedouin families living here.

62 Dragonfly of the genus *Sympetrum* in the Nasib oasis.

63 At Bir Nasib in the Wadi Nasib the ancient Egyptians operated a big copper smelting centre. A huge slag heap (part of it visible in the foreground) testifies to the large-scale production of copper. Alongside there is now a Bedouin cemetery.

64 Several years ago, near the slag heap of Bir Nasib, Beno Rothenberg discovered a hitherto unknown rock inscription of the New Kingdom. This shows two royal officials of an expedition facing one another and paying homage to the name of one of the Ramesses kings in the cartouche.

65 On the flat mountain top, visible in Plate 63, Georg Gerster discovered, a few years ago, a Proto-Sinaitic inscription of the 15th century B.C.—probably the earliest alphabetic script known so far. It reads (according to A. F. Rainey): "Praise be to 'Addu, commander of the camp . . .''.

66 Bedouin tent in the Wadi Zaghra. The dry tangle of scrub offers protection against the wind and serves as fuel for the camp fire.

67 Black is the colour of the women's dress in the desert.

61

62

Turquoise, Copper and Pilgrims

Archaeology of Southern Sinai

MINING AND PRAYERS IN THE DESERT The huge plateau of Badiet el Tih, the "Wilderness of Wandering", comes to an abrupt end in the south at a high and steep rock cliff which projects in the form of a triangle into the territory of southern Sinai. Descending one of the passes which lead down as a serpentine path, one finds oneself in a broad belt of sandstone—known as Debbet er Ramla—which extends from the Gulf of Suez to the Gulf of Elat-'Aqaba between the Tih plateau and the high granite mountains of the south. This sandstone belt contains deposits of turquoise and copper which have attracted settlers into the south of Sinai since time immemorial. Copper ore was found also further to the south, in the area of the Precambrian schists and granites of the high Sinai mountains. A glance at the distribution map of early settlements reveals that the majority of these settlements are concentrated in the areas of mineral deposit or along the roads leading to them and it is obvious that they owe their origin to the attraction of the natural resources of the south.

If it was tribes or family groups that moved southwards in prehistoric periods, we find a considerable settlement scatter, often over quite considerable distances from the ore deposits. These were the "logistic hinterland" of the miners, who also had to provide their own food and their stone tools and who left traces wherever environmental conditions were favourable—water, soil, game, grazing and flint. If, on the other hand, we are dealing with Pharaonic mining expeditions that arrived in the region well-equipped and supplied with the necessary food, they invariably settled close to the turquoise deposits or the copper mines and smelting camps. In consequence, during the dynastic period of Egypt, there were only workmen's camps in southern Sinai and not a single genuine settlement. For the Pharaohs, Sinai always remained a hostile desert, beyond the bounds of civilization.

In later periods we again find large numbers of people taking the laborious road to southern Sinai—hermits and pilgrims—but these were concerned mainly with the "heavenly Sinai" of biblical tradition; they lived in caves and huts or built chapels, monasteries and roads for the pilgrims. We may therefore distinguish two different motivations or, if one may put it so, two "levels" of human activity that made this remote and enigmatic sandy and stony wilderness so attractive—they may be labelled "mining" and "prayer". It is this coincidence of an earthly quest for the riches of this world and a devout quest for a holy life that lends the desert landscape of southern Sinai its unique character and its unparalleled history and archaeology.

NEOLITHIC MINERS In southern Sinai the history of settlement—insofar as this has been attested by archaeological finds—did not begin until the Pre-Pottery Neolithic B period, when small groups moved in from the north and the east to mine flint, turquoise and malachite. We must not, however, see those mining activities as genuine "expeditions", as in subsequent periods, but as a slow penetration into the south in a ceaseless search for pastures and water.

The direction of the advance of the Neolithic intruders may be traced from Gebel Khashm el Tarif and Qa'el Naqb in the mountains west of the 'Araba on the strength of what are often quite extensive remains of settlement stone enclosures for men and beasts—through the great wadis of southern Sinai, past 'Ain Hudera, 'Ain el Akhdar, the Wadis Zeleqa, Mara, Saal, Zaghra and across the Watia Pass into the mineral regions of the south. In some way this movement must have been purposeful: the Pre-Pottery Neolithic settlers stopped when, at the end of their long journey, they had reached deposits of turquoise, malachite and flint.

The aims of these movements, as mentioned above, included the extensive flint deposits at the southern end of Gebel Egma and the flint deposits that were even more conspicuous—on account of their extreme remoteness—in the Wadi Geba' (N. 481) on the western side of Wadi Serbal. This narrow steep wadi is actually a series of successive natural pools containing drinking water all the year round—a centre of attraction for game and hunters, and also for the establishment of an extensive Neolithic flint industry which left behind an incredible number of stone tools and flakes on the wide banks along both sides of the *wadi* estuary.

Other Neolithic groups, travelling southwards along the western watershed, left traces of encampments and typical flint tools in the turquoise mining area of Maghara, in the neighbourhood of Serabit el Khadim (N. 532, 702) and on the temple mountain itself. Pieces of turquoise have been found at a few settlements of the Pre-Pottery Neolithic B in southern Sinai and these were without doubt left by the earliest turquoise miners in Sinai.

It is of great interest that the sites of the Pre-Pottery Neolithic B discovered by the author, with fragments of malachite and the stone tools typical of that period, at the malachite deposits themselves, were long-lived settlements. Site N. 590 in the Wadi el Ahmar, a lateral branch of the Wadi Zaghra (northeast of St. Catherine's Monastery), one of the most important copper deposits in Sinai and subsequently intensively worked by copper smelters, was originally discovered by C. T. Currelly, who reported finds of flint arrow-heads together with copper smelting slag.[1] Our expedition examined that site in 1971[2] and found a large settlement of the Pre-Pottery Neolithic B there, with extensive remains of buildings, immediately next to a malachite deposit. We have indisputable archaeological proof of Neolithic malachite mining; the mineral must have been used for ornaments, pigment or cosmetics, since the metallurgical ores, slag and fragments of smelting-furnaces—which were also found by our expedition at the site—naturally belong to a much later period, to the Bronze Age Timnian period.

THE EARLIEST COPPERSMITHS—DURING THE ELATIAN PERIOD? As during the Neolithic Age, the settlers of the Elatian period in Sinai presumably also came from the north and the east, using the same routes to the south, across watersheds and through the big *wadis*. There is a great concentration of Elatian settlements around the flint deposits of Gebel Egma, and the manufacture of flint tools must have been the principal industry of Sinai at that time. Although several Elatian settlements have been found in the copper ore area of the Wadi Zaghra— and at one of these settlements even lumps of copper ore—no finds such as slag or remains of furnaces have so far come to light which would prove that copper was smelted at that early period. If copper was indeed mined in Sinai at that time, it must have been relatively small quantities of copper ore, which was subsequently smelted elsewhere. Copper ore and small copper objects, possibly originating from southern Sinai, have been discovered at contemporary sites on the north coast of Sinai and in Egypt. Similarly, no traces of metallurgy of the Elatian period have been found in the 'Araba or, more especially, at Timna, where the author has been systematically excavating ancient mines and copper smelting camps for a great number of years. There, as in Sinai, copper smelting began in the early Timnian period. Nor have any traces of the Elatian culture so far been found in the turquoise regions of Maghara or Serabit el Khadim, although a small group of Elatian settlements situated in the Wadi Feiran—at the entrance to the Wadi Mukattab, through which the road runs to the turquoise mines—were possibly connected with turquoise mining.

A totally new and unexpected aspect of mining in Sinai was revealed, however, when our expedition discovered native copper in the Wadi Ba'ba', west of Serabit el Khadim. There, small quantities of native metallic copper were found in a steep rock face which showed primitive hammer marks, and this discovery instantly suggested a connection with the finds of small objects made of native copper—and turquoise—in Badarian Egypt of the 4th millenium B.C. We consider it probable that the settlers of the Elatian period, who left traces not far from the Wadi Ba'ba', dug the native copper out of the rock in order to work it into small objects.

In spite of these finds, it must be said in conclusion that the inhabitants of Sinai during the Elatian period displayed no great interest in the mineral deposits of the south, and that they were essentially semi-nomadic hunters and shepherds, whose principal pastures were on the Tih plateau.

COPPER AGE AND BRONZE AGE COPPER INDUSTRIES—THE
TIMNIAN PERIOD   During the Timnian period, southern
Sinai was also densely populated. As in the north, groups
of small stone buildings and enclosures, with the flint implements and the pottery typical of that period, existed
wherever there was water, grazing and game. In
southern Sinai, too, we can find Timnian settlements
wherever good flint occurs. In the Wadi Geba', where an
extensive flint workshop existed in Pre-Pottery Neolithic
B, large quantities of flint implements and flakes, as well
as remains of buildings of the Timnian period were
found, and so indeed were some in the distant southern
tip of Sinai, immediately north of Ras Muhammad
(N. 434), as well as in the Wadi Letih (N. 437, 438, 441),
where there is also a large central burial ground of that
period. There, at the southern tip of the peninsula,
fishermen also lived and worked at that time, and in
some of their settlements (such as N. 482) whole mounds
of the shells of the *Lambis truncata sabae* snail, which
were probably "exported" from there to all parts of the
north, have been found.

Timnian remains are found in the Maghara region and
in the neighbourhood of Serabit el Khadim, and it can
be proved conclusively that turquoise was mined there
by Timnian settlers. But the most important industry of
the Timnian period, in terms of the economy and the history of settlement, was copper mining and copper smelting. Wherever geologists—and also the author's expedition—found evidence of copper smelting in southern
Sinai, there were also settlements and traces of metal-
working from both phases, I and II, of the Timnian culture. A glance at the settlement distribution map of that
period shows the densest concentration of Timnian remains in southern Sinai in the immediate neighbourhood of the ore deposits, and it is obvious that the search
for copper ore and ore smelting was the direct cause of
that population density.

During the Timnian period southern Sinai was an extensive mining area where, ever since the earliest phase of
that period, somewhere around 3800 B.C., copper ore
was smelted.

Our expedition found Timnian mining settlements with
remains of furnaces and copper slag in northeastern Sinai, not far from the ore deposits of the 'Araba, but more
especially in the south, in the area of the Wadi Riqeita,
to the northeast of St. Catherine's Monastery, and also
further south, a large copper smelting settlement in the
Wadi Shellal, southeast of the Monastery, and in the
copper ore area of Gebel Samra, in the far southeast of
the peninsula. Copper smelting works of this period also
existed in the west, e.g. at the entrance to the Wadi
Nasib, between Serabit el Khadim and the Wadi Ba'ba'.
It is possible to distinguish three stages in the development of the copper smelting technology within the Timnian period. Initially, during Phase I,[3] the copper ore
was smelted in simple bowl-shaped smelting pits dug in the
ground. The charge consisted mainly of malachite nodules and iron oxides (as a flux); the "furnaces" were
fired with charcoal from local acacia trees and presumably ventilated by means of primitive goat-hide bellows.
At the end of the smelting process, when the pit became
filled with slag, this was removed from the furnace after
cooling and broken up to recover the entrapped metal
globules—a primitive process which nevertheless
yielded surprisingly good copper.

Later, the smelting pits—actually no more than a hole in
the ground—were replaced by stone-lined smelting furnaces and this change was accompanied also by progress
in the smelting technology. The furnaces were made of
fire-resistant sandstone, which frequently had to be
transported to the smelting centre over considerable distances. One such sandstone furnace was excavated on
the granite rocks of site N. 590 in the Wadi Ahmar.
When these furnaces were filled with slag at the end of
the smelting process proper, they were kept hot for several hours more to give the copper globules time to sink
down to the furnace bottom. Then the front of the furnace was broken open to let the slag run out, with the result that a flat "plate" of slag formed on the ground. This,
together with the slag remaining in the furnace, was subsequently broken up to extract the copper prills. On the
furnace bottom, a copper ingot formed under the slag

68 The Wadi Umm Sideira above the Gulf of Elat-'Aqaba. In this narrow gorge in the "Nubian" sandstone, not far from the "pilgrims' way" to southern Sinai, Beno Rothenberg discovered, in 1956, numerous Nabataean, Greek and Arabic inscriptions.

69 A Jewish *menorah* (seven-branched candlestick) cut into a rock face in the Wadi Umm Sideira is proof that this road was also used by Jewish travellers from Palestine, possibly pilgrims to the Mountain of Moses. The Latin inscription from the Roman Imperial Period written across the *menorah* ("Victoria augusti Caesaris"—"Victory of the illustrious Caesar") dates the *menorah* as belonging to the early centuries A.D. Higher up, the personal name "Akrabos" is cut into the rock in Greek script.

70 The Bedouin sculptor Salem lives near the Wadi Umm Sideira. He sells his highly interesting stone sculptures to visitors to the "Wadi of Inscriptions".

71 Geziret el Fara'un ("Island of the Pharaohs") south of Elat has the only natural harbour in the Gulf of Elat-'Aqaba. The island was first investigated by Beno Rothenberg in 1956 and identified with King Solomon's harbour of Ezion-Geber. But even before King Solomon, who sent his merchant ships from Ezion-Geber to the legendary land of Ophir, this was the port of Egyptian mining expeditions into the 'Araba. The fortifications on the hill are from the time of Saladin (12th century).

72 'Ain Hudera, an oasis at the western end of the sandstone belt below the Tih plateau, seen here in the rays of the early sun.

73 The great Roman highway from Aila (Elat) through Pharan (Feiran) to Clysma (Suez) climbs from the Red Sea up to the Tih plateau in the Wadi Tueiba, south of modern Elat. Here, numerous Nabataean, Thamudic (= old northern Arabic), Greek and Arabic inscriptions have been found, as well as one of the very rare Latin inscriptions in Sinai. This reads (according to E. D. Kollmann): "Wanderer stop here! Here worked and died T. Atilius Turbon of the III Cyrenaican Legion of the *centuria* of Antonius Valens"—a memorial to a Roman soldier who worked in the quarry of the Wadi Tueiba and died there.

74 Nabataean hunting scene in the Wadi Tueiba. Hunting was done on foot or on a saddled camel, the game was the ibex *(Capra ibex nubiana,* see Plates 99 and 102).

75 The almost deserted "ghost oasis" of 'Ain Hudera. Although the Bedouin in southern Sinai also build stone houses, these are usually not lived in but serve as storage sheds or shops.

76 Early Bronze Age IV settlement in the Mittla Pass area—an enclosure of low angular unhewn boulders; frequently two monoliths serve as doorposts.

◁ 72 73 74

and this was recovered after the liquid slag had been tapped out of the furnace. Neither at site N. 590 nor at any other smelting centre of that phase of the Timnian culture have any remains of bellows or tuyeres been found, nor indeed any furnace lining.

These features of advanced furnace and smelting technology, however, soon appeared at Timnian II smelting centres, presumably imported by Egyptian metalworkers, who were by then working in Sinai. At two quite extensive sites of the Timnian II period, N. 229 in the mountains west of the Timna Valley and N. 701 in the Wadi Ahmar, opposite the above-mentioned site N. 590, numerous copper smelting remains were found, which make it possible for us to reconstruct the smelting process. Site N. 229 had pear-shaped furnaces lined with clay. Small pluglike tuyeres, about 8 cm (over 3 inches) wide, testify to the use of advanced bellows. Moreover, the slag was tapped out of the furnace upon completion of the smelting process and shows the typical flow structure of primitive tapping slag. The temperatures achieved in these furnaces were around 1,200° C—high enough to ensure that at least a considerable part of the metallic copper would sink to the furnace bottom. However, some of the metallic copper still remained enclosed in the slag and had to be recovered from it by mechanical means.

Site N. 229 must be dated, by its architecture, typical flint implements and pottery, as belonging to the Timnian II period. However, a few Proto-dynastic Egyptian potsherds and a few fragments of Canaanite pottery of the Early Bronze Age II, of the Arad type, were also found there. This fact was important not only for dating the site as belonging to Timnian II but also as evidence of relations between Sinai and Canaan at that period. These relations will be discussed in the next section.

Similar metallurgical finds—furnace linings, primitive tapped slag and tuyeres—were also made at site N. 701, in the Wadi Ahmar. This site is of particular interest because it contained not only archaeological and metallurgical remains of Timnian II but also of the Egyptian Old and New Kingdoms, and hence supplied clear proof that

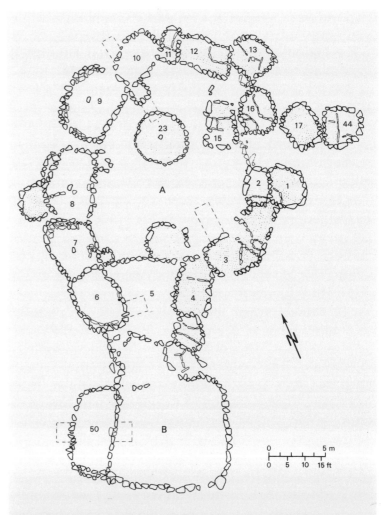

Fig. 29: Part of the settlement of Sheikh Nabi Sala of the Early Bronze Age II (after I. Beit Arieh).

both early and late dynastic Egypt were interested in the copper ore regions of southeastern Sinai. Careful investigation of all the smelting centres in Sinai showed that the pluglike tuyeres, which were most expertly manufactured from very sandy and hence fire-resistant clay, did not come into use in Sinai prior to the Timnian II period and that they were everywhere accompanied by Egyptian pottery. We may therefore assume that the progress in smelting technology, as observed at these sites and subsequently traced in the smelting industries of the Middle and New Kingdoms—in Sinai, in Nubia and in the 'Araba, as well as in Egyptian pictorial representations—was introduced into Sinai with the progressive "colonization", i.e. decimation of the local Timnian II population by the early-dynastic kings of Egypt.

METAL-HUNGRY CANAANITE INTRUDERS   As a result of Proto-dynastic Egyptian subjugation of the local inhabitants of the north and east, a settlement vacuum arose in southern Sinai. During the Timnian II period only few settlements existed there, compared with the preceding Timnian I, and those few were concentrated chiefly in the copper ore deposit regions of the Wadi Riqeita. Into this vacuum there now penetrated new arrivals, whom it has been possible to date on the grounds of pottery and architecture, to the Early Bronze Age II, the beginning of the 3rd millenium.

The first and largest of these settlements, N. 380, was discovered by the author in 1968 near the tomb of Sheikh Nabi Sala in the Wadi el Sheikh, north of St. Catherine's Monastery.[4] This settlement was later partially excavated by I. Beit Arieh.[5] Further settlements of the "Nabi Sala" type have been found during the past few years and it would appear that, with the exception of a few camping sites between the Negev and southern Sinai, this wave of intruders settled about 10–15 km (6–9 miles) west of the copper ore region of Wadi Riqeita.

The Early Bronze Age immigrants did not found entirely new settlements, but instead settled at the abandoned sites of the earlier Timnian I period, building their own dwellings and corrals above and alongside the earlier remains, making use of the stones they found there. All the excavations of "Nabi Sala" settlements by I. Beit Arieh produced architectural remains, ashes, flint tools and also pottery fragments of two layers of settlement, of which the earlier and lower layer must, in our opinion, be assigned to the Timnian period. The large quantities of ashes found by the excavators beneath the floor and walls of the Early Bronze Age buildings make it seem probable that the earlier Timnian I structures had been destroyed by force, possibly in the course of the fighting for the "unification" of Egyptian territories.

What makes these Early Bronze Age settlements in Sinai especially interesting is the fact that a large part of the pottery and at least some of the flint implements found in living quarters and workshops had been imported from Canaanite southern Palestine and that many finds excavated in Canaan originated in southern Sinai. Shortly after the discovery of Sheikh Nabi Sala, the pottery found there was petrographically compared by A. Slatkin—and after the excavations of I. Beit Arieh, also by J. Glass—with the pottery of Canaanite Arad, a large fortified town of the Early Bronze Age II in the south of the Land of Canaan[6]; and it has been possible to prove that a substantial part of the "Nabi Sala" pottery is identical with the pottery of Arad and also that hand-made cooking pots from southern Sinai were used at Arad. These reciprocal pottery relations between a big city of Early Bronze Age Canaan and a group of settlements in southern Sinai make it appear highly probable that the immigrants were in fact Canaanites who had left southern Palestine for southern Sinai and settled there near the Timnian II copper smelting centres.

It seems likely that such interrelations existed not only between Arad and the "Nabi Sala" settlements of southern Sinai but that small Early Bronze Age settlements scattered over a wide area of the Levant maintained intensive trade relations with the major towns of that period. It may now be regarded as established that the "Nabi Sala" settlements can be attributed to the cultural zone of southern Canaan. The Canaanite character of the "Nabi Sala" settlements may also be shown by their architecture. Wide rectangular rooms (about 5 x 3.5 m or 16.5 x 11.5 feet), sometimes with stone benches, door substructures and column pediments in the centre of the rooms, are identical with the typical buildings of Early Bronze Age Arad. At Sheikh Nabi Sala the rooms are arranged in circular groups, giving the impression of a palisade.

The group of "Nabi Sala" settlements is about 10 km (6 miles) to the west of the copper ore deposits of the Wadi Riqeita, yet at none of the settlements have traces of copper smelting, i.e. smelting slag, been found. On the other hand, there were a few fragments of crucibles, casting moulds, and shapeless lumps of copper, as well as a few locally manufactured copper implements. We regard these finds as evidence that the "Nabi Sala" settlers were coppersmiths but not copper smelters, and clearly did not produce any copper themselves. We therefore assume that the Canaanite "Nabi Sala" settlers, coming from a country where copper had never been smelted, therefore lacked the extensive metallurgical experience indispensable to the production of copper and that they acquired their unwrought copper from the Timnian II settlements which, during that same period, produced unwrought copper in the nearby copper mining and smelting area of the Wadi Riqeita. Judging by the finds, the copper-working skills of the "Nabi Sala" settlers were rather primitive, and the exceedingly rare metallurgical traces make it seem unlikely that any important copper casting or copper working activities took place here. At none of the "Nabi Sala" settlements were any tuyeres or other bellows-parts found together with the remains of metalwork, although these were by then in use in all the metal producing sites both for smelting furnaces and for the crucible furnaces of coppersmiths, and it is therefore obvious that we are here dealing with a primitive copper-working technique that lagged considerably behind the highly developed technology of the Timnian II metallurgists.

The "Nabi Sala" settlements in southern Sinai were evidently trading posts engaged in a lively metal trade with the native Timnian II metallurgists, but who also transported by caravan other raw materials, such as shells of various kinds and perhaps also pottery to Canaan. It is important to point out in this context that the few Egyptian pottery vessels found at "Nabi Sala" settlements were invariably large storage vessels intended for transport and that fragments of Canaanite jars—possibly the containers of Canaanite oil and wine deliveries—have also been found at certain Timnian II settlements in southern Sinai.

These trade relations between southern Sinai and southern Palestine were only a small part of the well-attested and intensive trade connections between Proto-dynastic Egypt and Early Bronze Age Canaan. The "Nabi Sala" invasion of southern Sinai, though archaeologically extremely interesting, was historically only a minor episode in the history of Sinai.

EGYPTIAN PHARAONIC MINING EXPEDITIONS—TURQUOISE AND COPPER The incorporation of the northern and eastern territories into Proto-dynastic Egypt, accomplished in the reign of Hor Aha (c. 2955–2925 B.C.) and consolidated by the subjugation of the Sinai nomads by Hor Den (c. 2870–2820 B.C.), brought the Timnian I period to an end. From then on we find, in settlements of the final Timnian phase (Timnian II), evidence of Egyptian copper smelting technology, as well as quantities of Proto-dynastic Egyptian pottery (e.g. site N. 701 in the Wadi Riqeita area). However, it took several more decades before, under the reign of Nebka (c. 2635–2620 B.C.), the first king of the Third Dynasty, the local Timnian II population of Sinai—and their Canaanite "guests"—finally vanished from the annals of Sinai history. Thenceforth and throughout the history of dynastic Egypt, with the exception only of the Intermediate Periods and periods of extreme domestic unrest, Pharaonic expeditions to south Sinai engaged in intensive turquoise and copper mining activities and maintained more or less amicable relations with the "Bedouin of the East". Although stelae on rock faces in the Maghara region and in the Wadi Kharig testify to further clashes with the local Semitic inhabitants, these hostilities gradually died down after the Fifth Dynasty; after the Twelfth Dynasty, Pharaonic memorials to victories over the "Asian nomads" also disappeared from Sinai's rock faces.

The Timnian culture in Sinai ceased to exist at the beginning of the Third Dynasty, but dynastic Egypt displayed very little interest in the vast desert region of central and southern Sinai. With the exception of the Pharaonic bases on the ancient military highway along the Mediterranean coast and one or two lesser locations of the Middle Kingdom in the Bay of El Markha, possibly

77 Jewish *menorah* (seven-branched candlestick), surrounded by a Hebrew inscription, of which it has so far only been possible to decipher the word "shalom" ("peace"). It was found by Beno Rothenberg near 'Ain Hudera, together with many other rock carvings (see Plates 79—82).

78 The oasis valley of 'Ain Hudera is one of the most beautiful landscapes in Sinai. Despite the date palms thriving there, and despite the good water, the Bedouin are compelled to move with their herds to better grazing areas. In consequence, the oasis is mostly deserted. The entire valley is bounded by two rifts belonging to the fault system of the Gulf of Elat-'Aqaba.

79 One of the many Nabataean rock inscriptions from the 'Ain Hudera neighbourhood. It reads: "In memory of 'Oyaidu and 'Abu'ausu and Borai'u the sons of Harisu". The Harisu family is mentioned in many southern Sinai inscriptions—especially near the turquoise mines.

80/81 Byzantine pilgrims' crosses near 'Ain Hudera testify to the passage of Christian pilgrims, presumably from the direction of the Holy Land to the Mountain of Moses.

82 Camel caravan—a Nabataean rock carving on sandstone near 'Aid Hudera.

83 Greek Orthodox chapel on Tell el Mekharet in the Wadi Feiran—at one time the only Nabataean-Romano-Byzantine town in southern Sinai. In the third century A.D. the first Christian hermits settled here in mountain caves (some of these can be seen in the background), and the first Christian monastery in Sinai was built here. All that is left of it today are the ruins, but until comparatively recently a solitary monk was still living in a well-tended garden below the remains of the ancient monastery. It was he who built the chapel in the foreground of the picture. Now everything is abandoned.

84 Feiran—formerly Pharan, often identified with biblical Refidim—is the largest oasis in Sinai. An ancient desert track used to run through it, as well as the Roman road from Aila (Elat) through Pharan (Feiran) and Clysma (Suez) to Egypt. Thousands of date palms and numerous wells enable a considerable number of Bedouin to lead a settled life here.

85 The Wadi Maghara ("Wadi of the Caves") is the famous valley of the turquoise mines. It was sought out by miners as early as the Neolithic Age and again during the Timnian period. The Egyptian Pharaohs of the Old and Middle Kingdoms sent mining expeditions to the Wadi Maghara; these left not only ruins of workmen's camps, stone tools and pottery vessels, but also many monumental inscriptions on the walls of the turquoise mines. The picture was taken from a steep, high hill situated in the turquoise region, which was developed, in the Old Kingdom, into a fortified workmen's camp (partly visible in the foreground). In the valley, an Egyptian workmen's camp and on the slopes, the spoil of the turquoise mines.

79

80

81

82

harbour installations, there was not a single Egyptian urban settlement or even Egyptian village throughout the territory of central and southern Sinai all through the long history of Pharaonic Egypt. To the Pharaohs, Sinai remained a strange no-man's-land that was left to the nomads so long as they kept the peace and worked on Egyptian mining enterprises. Only there, in the turquoise mining area, are remains found of fortified Pharaonic labour camps, monumental rock drawings and a large Egyptian temple.[7]

Sinai's earliest *turquoise mines* are in the region of *Maghara* ("the caves"), on the western side of the sandstone belt south of the Tih escarpment, on a mountain about 150 m (500 ft) high—Gebel el Maghara—in the Wadi Qenaia. There, turquoise was mined even in prehistoric times, and Pharaonic mining expeditions are attested from the beginning of the Third Dynasty onwards, through the centuries of the entire Old Kingdom, during the Middle Kingdom (Twelfth Dynasty) and even for a short while under the New Kingdom, by monumental rock inscriptions and by the living-quarters of the miners. The ancient mines can now scarcely be identified on account of the continued exploitation by Bedouin, who have used explosives to drive huge galleries into the mountain. However, the mining methods may be reconstructed from old accounts of travels and from the publications of H. Bauerman[8] and Flinders Petrie: as the turquoise occurs in several strata lying one above the other in the sandstone formation of Gebel el Maghara, low galleries were driven into the sandstone horizontally. The turquoise occurred in narrow seams and these were followed by the miners over long distances, with the result that the galleries were enlarged into very large cavities, in which pillars were left standing to support the roof. Chisel and hammer marks can still be seen on the walls today. The broken rock was taken to the gallery entrance and the small white or ochre-coloured turquoise nodules were picked out there in the daylight. Large tips of waste rock still cover the mountain-side. On the rock face of Gebel el Maghara large rock inscriptions of the Pharaohs were found, enabling the mines to

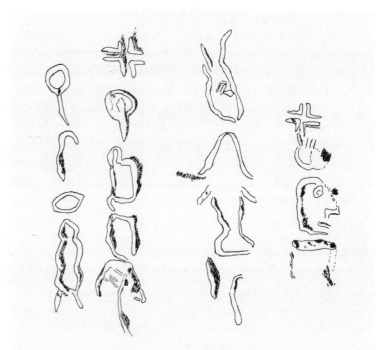

Fig. 30: Proto-Sinaitic inscription at Bir Nasib (after A. F. Rainey).

be dated. The first workmen's camps of the Old Kingdom were built, presumably for reasons of security, on a high plateau rising to about 70 m (230 ft) between the Wadi Qenaia and the Wadi Iqna. Later, the camps were set up on the *wadi* slopes, but they are all protected by walls surrounding the living and working quarters of the miners and officials.

In some of the workers' camps fragments of coppercasting moulds were found, presumably for the manufacture of miners' tools from copper which was actually produced elsewhere in Sinai.

At the time of the Old Kingdom the "principal god" of the expeditions was Thot, possibly an Egyptianized version of the local moon god. Later, during the Middle Kingdom, the goddess Hathor, the "House [= mother] of Horus", appeared as a "female partner" in the Maghara pantheon.

Serabit el Khadim is a plateau approximately 850 m (2,800 ft) high, displaying the same geological formation as the Maghara region, except that the upper sandstone

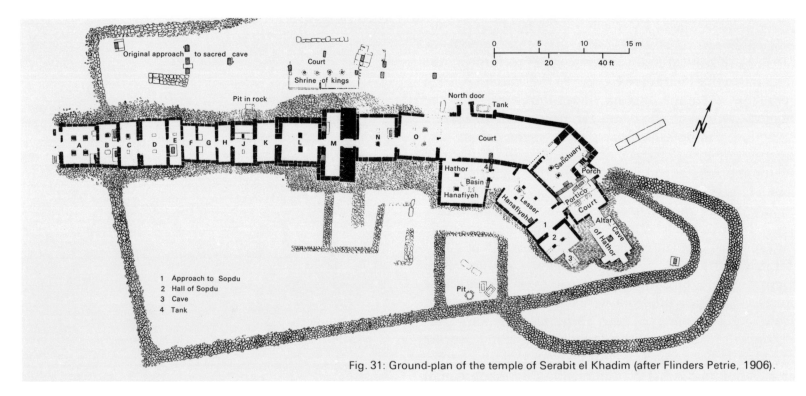

Fig. 31: Ground-plan of the temple of Serabit el Khadim (after Flinders Petrie, 1906).

formations have been totally eroded there, so that the turquoise-bearing schist layer is almost at the surface of the plateau. Here, too, as at Gebel el Maghara, clear traces have been found of prehistoric and Timnian mining. The Egyptian miners drove short vertical shafts down to the turquoise-bearing horizons; these served as the entrance to the workings as well as for ventilation and light, and it was in these shafts that archaeologists found hieroglyphic records of the expeditions. Occasionally, when erosion had laid bare the turquoise-bearing schist layer, the gallery opening was horizontal, as at Gebel el Maghara. The galleries of Serabit el Khadim were very similar to those of the Maghara area, except that the masonry is noticeably more careful, due presumably to the use of good-quality bronze tools instead of the earlier copper chisels. These implements were manufactured locally at Serabit el Khadim, a fact attested by finds of crucibles, moulds and pot-bellows.
In these dark galleries of the turquoise mines a discovery was made in 1906 which for a long time kept scholars in

suspense. The walls revealed inscriptions in a hitherto unknown script, which bore a marked similarity to Egyptian hieroglyphics and which is nowadays called the *"Proto-Sinaitic"* script. Similar inscriptions were also found by Flinders Petrie on votive objects in the temple of Serabit el Khadim. Although he was unable to decipher the inscriptions, Petrie realised that it was a Semitic alphabetic script—in fact the earliest alphabetic script found so far[9]. Petrie dated the inscriptions as belonging to the 15th century B.C. and regarded them as votive writings by the Semitic miners labouring in the Pharaoh's turquoise mines, using the alphabetic script they had developed from hieroglyphic signs. It is not surprising that such ideas were immediately connected with biblical events and caused a great deal of excitement.
At the eastern end of the plateau are the famous ruins of the temple of *Serabit el Khadim*. Initially, at the time of the Twelfth Dynasty, this had been no more than a small cave, equipped as a rock shrine to the goddess Hathor, the "Lady of Turquoise". Two chambers were

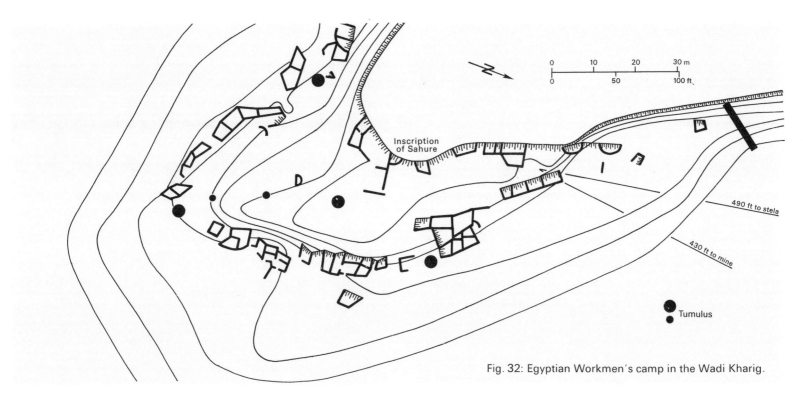

490 ft to stela
430 ft to mine

Tumulus

Fig. 32: Egyptian Workmen's camp in the Wadi Kharig.

subsequently added, dedicated to the god Sopdu. Sopdu, the "Lord of the Eastern Desert" or "Ruler of Foreign Lands", as he is called in the inscriptions, was presumably a local god of Sinai.

Still at the time of the Middle Kingdom, the "Shrine of Kings" was built, but it was not until the period of the New Kingdom, following the Hyksos period, during which no Egyptian expeditions appeared in Sinai, that a new period of construction gave the temple its present form: starting at the great eastern Court, the kings of the Eighteenth Dynasty added a long series of spacious chambers (O–C in the plan), in which numerous stelae describe in great detail the history of the Pharaonic mining expeditions. The interior walls of the temple were everywhere also covered with hieroglyphic inscriptions and pictorial representations. The last two rooms (B and A) were added during the Ramesside period; the last Pharaoh represented here is Ramesses VI.

The temple chambers yielded an exceptional number of small finds, including votive objects, jewellery and figurines, most of which had been brought from Egypt to Serabit el Khadim to ensure the help of the gods in the mining activities. The finds also include the sculptured figure of a female sphinx which, besides the hieroglyphic name of Hathor, also bore a votive inscription in Proto-Sinaitic script, in which the name "Ba'alath", probably the Semitic name of the goddess Hathor, is mentioned. This find shows unequivocally that the Egyptians and the Semitic miners performed their rituals in the temple of Serabit el Khadim together—a situation known to us also from the Egyptian-Midianite miners' sanctuary at Timna.[10] It may therefore be assumed that by the time of the Middle Kingdom the Semitic miners were free workers and not prisoners or slaves. This fact is also confirmed elsewhere in the temple of Serabit el Khadim. There has been much discussion about the origin of those Semitic workers, and various regions—Palestine, Syria, the Arabian Peninsula—have been suggested as their homeland, but the early history of Sinai, as it is understood now, makes it seem probable that they were semi-nomadic native inhabitants of the Sinai peninsula itself, descendants of the Timnian settlers of earlier centuries. Only in this way can we explain the fact that a local god—Sopdu—was venerated together with the Egyptian Hathor = Ba'alath, both by the Egyptians and by their Semitic "partners".

Copper ore was mined and smelted in southern Sinai already during Egypt's Proto-dynastic period. In the Wadi Riqeita area, in the east, Proto-dynastic and Old Kingdom pottery have been found in at least seven smelting camps which had already existed in the Timnian period, together with primitive tapped slag and the typical tuyeres and architecture of those periods. At some of these settlements, such as site N. 701, the metallurgists of the New Kingdom also left their own unmistakable slag and tuyeres, such as are known from other New Kingdom smelting camps in Sinai and in the 'Araba (e.g. at Timna). There evidently existed a rather long tradition of local copper production, but the quantities of copper produced in the Wadi Riqeita area never amounted to more than a few hundred kilograms in any of the periods referred to. At that time copper must therefore have been an expensive luxury material.

Flinders Petrie's explorations resulted in only the turquoise mining areas of Maghara and Serabit el Khadim being recognized as Egyptian mining centres. For this reason there were constant discussions on whether the Egyptians had, in fact, actually produced any copper in Sinai. It has now been possible to give a definitive answer to this question, thanks to our discovery of a hitherto unknown Egyptian mining centre in the Wadi Kharig, a lateral branch of the big Wadi Ba'ba', in the immediate vicinity of an ancient copper mine, as well as of remains of smelting furnaces and slag. The official Egyptian map of Sinai records an "ancient mine" in the Wadi Kharig, described by 19th century travellers, which still contained manganese and iron ore. The mine is exceedingly irregular, sunk obliquely into the ore horizon, about 100 m (330 ft) long, 10 m (33 ft) wide and 2 m (nearly 7 ft) high. The miners of those days evidently left the manganese and iron ores untouched and mined only the copper ore which, throughout western Sinai, occurs together with manganese and iron in the same horizon. On the mountain above the mine there lies a stela of King Sesostris I of the Twelfth Dynasty which, when it stood upright in antiquity, was visible from a great distance, marking the location of the copper mine. On the stela, Hathor—"the Lady of Turquoise"—is described as the patron deity of the king.[11]

About 150 m (500 ft) south of the stela of Sesostris I the author discovered a typical Old Kingdom workers' camp. This is a long row of adjoining rooms, constructed in a semi-circle against a steep rock face. On that rock face, in the middle of the camp, there is a carefully executed monumental hieroglyphic inscription of King Sahure of the Fifth Dynasty. In the camp itself, potsherds were found, together with some copper casting slag and fragments of crucibles. We have here a third centre of dynastic Egyptian activity in Sinai, in fact the earliest metallurgical workers' camp of the Old Kingdom, built, as was the big camp of Maghara, on a steep hill, no doubt for the sake of security. The security problems of Pharaonic expeditions to Sinai are reflected also in the inscription in the Wadi Kharig: "Toth, Lord of Fear, who conquers the land of Setjet [Asia]."

We now know that copper was produced and cast in western Sinai already during the Fifth Dynasty—but the first great "copper king" of the Egyptians was presumably Ammenemes III (1842–1798 B.C.), the last important ruler of the Twelfth Dynasty. Whenever the stelae of Egyptian mining expeditions in Sinai mention copper, and wherever copper slag has been found in workers' camps of the Maghara region, the name of Ammenemes III occurs. In order to be able to practise such extensive copper mining, Ammenemes III had to recruit additional local labour. That may be the reason for the evident pacification of the eastern neighbours—the "men of Retjenu"—who are represented at Serabit el Khadim as free, arms-bearing "partners" under the leadership of "the brother of the Prince of Retjenu".

It is also Ammenemes III whose stela was hewn into the rock on a mountain ridge above the large heaps of cop-

Fig. 33: Situation-plan of large copper smelting works at Bir Nasib.

per slag at *Bir Nasib*. Bir Nasib was the most important copper smelting centre in Sinai: the huge slag heap near the ancient well has been calculated at 100,000 tons—for that period of antiquity a vast copper industry.

The slags of Bir Nasib represent at least two different smelting processes and they cover a large part of the wide valley floor, where two ancient wells still yield plenty of water. Today there is also a big Bedouin village there. The ruins of two buildings near the slag heap could be dated to the New Kingdom. On the slag heap were found not only two different types of Egyptian tuyeres but also Egyptian pottery, some of which was also manufactured locally. According to calculations by H. G. Bachmann[12], the total production at Bir Nasib amounted to about 5000 t of metallic copper. Such an extensive copper production required large quantities of copper ore—and this was until recently one of the great problems of the archaeology—and geology—of Sinai. Our expedition succeeded in solving this problem by the discovery of a large number of hitherto unnoticed smaller copper ore mines in the manganese horizon in and around Bir Nasib. In all these places there are small galleries around which manganese and iron ores were left untouched, because at that time only the copper ore—chiefly malachite and paratacamite—were of interest.

Inscriptions found near the copper mines testify that from the Middle Kingdom onwards, Bir Nasib was important at certain times as a mining and metallurgical centre. Near the stela of Ammenemes III, the Swiss traveller G. Gerster[13] found two Proto-Sinaitic inscriptions; one of these was dedicated to the "commander of the labour camp"[14]—see Plate 65—which presumably meant the copper smelting camp in the valley of Bir Nasib. Potsherds recovered during the author's excavations of the slag heap of Bir Nasib in 1978 date back to the period of the New Kingdom, but, in view of the stela of Ammenemes III, we assume that somewhere at the bottom of the slag heap, remains of the Middle Kingdom are to be found.

On a rock face in the immediate neighbourhood of the slag heap, the author found yet another monumental rock carving of the New Kingdom. This shows two male Egyptians facing each other, and between them a cartouche of one of the Ramesside kings, presumably Ramesses IV. The two men are identified by hieroglyphic inscriptions as "Paenrai, the commander of the troops and overseer in the mountain land" and "Neferroupe, the royal butler"[15], i.e. they were the Pharaoh's commander and official at Bir Nasib.

A few Nabataean inscriptions found on a rock at the southern end of the slag heap, and a fine Nabataean inscription at the entrance to a small copper mine on the western side of the Bir Nasib valley, testify to the continuity of copper production at Bir Nasib down to Nabataean-Roman times.

Our researches in Sinai and the 'Araba have yielded an entirely new picture of the highly developed mining and metallurgical industry in the New Kingdom. At nearly all locations in southern Sinai where copper was mined and smelted at various Pre-dynastic and Proto-dynastic periods, the typical metallurgical remains of the New Kingdom were also found. In addition to the large copper industry in the Wadi Nasib, the New Kingdom also smelted copper in the Wadi Ba'ba', in the Reqeita region, in the Wadi Shellal and in the mountains west of the 'Araba.

Although the Pharaohs of the New Kingdom continued to take an interest in the turquoise mines, the centre of industrial activity clearly shifted to the production of copper. The archaeological finds in Sinai and in the 'Araba—as well as the descriptions in the Harris I papyrus scroll—indicate that Ramesses III was Egypt's last great "copper king".

ANCIENT ROADS—FROM THE NEOLITHIC TO THE MIDDLE AGES When we speak of an ancient road through the desert, we must not think of anything like a regular highway. Often a desert road is not much more than a pathway, a strip of land or a watershed through which hundreds of narrow tracks run in one direction, or a narrow *wadi* where many beaten tracks from all directions converge, to continue jointly to their destination. Mostly a desert road is determined by the topography of the terrain, but it is always the sources of water—springs, wells and cisterns—that attract the desert traveller and his pack animals over great distances and thus determine the route. That is why desert routes have remained unchanged since time immemorial.

The oldest "road" in Sinai is the *Darb esh Shawi*, which runs right through the great Tih wilderness, linking the Gulf of Elat-'Aqaba with the Gulf of Suez. Climbing the Sinai plateau from the east, the ancient roadway first runs through territory that has been well populated since earliest times, extending from the mountains west of the 'Araba to the vicinity of Bir el Themed. As everywhere along the edges of the Badiet el Tih, there is a relative abundance of water and, in consequence, settlements and camping sites of all the prehistoric and historic periods of Sinai: a few stations of the Pre-Pottery Neolithic and of the Elatian periods, and a remarkably large number of Timnian settlements, in some of which remains of the Early Bronze Age IV have also been found. Then for a long time there was nothing at all—except possibly Bedouin occupation, but these nomads leave no datable traces—after which the remains of the New Kingdom appear near small copper ore deposits and smelting camps in the metamorphic rock of the region. No doubt the mining expeditions of the New Kingdom passed through on their way to the big copper mines of the 'Araba. At some settlements Romano-Byzantine and early Arab pottery fragments have also been found.

To the west of Bir el Themed, for approximately the next 120 km (75 miles), the road runs through arid desert country where no human traces have been found, apart from an occasional cairn grave. However, habitation remains immediately appear again when the road enters the well-watered region of the Wadi Sudr. Here, as also in the Wadi Raha, which leads down from the Tih plateau south of Gebel Raha to the Gulf of Suez, there are a number of springs and again numerous settlements from different periods of early Sinai history.

Every devout Muslim, man or woman, is expected to make at least one pilgrimage to Mecca in his or her lifetime. For this reason the early caliphs, both for religious and for political reasons, built pilgrims' roads—*"Darb el Hagg"*—which have been used repeatedly for a thousand years by believers from all Islamic countries.

The "Egyptian Hagg road", which runs from Suez to 'Aqaba across the Tih desert and has served pilgrims from North Africa, Egypt and Spain, was constructed in the year 875 A.D. by the Egyptian governor of Caliph Ahmed Ibn Tulun. At first little more than a few narrow parallel tracks between resting and watering places, it was soon worn by the feet of pilgrims and their pack animals upon the stones of the roadway into a broad glistening band across the desert. This can still be seen today, even though the Darb el Hagg was developed in 1816 by Ibrahim Pasha, the son of Muhammad 'Ali, into a road suitable for vehicles. Along the Darb el Hagg there were a number of halts with not only cisterns and large open water pools or dams, but also with rest-houses—and in their vicinity "densely inhabited" cemeteries.

The Darb el Hagg begins at 'Ajrud in the Suez area, and runs north of the Mittla Pass, and parallel to it, across the Wadi el Hagg into the Wadi el Qubab. At that point there once stood a most interesting station, which was investigated by the author in 1972. Strangely enough, the "Survey of Egypt" map has the sign for "chapel ruin" at that point. Instead of the expected Byzantine chapel, the author's expedition found a domed Muslim tomb there and a complicated system of retaining dams and water reservoirs for the storage of rainwater. We found no well of any kind and it seems that this station depended solely on its dams. These were probably constructed by the Mameluk Sultan Hasan (1347–1357).[16]

About 80 km (50 miles) east of the Wadi el Qubab, in the middle of the great Tih desert, stands the main station of the "Egyptian Darb el Hagg"—namely, the "Qal'at [fortress] el Nekhel". This was built by El Malik el Dynkandar in 1331 and subsequently enlarged by Kansuh el Ghawri (1509) and 'Ali Pasha (1551). The wells and water reservoirs of Nekhel (Nakhl), however, were known as early as the 13th century and it is assumed that they were built by Sultan Hasan.

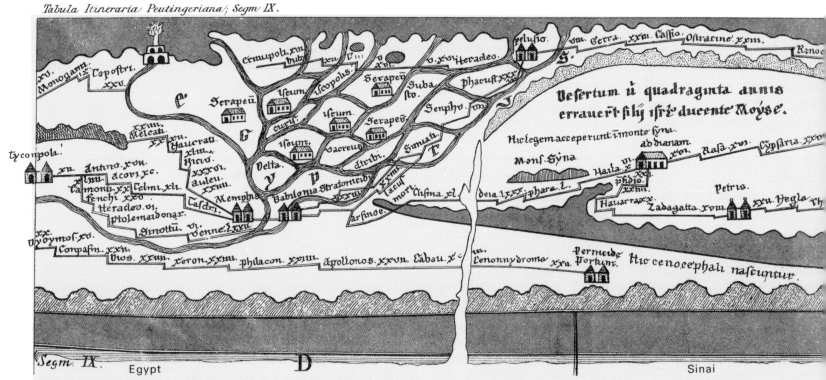

Tabula Itineraria Peutingeriana; Segm IX.

Segm. IX.   Egypt   D   Sinai

Fig. 34: Detail from the Tabula Peutingeriana (Peutinger Table). In the lower part, the road leading from Aila——"Haila" on the map——to Pharan in the

The fortress of Nekhel (Nakhl) was built to protect the precious water supply and it had a well within its walls, but it was at the same time a military and supply post. Inside the fortress there were a two-storeyed caravanserai and a small mosque. The fortified wall was remarkable for its careful masonry and had four circular corner towers; above the gateway, a few circular Arabic cartouches were inset as historical records. To the desert traveller who had just traversed the long road across the flat and utterly desolate Tih plateau, this fine building must have seemed like an incredible mirage. Unfortunately it was destroyed in the Sinai war of 1956.

No less impressive is the 'Aqabat el Urqub rock passage 180 m (590 ft) in length cut through white limestone along the Darb el Hagg to the east of Themed; it was discovered by the author in 1967.[17] On the south wall of this passage, which is 15 m (49 ft) wide, two monumental Mameluk Arabic inscriptions are carved in the rock; one of these is a cartouche of Sultan Kansuh el Ghawri, dating the rock passage to the years 1508 to 1510.[18] The

'Aqabat el Urqub is most impressive and surprising—but it is not easy to explain why such immense labour was invested at that spot since, fundamentally, the passage does nothing to improve the roadway. Possibly it was envisaged merely as a monumental memorial to the Sultan's great road-building project.

Some 50 km (30 miles) further to the east, the Darb el Hagg runs into the magnificent and steep descent to the Red Sea—called "Naqb el 'Aqaba"—constructed by Ahmed Ibn Tulun in 875 A.D. Here, on the summit of the pass, there are inns and resting places for pilgrims' caravans and also the camping sites of the builders of this superb roadway serpenting down from the mountains. Only Muslim remains are found along the Darb el Hagg and there is no doubt that this road did not come into existence until the Muslim period, unlike the Darb esh Shawi further south, which was important mainly during earlier periods of settlement in Sinai. But where is that great Romano-Byzantine road which, according to the Tabula Peutingeriana[19], ran from Aila ('Aqaba) to Clys-

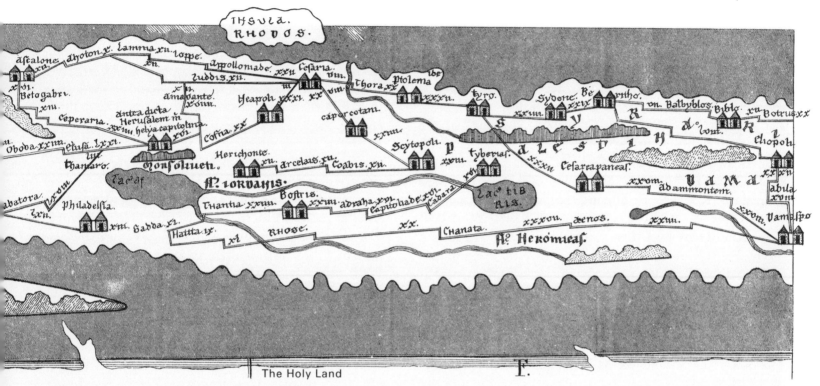

The Holy Land

F.

south of the Sinai mountains and thence to Clysma (Suez) can be recognized; on the upper margin of the map the coast road from Askalon to Pelusium.

ma (Suez) and which has until recently been marked on historical maps as running right across the Tih desert? This "table" of Romano-Byzantine roads compiled by the Roman cosmographer Castorius in the second half of the 4th century A.D., shows an important road with stations, but neither the Darb esh Shawi nor the Darb el Hagg can be regarded as a Roman road.

When the author's expedition embarked on its work in southern Sinai, it was looking for the ancient road from the Gulf of Elat-'Aqaba to the turquoise and copper mines in the south. It soon became clear that, strictly speaking, there had always been only *one great line of communication* in all the periods of Sinai history. This roadway climbed up to the Tih plateau from the coast to the south of present-day Elat, through the Wadi Tueiba or one of the *wadis* parallel to it and thence ran south, with some bifurcations and local alternatives, through the *wadis* parallel to the coast as far as 'Ain Hudera. From there, the route ran through the Wadi Saal and the Wadi Zaghra into the central ore-bearing massif in the

south. The big oasis in the Wadi Feiran was the southern-most point on this route; from there, several tracks led to the ore deposits of Maghara, Bir Nasib, Serabit el Khadim, etc. From the Wadi Feiran, where the principal station of the ancient route was found, the track led to the north, up to the Tih plateau and then followed the watershed towards the north to Clysma = Suez. All along this route the expedition found settlement remains of early periods—from the Neolithic period to the New Kingdom.

When, about the middle of the twelfth century B.C., the Egyptians withdrew to the Egyptian heartland and also evacuated Sinai, numerous Early Iron Age newcomers appeared in the region and made their temporary homes along that route in earlier settlements that had been abandoned. Again it was a settlement vacuum—the withdrawal of the Egyptians—that attracted new immigrants. Traces of these Early Iron Age arrivals have also been found in the copper ore region of the Wadi Riqeita and in the turquoise region of the west—but we have no direct evidence so far that these people practised mining or smelted copper. The historic, and above all the ethnic, background to the emergence of Early Iron Age pottery in Sinai has so far remained unsolved—though biblical traditions here encourage bold speculation.

The most striking features of the route described above are the incredible number of Nabataean to Byzantine rock drawings and inscriptions scratched or chiselled everywhere on the rock faces in the wadis, and the large number of Romano-Byzantine camping sites along that road. There are, it is true, also many rock inscriptions, on high mountains and in remote wadis, that are not in direct connection with the road or with the ore deposits —we assume that they were the work of shepherds—but the great concentrations of rock drawings indicate clearly the route of the great highway into the Wadi Feiran and thence into the several ore bearing regions in the east and west of southern Sinai.

The Nabataeans, whose kingdom extended over the territory of Jordan, the northwest of Saudi Arabia and the Negev, and who built settlements and cities there and left numerous rock drawings and inscriptions on the cliffs, also wandered about Sinai for several centuries and thence into Egypt. Wherever there were ore deposits there also were Nabataeans—both in the heartland of their own empire and in Sinai and eastern Egypt. Our expedition found unequivocal evidence that the Nabataeans mined both turquoise and copper—or at least traded in these commodities. Perhaps their possession of minerals and metals and their trade in them was the reason for the wealth of their state—and for that matter the cause of its downfall?

Not only the Nabataeans, but also Judaeans from Palestine, travelled along the Aila–Clysma road and there, at a number of places, they left not only Aramaic-Hebrew inscriptions but also the Jewish symbol of the seven-branched *menorah*. The Nabataeans—and Judaeans—continued to be present in Sinai even after the Nabataean empire had been wiped out as a result of its "annexation" by the Romans; datable Nabataean inscriptions were still found in the Byzantine period.

The Romans themselves displayed little more than a rudimentary interest in southern Sinai; their main interest was in the Mediterranean coastal road from Egypt to Palestine. Whereas a few Late-Roman fortlets existed in the 'Araba and inscriptions of the Third Legio *Cyrenaica*, only one single settlement with Roman remains has been found in southern Sinai—on Tell el Mekharet in the Wadi Feiran—and here and there a few traces at the ore deposits. They also produced a little copper but, as the processing of the archaeological material has shown, such production was of purely local significance. For the Roman Empire, Sinai was a remote desert territory of rather minor economic or military importance. With the birth of Christian traditions, hermitages, monasteries and chapels came into existence around the "Mount of the Revelation" and the rather laborious Aila–Clysma route became a much-travelled pilgrims' road. Now Christian symbols and Byzantine inscriptions were scratched on the rock face—a new aspect of cultural history recorded on the rocks of the Sinai desert.

Camping sites and tombs, inscriptions and potsherds along the Aila–Clysma road investigated by our expedition now make it possible to identify the "stations" mentioned in the Peutinger Table: *Aila*, spelt "Haila" in the table, is generally assumed to have been in the vicinity of present-day 'Aqaba, where ruins with Romano-Byzantine potsherds have been found. *Phara*, presumably present-day Feiran, is identified as Tell el Mekharet, where a fortified town with a big monastery and a large Christian community was situated in the Byzantine period. *Deia*—possibly "Medeia"—is up on the Tih plateau and is identified by the author with the big desert station N.690 in the Wadi el Khuteimiya, the continuation of the vast Wadi Umm Gidla. The end of this road, *Clysma*, is to be sought in the Suez area.

The history of mining and settlement in southern Sinai was superseded by Christian monastic and pilgrim traditions and the "earthly" history of industry, settlement and warfare was transformed into a chapter of religious history—marking the end of Sinai research proper.

Beno Rothenberg

Notes

1 In: W. M. Flinders Petrie, Researches in Sinai, 1906, p. 239–240, Fig. 170, 171.

2 B. Rothenberg, Sinai Explorations 1967–1972, Bulletin, Museum Haaretz Tel Aviv, 1972, p. 35.

3 'B. Rothenberg, R. F. Tylecote, P. J. Boydell, Chalcolithic Copper Smelting, Archaeo-Metallurgy I, 1978.

4 B. Rothenberg, An Archaeological Survey of South Sinai, Palestine Exploration Quarterly, 1970, p. 27.

5 I. Beit Arieh, An Early Bronze Age II Site at Nabi Salah in Southern Sinai, Tel Aviv Vol. 1, 1974.

6 R. Amiran, Early Arad, 1979.

7 W. M. Flinders Petrie, Researches in Sinai, 1906; A. H. Gardiner, T. E. Peet, J. Černy, The Inscriptions of Sinai, 1955.

8 H. Bauerman, Quarterly Journal of Geological Society, 25, 1869.

9 W. F. Albright, The Proto-Sinaitic Inscriptions and their Decipherment, 1969. Albright dates the inscriptions between 1525 and 1475 B.C.

10 B. Rothenberg, Timna, 1972.

11 A. Schulman, The Egyptian Inscriptions from Bir Nasib and Wadi Kharig, in B. Rothenberg (Ed.), New Researches in Sinai (in preparation).

12 B. Rothenberg (Ed.), New Researches in Sinai (in preparation).

13 G. Gerster, Sinai, Land der Offenbarung, 1961.

14 A. F. Rainey, Notes on some Proto-Sinaitic Inscriptions, Israel Exploration Journal, 25, 1975.

15 A. Schulman, in B. Rothenberg (Ed.) New Researches in Sinai (in preparation).

16 In the tracks of the author's expedition, the Arabist S. Tamari investigated a few stations along the Darb el Hagg. See S. Tamari, Darb el Hagg in Sinai: Al Qubab, Arabic and Islamic Studies 2, Bar Ilan University, 1977.

17 B. Rothenberg, An Archaeological Survey of South Sinai, Palestine Exploration Quartely, 102, 1970 (Site N. 335).

18 S. Tamari, An Inscription of Qansun al-Gauri from 'Aqabat al 'Urqub, Atti della Accad. Naz. dei Lincei, Roma, 1971.

19 See K. Miller. Die Peutingersche Tafel, 1962.

86 Greek monk from St. Catherine's Monastery. At present the monastery houses about a dozen monks.

87 The fortified Monastery of St. Catherine was built in the 6th century by the Emperor Justinian (527—563) to protect the monks against the raids of hostile Saracens. In spite of numerous restorations and new buildings (library and pilgrims' rest-house) a large part of the original building still survives; the monastery has been inhabited continuously since its foundation in the 6th century. In the courtyard, beside the church, stands a mosque——an unusual sight. To the right, in the monastery orchard, is the charnel-house.

88 The summit of the Mountain of Moses——Gebel Musa——with its small chapel.

89 The basilica of St. Catherine's Monastery is the oldest Christian church to have had divine services conducted in it uninterruptedly since its foundation. It is built in the early Byzantine style and adorned, in the Greek Orthodox manner, with precious votive gifts from different periods and from all over the world.

90 The monastery bell which summons the monks to prayer.

91, 95—97 The monastery walls are decorated with numerous reliefs representing Christian symbols. The external wall has embrasure-like openings which probably served as look-outs and which are surmounted by stone coats-of-arms and monograms.

92—94 The Crusaders left their coats-of-arms and memorial inscriptions on the walls and gates of the monastery.

98 In the gorges of the granite mountains, shallow pools of water or springs of clear refreshing water are often encountered. At the edge of these pools grow thick clumps of sea rushes *(Juncus maritimus)*, which is processed into ropes and cords.

87
88

95

96

97

Land Bridge Between Asia and Africa

Archaeology of Northern Sinai
up to the Classical Period

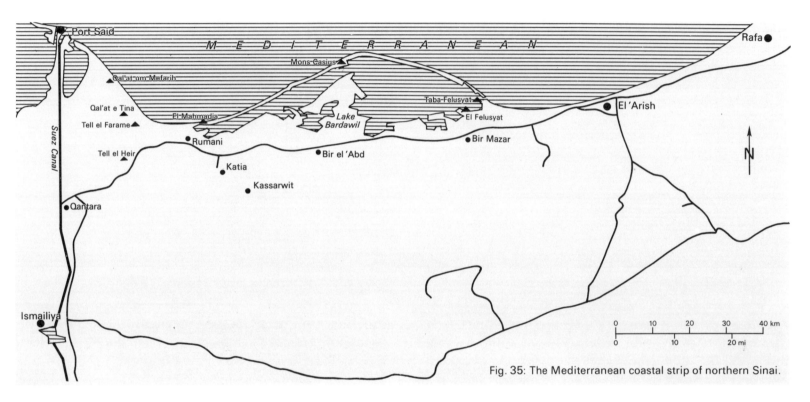

Fig. 35: The Mediterranean coastal strip of northern Sinai.

The Mediterranean coastal strip of the Sinai peninsula, stretching between the Suez Canal and Gaza, was undoubtedly the most important land bridge linking Egypt and Canaan from Pre-dynastic times onwards. The well-travelled highways of North Sinai facilitated the military expeditions of the Egyptian pharaohs on their way to Canaan and Asia, as well as of the invading armies of Persia, Greece, Rome and others who set out to conquer Egypt. In 1920 the eminent Egyptologist, Sir Alan Gardiner, concluded his study on the ancient military road in North Sinai with the words: "There can be little or no doubt that the road from El Kantara [the starting point on the east Delta frontier] to Gaza via Rafa has witnessed the marches of nine-tenths of the armies that sought to invade Palestine from Egypt, or Egypt from Palestine, along the land route."

Because of its strategic, political and economic importance the history of North Sinai is well documented in ancient records and maps. Greek and Roman historians and geographers, such as Herodotus, Strabo, Pliny,

Josephus and Ptolemy, provide valuable information on the early history of North Sinai. Additional data are available from maps and itineraries, such as the Tabula Peutingeriana, the Madaba Map, the Antonine Itinerary and the Notitia Dignitatum. These sources, however, are concerned primarily with the lines of communication and stations in North Sinai, disregarding such aspects as settlements and population, their cultural background and economic activity. Moreover, in spite of the close political and cultural links between Egypt and Canaan through North Sinai for nearly 2,000 years, the written evidence prior to the classical period is indeed very limited. This is actually confined to the "map" of the "Ways of Horus"—the military road of North Sinai— and the chain of stations and forts along it which was carved on the exterior north wall of the great Hypostyle Hall in the temple of Amun at Karnak during the early reign of Sethos I of the XIXth Dynasty. This relief is complemented by the itinerary of the military highway as detailed in the geographical section of the Papyrus

Fig. 36: Relief from the Temple of Amun at Karnak, showing the eastern canal and the line of fortifications along the military highway.

Anastasi I, which is assigned to the reign of Ramesses II. The earliest "map" and itinerary of the military road thus form the most comprehensive Egyptian document attesting the strategic importance of North Sinai as a land bridge between the Egyptian Delta and the northern provinces of Canaan and Syria. The reference to the "Ways of Horus" in the Sinuhe story of the Middle Kingdom period (20th century B.C.) would imply an even much earlier date for the establishment of this essential highway between Egypt and Asia. Occasional references to North Sinai in some New Kingdom papyri as well as in Assyrian records of the Egyptian campaigns, and Herodotus' testimony on the Persian invasion of Egypt under Cambyses provide some additional data concerning the inhabitants—"Shasu" and "Arabians" respectively—and the rôle they played in assisting the invading armies on their passage through North Sinai.

Ever since the beginnings of modern scholarship, North Sinai has attracted travellers and explorers. The literature, as a result, abounds in studies of the topography, flora and fauna and the local inhabitants—the Bedouin. To the student of Biblical history, North Sinai is of special significance because it was here, as argued by many scholars, that the Exodus from Egypt took place. Indeed, some of the more prominent landmarks in the Exodus itinerary have been almost universally located in North Sinai, i.e. *Migdol* (Tell el-Heir), *Yam Suph* (Lake Bardawil), *Baal Zephon* (Mount Casius), etc. Yet despite the historical importance of this region it had, until recently, hardly been explored. The present state of research is perhaps best illustrated by Gardiner's article quoted above. In this classic study, Gardiner skilfully analysed all available written sources for the identification of the Egyptian forts along the ancient military highway in North Sinai. The location of these forts, however, and consequently the alignment of the ancient road, is not founded on any archaeological evidence whatsoever and must therefore be regarded purely as a working hypothesis. Similarly, nearly fifteen years of pioneering research in the eastern Nile delta and along the coast of northern Sinai by the French archaeologist Jean Clédat (1910–1924) have certainly yielded most valuable data on the history of the region in Roman and Byzantine times but hardly, if at all, on the long period of settlement prior to the Hellenistic period. In spite of its very important rôle as a major link between the two great civilizations, North Sinai has, until recently, remained *terra incognita* to archaeology and history.

Since January 1972, the North Sinai Expedition of Ben-Gurion University of the Negev, under the direction of the author has been conducting a systematic archaeological survey between the Suez Canal and the Gaza Strip. The aim of the survey was to record all ancient sites in this area, to analyse the distribution and pattern of the settlements and their cultural affinities, as well as to examine the problem of cultural interaction between Egypt and Canaan against the background of the North Sinai sites. Thus far (1978) the North Sinai Expedition has explored and recorded over 800 sites, ranging in time from the Chalcolithic period in the fourth millennium B.C. to medieval times. These include roads, ancient waterways and irrigation systems, large settlements, villages, forts, caravan stations, cemeteries, industrial complexes and seasonal encampments. A number of these sites have also been excavated to enable us to control the dating of the sites throughout the region.

The most intensive periods of occupation were in the Early Bronze Age I–II or the Egyptian Proto-dynastic period, the Late Bronze Age or New Kingdom period, and the Persian to early Islamic period. The results of our survey have demonstrated clearly that, except for certain intervals of decline or hiatus, the coastal strip and sand-dune region of North Sinai not only acted as a corridor between Egypt and Canaan, but was also densely populated almost throughout its history. The material culture in the different periods of occupation in North Sinai reflected, in fact, the cultural intercourse between the civilizations which flourished at either end of that land bridge. At the same time the sites yielded ample evidence of the development of a local, indigenous, material culture stemming from the long period of permanent settlement. The following chapter summarizes the history and archaeology of North Sinai prior to Cambyses' invasion of Palestine and Egypt in 525 B.C. and the beginning of the classical era.

THE EARLIEST SETTLEMENTS IN NORTH SINAI   The earliest sites recorded to date in North Sinai belong to the Chalcolithic or Egyptian Pre-dynastic period in the fourth millennium B.C. In the light of the occurrences of Upper Paleolithic, Epi-Paleolithic and Neolithic settlement sites in Gebel Maghara and Gebel Lagama to the south of the surveyed area, as well as at both ends of it—in the Gaza Strip and the Egyptian Nile delta—it would seem most likely that the absence of sites earlier than the Chalcolithic period is due to some morphological changes that took place along the Mediterranean coast between the Nile delta and the Gaza Strip. The dozen sites of the Chalcolithic period were actually seasonal encampments comprising the remains of hearths and scattered bones, pottery and flint tools. The pottery falls under the same categories as best exemplified in the Beer-Sheba Culture, i.e. churns, painted bowls and jars, and even fragments of fenestrated and pedestalled basalt bowls. These are accompanied by Egyptian Late Pre-dynastic pottery types which are paralleled in some Deltaic sites such as Ma'adi.

More than one hundred sites belong to the Early Bronze Age I–II or the Egyptian Proto-dynastic period in the early third millennium B.C. These sites are distributed equally over the entire stretch of dunes in northern Sinai, though none has so far been encountered along the Mediterranean coast or on the sand bar of Lake Bardawil. The sites are usually clustered in groups of five to ten over an area of a few kilometres and are only 50–400 metres (160–1,310 ft) apart. They are located on the slopes of stationary sand dunes and shallow depressions between dune ridges. No architectural remains have been recorded at these sites, implying, perhaps, the use of huts and tents as dwellings. Judging by the remains of cooking and baking installations, i.e. clay ovens and baking bowls, as well as a large collection of stone tools and pottery vessels, it is conceivable that most of these sites were seasonal encampments while some, especially the larger ones, were permanent settlements or villages. It is of some interest that the location and distribution of the sites under review correspond very closely to those of present-day Bedouin settlements. It is argued, therefore, that a similar pattern of settlement—seasonal and permanent encampment, as well as villages—has prevailed in this region from as early as the fourth millennium B.C.

The early Bronze Age sites yielded stone tools and containers, flint tools, metal objects and large quantities of Egyptian and Canaanite pottery vessels. The impressive collection of Egyptian pottery included categories which are very common in Proto-dynastic contexts in Egypt, i.e. Gizeh, Saqqarra, Tarkhan, Abusir el Meleq, Abu Roash, Abydos, etc., as well as in Early Bronze Age I–II sites in southern Canaan, i.e. En Besor, Tell Halif, Tell Erani and Arad. The most popular type of vessel is the tall, elongated jar with scalloped design—Petrie's "Wavy Handle"—on the shoulder, and occasionally also a *serekh* inscription. Another type frequently recorded is the cylindrical vase with plastic or incised rouletted design below the rim, and sometimes also with a lattice pattern painted in red or brown. Other vessels include Petrie's "Red Polished" and "Rough Faced" as well as examples of his "Fancy" class.

The Canaanite assemblage is typified by the ledge-handled storage jars and jars with arched spouts and pillared handles. The majority of the Egyptian pottery belongs to the earlier part of the First Dynasty period. Accordingly, the Canaanite material is confined to the Early Bronze Age I–II types.

Since characteristic Early Bronze Age II elements such as platters and "Abydos" metallic ware are hardly represented in the North Sinai collection, we may argue that the *floruit* of our sites is limited to Early Bronze Age I and the beginning of Early Bronze Age II, corresponding with the late Pre-dynastic and First Dynasty periods in Egypt. It is worth noting that the proportion of Egyptian to Canaanite pottery throughout North Sinai is about 5:1. At the same time the areas on the fringe of the eastern Delta, like those to the east of the Wadi el 'Arish, are represented by sites in which Canaanite material was actually predominant. This observation seems to be an essential factor in understanding the nature of Canaanite–Egyptian confrontation during the period under review.

The collection of flint tools included ripple-flaked knives, serrated sickle blades, fan scrapers, transversal arrow-heads and other types which are best matched in

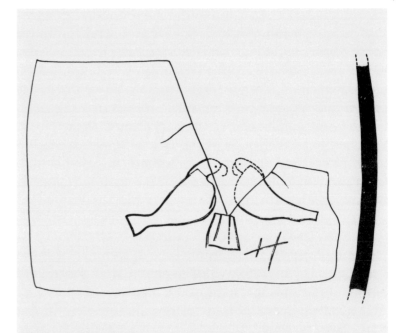

Fig. 37: Pottery fragment with the Serekh sign (see Colour Plate 57), found in Sinai.

archaic contexts in Egypt and in Early Bronze Age I–II deposits in Canaan. A number of sites near El 'Arish and Nahal Yam yielded copper ores and implements which are likewise paralleled in First Dynasty graves and settlement sites in Egypt. Preliminary results of the metallurgical analysis indicate that the source of the copper was neither Sinai nor the 'Araba Valley. This discovery is of great significance, particularly in the light of recent explorations in southern Sinai, where some Early Bronze Age II sites, i.e. Nabi Salah and Sheikh Moshin, produced evidence of local copper working. These sites are closely related to those of southern Canaan, but had very little to do with Egyptian material culture.

The data gathered in the survey of North Sinai provide the missing link of evidence for the intensive connections across North Sinai between Egypt and southern Canaan at the very beginning of the Dynastic age. The predominance of Egyptian material in northern Sinai and the large quantities of Egyptian pottery which has lately been turning up in southern Canaan, coupled with the growing ensemble of Canaanite artefacts in North Sinai and Egypt, must undoubtedly reflect the lively cultural interchange between Egypt and Canaan through the North Sinai (Egyptian?) settlements. Furthermore, the new evidence from northern Sinai supports the hypothesis that the occurrence of Canaanite materials in Egypt and Egyptian artefacts in Canaan can no longer be viewed as the result of trade relations only. In all likelihood, Egypt used northern Sinai as a springboard for forcing her way into Canaan, with the result that this area and perhaps also southern Canaan became an Egyptian domain linked up geographically and culturally with the Egyptian Nile delta.

The archaeological evidence from North Sinai concerning the history of Canaanite-Egyptian cultural exchange is in full agreement with that from Egypt and Canaan. The ever-growing body of material indicates that contacts which began in Pre-dynastic times were most intensive during the First Dynasty period, and became minimal or even interrupted altogether in the Second Dynasty, only to be resumed again with the rise of the Old Egyptian Kingdom. Judging by the absence, in northern Sinai and southern Canaan, of Egyptian material later than the First Dynasty period, it is not unlikely that the resumption of relations between Egypt and Canaan at the beginning of the Pyramid Age was facilitated by direct maritime traffic, avoiding this troublesome and inhospitable area of North Sinai altogether.

Similarly, the rarity of Egyptian pottery in the Early Bronze Age II copper working sites in southern Sinai suggests that the founders of dynastic Egypt had no direct access to the copper mines of Sinai. Indeed, as evidenced by the Egyptian monuments in Sinai, it was not until the Third Dynasty that the Sinai mines were systematically exploited by Egyptian expeditions. The discovery of copper ores in North Sinai sites may, accordingly, suggest that copper was imported into Egypt from the east and from the north via the land bridge of northern Sinai.

The contribution of the North Sinai survey is not merely the discovery of many First Dynasty sites, but particular-ly that it provides the archaeological background for a better understanding of the cultural interchange and political relations between Archaic Egypt and Early Bronze Age Canaan. The North Sinai settlements must, accordingly, be regarded as an eastern extension of Archaic Egypt, serving as a springboard for Egypt's advance into southern Canaan in the early Proto-dynastic period. At the same time the occurrence of a relatively large number of Canaanite objects in northern Sinai, particularly at sites where Canaanite material is predominant, as well as at Egyptian sites, in all probability reflects a two-way traffic, in the course of which Canaanites and Canaanite culture entered Egypt, influencing Egyptian material culture and leaving its impact on the Egyptian language and religion.

NORTH SINAI BETWEEN THE FIRST AND SECOND INTERMEDIATE PERIODS Not a single site which could be ascribed to the Old Kingdom has so far been recorded in northern Sinai. The number of sites dated to the First Intermediate period or Early Bronze Age IV, c. 2250–2000 B.C., is relatively small, and most of them have been encountered to the east of the Wadi el 'Arish, the biblical "Brook of Egypt". At one site near Bir el 'Abd the remains of structures built of local rock from the seashore were explored. All other sites were apparently seasonal encampments. The pottery and flint tools from these sites are very much the same as those found in Early Bronze Age IV (Albright's Middle Bronze Age I or Kenyon's Intermediate Early Bronze—Middle Bronze Age) settlements throughout the Negev and recently also at Gebel el Meghara and Gebel Hilal. It must be emphasized that at North Sinai sites, as at their counterparts in Canaan, not a single object has been identified as Egyptian. Similarly, Canaanite Early Bronze Age IV material is completely absent in Egyptian First Intermediate contexts. It must be concluded, therefore, that the settlements of northern Sinai were practically cut off from Egypt and should be regarded as an integral part of the Early Bronze Age IV culture of Palestine and in particular that of the Negev region.

One of the most surprising results of the North Sinai survey was the scarcity of sites from the Middle Kingdom period, c. 2000–1750 B.C., and the total absence of sites which could be assigned to the Second Intermediate period, c. 1750–1550 B.C. This is even more astonishing in the light of the close links that existed between Egypt and Canaan during the so-called "Hyksos period", when Lower Egypt was ruled by the foreign Hyksos dynasty and large quantities of Egyptian artefacts, pottery, alabaster, faience, royal scarabs, etc. turned up in many Middle Bronze Age II sites in Palestine, and Canaanite objects, including Tell el Yehudiyeh containers, are very common at Egyptian sites.

The few sites of the Middle Kingdom period were encountered mainly in the eastern Delta, just to the east of the Suez Canal. One site, located halfway between El 'Arish and Bir el 'Abd, yielded stone tools, Egyptian pottery and a number of Canaanite Middle Bronze Age IIa vessels. A group of Middle Bronze Age IIc settlement sites with characteristic Tell el Yehudiyeh ware and Cypriote White Painted sherds was recorded in the Rafa region, belonging in all probability to the Canaanite settlement of southern Palestine (Tell Ajjul, Tell Fara and Tell Abu-Sleimeh) during that period.

The scarcity of Middle Kingdom sites and the absence of Second Intermediate sites between the Suez Canal and Wadi el 'Arish would argue that the contacts between Egypt and Palestine were maintained by maritime traffic only. The only reference to North Sinai is found in the story of Sinuhe of the early Middle Kingdom period. The nobleman Sinuhe, according to this document, was returning to Egypt, probably via North Sinai, from his exile in Palestine. After reaching the "Ways of Horus"—Sile near Qantara—he was taken by boat to the royal residence in Memphis. This revealing testimony would clearly indicate that Sile on the eastern fringe of the Delta was linked by a navigable waterway with the heart of Lower Egypt. It is highly plausible that the eastern frontier canal, discovered recently near the Suez Canal, was already completed in the early years of the Middle Kingdom period.

NORTH SINAI DURING THE NEW KINGDOM PERIOD Following the rise of the Eighteenth Egyptian Dynasty, and particularly as a result of Tuthmosis III's Asian campaigns, the coastal strip of northern Sinai became the most vital land bridge between the Egyptian Delta and the provinces in Palestine, Syria and beyond. It was during this period that the major highway, the Egyptian "Ways of Horus" or the biblical "Way of the Land of the Philistines", was established officially to facilitate the movement of Egyptian armies and to control merchant caravans between the Egyptian Delta and Canaan. From the Karnak relief and Papyrus Anastasi I we learn that a chain of forts, each named after the ruling Pharaoh, was built at certain intervals along the military highway, and arrangements were made for supplies of food and water. The first leg of Tuthmosis III's military campaign to Asia, that from Sile to Gaza (240 km = 150 miles) in a mere ten days, strikingly demonstrates how well guarded and well provided was the military highway during the New Kingdom period.

In the course of Ben-Gurion University's survey, more than eighty sites have been explored. Most of them are located in the eastern Delta, between Qantara and Rumani, including settlements and caravan stations that once made up the most densely populated part of the Delta plain. A number of sites were recorded along the eastern frontier canal, which marked the border of Egypt in antiquity and provided a direct link between Lower Egypt and the Mediterranean Sea. The freshwater canal which is also represented on the "map" of the military highway should in all probability be identified with the newly discovered frontier canal. This waterway is named in the Karnak relief *Ta-denit*, i.e. "the dividing waters", "ditch" or "canal", separating the fertile eastern Delta from the Sinai desert on the east. The same canal is also referred to in the Bible as *Shihor*, i.e. the Hebrew form of the Egyptian "Waters of Horus", which is taken as a landmark for the easternmost corner of Egypt (I Chronicles 13:5; Joshua 13:3). The occurrence of New Kingdom sites along the eastern canal argues an early date for the construction of this enormous project, even

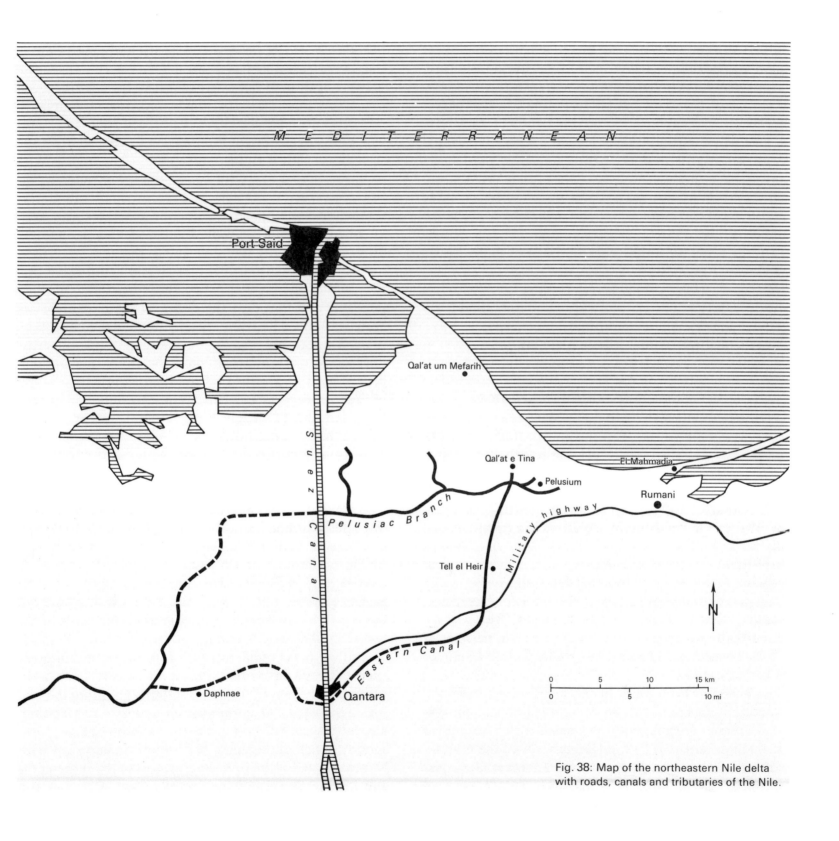

Fig. 38: Map of the northeastern Nile delta
with roads, canals and tributaries of the Nile.

though, as suggested above, the initial excavation of the canal could already have taken place during the early days of the Middle Kingdom.

The sites of the New Kingdom period are well represented throughout the surveyed area, though some larger groups of sites are clustered at Bir el 'Abd, Nahal Yam, Bir Mazar and El 'Arish. The sites yielded architectural remains in stone and mud-brick, cooking and baking installations, stone tools and containers, large quantities of Egyptian as well as Canaanite, Mycenaean and Cypriote pottery, alabaster and faience vessels, scarabs and sherds impressed with Egyptian seals. Systematic exploration at some of the sites, especially the one near Bir el 'Abd, enabled us for the first time to understand the magnitude of the Egyptian military and commercial activity in northern Sinai.

The site of Bir el 'Abd is about 50 dunams (16 acres) in size and its surface was heavily strewn with building materials and pottery of the New Kingdom period. The northern part of the site was slightly raised above its surroundings and it was here that we uncovered the remains of a massive mud-brick wall, 1.5 m (5 ft) thick. This wall was part of a fortified enclosure, some 40 × 40 m (130 × 130 ft) in size. The size of the bricks and the building technique are paralleled in the public architecture of New Kingdom Egypt. On the beaten-earth floor along the wall of the enclosure many domestic Egyptian vessels were found, including storage jars, ring stands, drop-shaped vessels and sherds painted in the typical Amarna style. Some 250 m (820 ft) to the north of the structure, certain depressions in the sandstone were noted lined with thick layers of silted material. This was apparently the site of the fort's water reservoir, perhaps of the type illustrated at Karnak together with the chain of forts and stations.

About 40 m (130 ft) south of the fortified structure, the expedition uncovered a well-preserved granary, consisting of four cylindrical chambers or silos, each nearly 4 m (13 ft) in diameter. The mud-brick walls of the granary were preserved to the height of some 2 m (over 6 ft) to just below the base of the dome which had originally covered the structure. The bricks of the walls and floors were of the same size as those used for the enclosure wall. Fortunately a section of the dome of one of the chambers was preserved, making it possible to reconstruct with accuracy the entire granary up to its domed roof. The dome was constructed of alternating circles of headers and stretchers, with a third course of upright bricks. With each successive course of bricks the space between the bricks grew wider; the circles became smaller in diameter the more the bricks inclined inward. Dark grey mortar filled the space between the bricks and covered the outer surface of the dome as well as the interior walls of the silos and the floors. The excavations indicated that the granary had originally been built in a large pit cut in the dune and that only the dome had remained visible above ground. This was perhaps designed to maintain an even temperature inside the granary. Soon after the domed roof had collapsed into the chambers, the granary was used as a refuse pit for the rubbish cleared out of the fortress near by. The chambers contained broken Egyptian vessels, such as blue-painted vases and bowls, "flower pots" and drop-shaped containers, together with Canaanite, Cypriote and Mycenaean potsherds.

The dating of the construction of the complex—the fortified structure and the granary—to the 15th century is confirmed by characteristic Egyptian, Canaanite and imported Mycenaean and Cypriote objects, as well as by Egyptian XVIIIth Dynasty scarabs and seal impressions. The latest datable object from the site of Bir el 'Abd is a jar-handle impressed with a seal bearing the name of Sethos I (1309–1291 B.C.)—the Pharaoh who ordered the North Sinai "map" to be carved on the walls of the temple of Amun at Karnak.

The site of Bir el 'Abd, together with the dozens of other sites explored in North Sinai, point clearly to a well-organized system of forts and stations guarding the major Egyptian line of communication to Asia and facilitating the passage of army expeditions and trade caravans. The evidence gathered so far argues an early XVIIIth Dynasty date for the founding of most of the settlements and forts in this region, apparently soon after, and as a

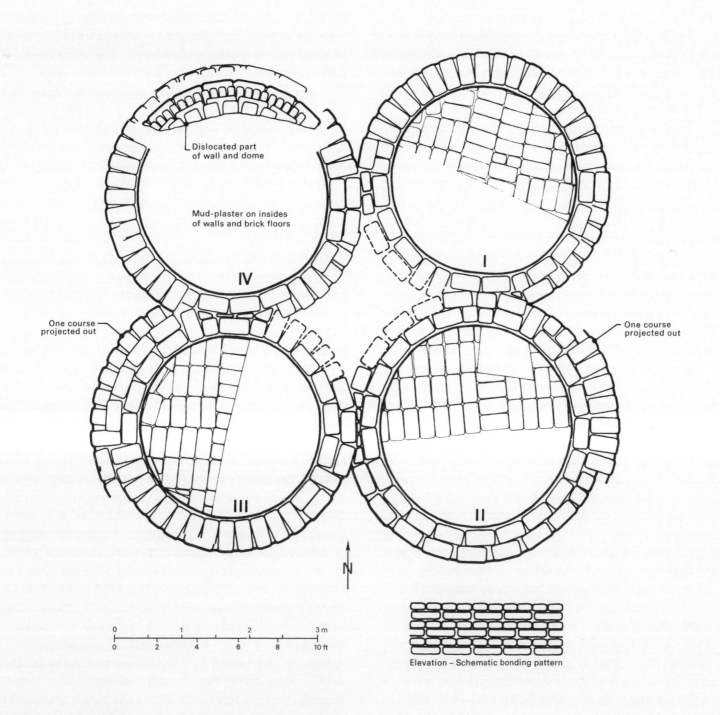

Dislocated part
of wall and dome

Mud-plaster on insides
of walls and brick floors

IV

I

One course
projected out

One course
projected out

III

II

N

0   1   2   3 m
0   2   4   6   8   10 ft

Elevation – Schematic bonding pattern

Fig. 39: Bir el 'Abd, ground-plan of the New Kingdom granaries.

result of, the Asian campaign of Tuthmosis III. Egyptian activity in North Sinai continued during the major part of the XIXth Dynasty and until Egyptian control over the Asian provinces was lost. One site near El 'Arish yielded a scarab of Ramesses III, suggesting that the Egyptian presence continued, or more probably was resumed, at the beginning of the XXth Dynasty.

It should be noted in conclusion that all New Kingdom sites were recorded south of Lake Bardawil. Not a single site has so far been found on the coastal strip or on the sand bar separating the Bardawil lagoon from the Mediterranean Sea. Furthermore, very careful exploration on and around Ras Kasroun—the traditional location of classical Mount Kasios or Egyptian and biblical *Baal Zephon*—have produced no New Kingdom sites. In fact, the oldest settlements in this area belong to the Persian period in the 5th century or the 6th century B.C. at the earliest. This evidence is of utmost importance for the controversy over the route of the Exodus in the 13th century B.C. In the light of the new data there seems to be no ground for placing the route of the Exodus along the Mediterranean coastal strip of northern Sinai—a theory to which many scholars subscribe. Nor is it possible to identify *Baal Zephon* with Ras Kasroun or biblical *Yam Suph* (Red or Reed Sea) with the Bardawil lagoon.

NORTH SINAI DURING THE SAÏTE PERIOD The number of Iron Age sites in North Sinai is indeed very small, and most of them were found east of the Wadi el 'Arish. Judging by the finds associated with these sites, it is evident that they are related rather to the material culture of southern Palestine. Petrie's excavations at Tell Abu-Sleimeh, halfway between Rafa and El 'Arish, have shown clearly that the Palestinian material culture of Iron Age I and II spread westwards to the Sinai coast. Biblical, Egyptian and Greek written sources, coupled with archaeological evidence from Egypt, have already demonstrated that, during the Saïte period in the 6th century B.C., Greek mercenaries, craftsmen and merchants settled in large numbers in frontier garrisons and trading colonies in the Egyptian Delta. The survey of North Sinai has recently produced new data, including burial customs, for the settlement of Greeks on the edge of the eastern Delta and perhaps even to the east of the Suez Canal.

The largest settlement from the period under review, T.21 on the Expedition Map, is located about one kilometre north of Tell el Heir and near the eastern frontier canal. The settlement included an unusually large fortress enclosed by massive mud-brick walls, 15–20 m (50–65 ft) wide. Inside the walled area some buildings and many installations for storage and industry were excavated. The excavations yielded large quantities of Egyptian vessels of the Saïte period, Syro-Palestinian pottery and a collection of east Greek containers, mainly wine amphorae from the islands of Chios, Samos, Lesbos, and also from Corinth. The evidence of copper ores, slags, crucibles and many arrow-heads would imply a very active copper-working industry, particularly for weapons, in this fortress. The assemblage of materials from T.21 points to a 6th century B.C. date for the occupation of the fortress and its destruction by fire in 525 B.C., apparently as a direct result of Cambyses' incursion into Egypt. The architecture and the associated finds are very similar to those of the Greek garrisons and settlements in the Delta, i.e. Naukratis, on the Canopic arm of the Nile delta, and in particular Tell Defenneh—Greek Daphnae and biblical Tahpanhes, on the eastern frontier canal. Written evidence coupled with archaeological data support the identification of the fortified site T.21 with biblical *Migdol*, which was located according to the Prophets Jeremiah (44 : 14, 46 : 14) and Ezekiel (29 : 10) on the eastern border of Egypt. *Migdol* is listed among the garrisons where Jewish refugees, including mercenaries, found asylum during the Babylonian invasion of Palestine. The fortress of *Migdol* is also mentioned by the Greek historian Herodotus (Book II, 159) when describing the military campaign of Pharaoh Necho to Syria in 609 B.C. Necho, according to Herodotus, first defeated the Syrians at *Migdol* and then proceeded to *Kadytis*, i.e. Gaza. Accordingly, *Migdol*, on the

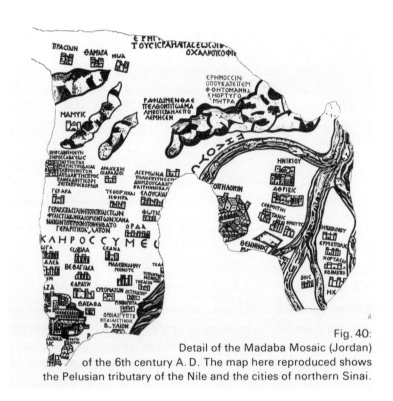

Fig. 40:
Detail of the Madaba Mosaic (Jordan)
of the 6th century A.D. The map here reproduced shows
the Pelusian tributary of the Nile and the cities of northern Sinai.

eastern border of Egypt, and Gaza, the southern gateway into Palestine, mark the two ends of the Egyptian military highway in North Sinai. During the reign of King Psamtik I, Greek mercenaries were settled in "camps" (Greek *stratopeda*) on either side of the eastern canal. It is suggested that the Greek "*camp*" is actually a direct translation of the Semitic name *Migdol*, i.e. "fort" or "camp". Herodotus' account is substantiated by the occurrence of many eastern Greek vessels, including local imitations, in both T. 21 and Daphnae. Moreover, the North Sinai Expedition has excavated a cemetery with cremation burial and eastern Greek vases near the fortress of T. 21. The number of sites with eastern Greek material explored in the area south of Lake Bardawil suggests that the communication with Palestine during that period was still by way of the ancient Egyptian military highway.

The invasion of Egypt by the Persian army in 525 B.C. brought about a drastic change in the pattern of settlement in northern Sinai, namely, the establishment of large trading centres, cities and port facilities along the coastal strip of the Mediterranean and on the sand bar of Lake Bardawil. Consequently, a new road, the "Coastal Highway", or *via maris*, as it is erroneously called, was built, replacing the ancient military road more to the south and becoming the major artery of communication between Egypt and Palestine. A series of large cities, i.e. Pelusium, Gehrrum, Kasion, Ostracina and Rhinocorura were founded, giving rise to a new mode of life in northern Sinai settlements.

Eliezer D. Oren

Selected Bibliography

Amiran, R., "The Beginnings of Urbanization in Canaan" in J.A. Sanders (ed.), Near Eastern Archaeology in the Twentieth Century (Essays in Honor of Nelson Glueck), New York 1970, pp. 85–89.
Gardiner, A.H., "The Ancient Military Road between Egypt and Palestine", Journal of Egyptian Archaeology, 6 (1920), pp. 99–116.
Hennessy, J.B., Foreign Relations of Palestine During the Early Bronze Age, London 1967.

Kantor, H.J., "The Relative Chronology of Egypt and its Foreign Correlations before the Late Bronze Age" in R.W. Ehrich (Ed.), Chronologies in Old World Archaeology, Chicago 1965, pp. 6–19.
Oren, E.D., "The Overland Route between Egypt and Canaan in the Early Bronze Age", Israel Exploration Journal 23 (1973) pp. 198–205.
Oren, E.D., "Bir el-Abd", Notes and News, Israel Exploration Journal 23 (1973), pp. 215–217.
Oren, E.D., "Biblical Migdol—Stratopeda? A Newly Discovered Fortress of the Archaic Period in the Eastern Nile Delta", Acts of the XI International Congress of Classical Archaeology, London 1978.

99 The native ibex *(Capra ibex nubiana,* see Plate 74*)*. From H. B. Tristram, Fauna and Flora of Palestine, London, 1884.

100 From the summit of the Mountain of Moses there is an incomparable view across the high granite mountains and deep gorges of southern Sinai. As a rule pilgrims set out before daybreak to climb the Holy Mountain in order to enjoy the spectacular sunrise there.

101 The chapel on the peak of the Mountain of Moses in the early morning light.

102 The granite mountains around St. Catherine's Monastery are populated by ibex *(Capra ibex nubiana),* which have become used to human beings and often approach to within a few feet of visitors. Our picture shows a female (see Plate 99).

103 The iconostasis and——behind it, partly concealed——the Holy of Holies, the chancel of the chapel on the summit of the Mountain of Moses.

104 "Draw not nigh hither: put off thy shoes from off thy feet, for the place whereon thou standest is holy ground" (Exodus 3:5). According to tradition the chancel of the Chapel of the Burning Bush in the Basilica of St. Catherine's Monastery is that "holy ground"——besides being the most ancient part of the Basilica. The tiles betray Arab influence.

105 In the charnel-house of the monastery, where the bones of the Sinai monks have been preserved since the very beginning, there to await the Resurrection.

▷

Monks, Pilgrims and Saracens

Sinai in Early Christian Times

Fig. 41: The monastery ruins in the Feiran / Pharan Oasis (after W. A. Bartlett, 1848).

SINAI IN EARLY CHRISTIAN TIMES Upper Egypt is the cradle of Christian monasticism. It was from there that Coptic monks travelled to the sandy and stony deserts of the Sinai peninsula in order to lead a strictly ascetic life in extreme seclusion from the world, in line with the "consilia evangelica". This "evangelical counsel" for the attainment of perfection is based on the Gospels and enjoins those who have chosen this particular form of Christian existence to practise absolute poverty, celibacy and unconditional obedience.

At first the hermits, who had turned their back on the world, settled in the valleys and on the slopes of the inaccessible Sinai mountains in the south of the peninsula and there founded small colonies of monks, each of them living alone in a hut built with his own hands or a cave in the rock. Later these scattered hermitages were joined by a few monastic communities under the leadership of an abbot who was responsible for a strictly regulated monastic life. The famous Saint Catherine's Monastery at the foot of the Mountain of Moses is a foundation of the Byzantine Emperor Justinian I from the 6th century. A monastic community, however, also existed at Rhaithou (now El Tor) on the Gulf of Suez (on the west coast of the Sinai peninsula), while in the oasis of Pharan (now Feiran) a bishop resided in early Christian days, with responsibility for the protection and spiritual welfare of the Sinai hermits and monks.

THE EXAMPLE OF THE EGYPTIAN FATHERS ANTONIUS AND PACHOMIUS The early Christian and early Byzantine monastic settlements in Sinai may be regarded as offshoots of the Egyptian monastic colonies in the desert of Thebes (Upper Egypt), in the wilderness of Sketis (Lower Egypt) and in the Nitrian mountain desert (Lower Egypt). A fundamental distinction must be made between two types of monastic life—the ideal of Saint Antonius and that of Saint Pachomius.

In his "Vita Antonii" the Church historian Bishop Athanasius of Alexandria (about 295–373 A.D.) describes the life and work of his elder contemporary. We learn from this biography that Antonius (who died in 356 A.D. and is also known as the "Father of Monasticism") was so impressed by Christ's injunction to the rich young man to give up all his possessions (Matthew 19:21) that around the year 270 A.D., he sold the 300 acres of his patrimony, lived as an ascetic in an empty tomb, and finally was "the first monk to penetrate into the desert" (though another source names Paul of Thebes as the first desert hermit), to live and die in total seclusion in the sandy desert between the right bank of the Nile and the Red Sea.[1]

Antonius' ideas were further developed by Pachomius (who died in 346 A.D. and whose name means "the Eagle"). About 320 A.D. he gathered the scattered hermits living in Upper Egypt and persuaded them to join together in a monastic community, in a close-knit and well-organized brotherhood. Thus the first monastery was founded at Tabennisi (north of Thebes), with another later at Pebou; by the end of his life there existed no fewer than nine Pachomian monasteries, with over 5,000 brethren. Prior to his conversion to Christianity Pachomius, the Eagle, had been a Roman legionary; this may explain why he drafted his monastic rules on a military model and demanded from the monks absolute obedience under the leadership of an abbot. This particular form of monastic communal life is called coenobitism (Greek *Koinobion* from *koinos bios* = communal life). "It was Pachomius' intention 'with his Koinobion to create a sphere within which as many as possible might atone for their sins and sanctify themselves to the glory of God without being exposed to those dangers by which anchorite [= hermit] life was found by experience to be attended'."[2] It is a fact that nearly all hermits—"anchorites" (from Greek *anachoretes* = recluse), "hermits" (from Greek *eremites* = he who lives in the desert) or "monks" in the strict meaning of the word (from Greek *monachos* = solitary, a person living alone)—have spoken of their spiritual temptations in the solitude, where they were ceaselessly attacked by desert demons and the Devil himself. That was why that great pastoral leader and Abbot of Saint Catherine's Monastery, St. John Climacus (Greek *klimax* = ladder, so called after his work "The Ladder of Paradise"), warned his monks against rashly leaving the monastery, with the complete protection it provided, and against hasty conversion to anchoretism. To recapitulate: Egyptian and Sinaitic monasticism was characterized by the two ways of life described; these had been founded, propagated and demonstrated by Antonius and Pachomius. "Antonius' ideal was anchoretism, that of Pachomius was coenobitism" (A. Adam).

THE CHRISTIANIZATION OF THE SINAI PENINSULA In much the same way as in the Egyptian monastic colonies, where anchorites settled in the Theban, Sketian and Nitrian deserts, so hermits were the first to establish themselves in the stony desert of southern Sinai. They grouped themselves around the two sacred mountains, Gebel Musa (Mountain of Moses, 2,285 m, c. 7,500 ft) and Gebel Katherina (Mount Catherine, 2,642 m, c. 8,585 ft), i.e. the place where, according to early Christian tradition, Moses came face to face with the desert god Jahve in the "burning but unconsumed bush", where the Old Testament prophet Elijah, fleeing from the Northern Israelite King Ahab and Queen Jezebel, hid in a cave on the Mount of God, Horeb/Sinai and, like Moses before him, waited for a theophany, and where, finally, according to legend, the bones of Saint Catherine of Alexandria were found after her martyrdom.

The transition from earlier anchoretism to coenobitism coincided with the foundation of the Burning Bush or St. Catherine's Monastery. The Emperor Justinian I (527–565 A.D.) ordered the construction of an impressive fortified monastery, on the one hand to protect the Sinai monks against continual attacks by pre-Islamic Saracens and on the other to guard the far-flung southern flank of the immense East Roman Empire. The monastery has preserved its original appearance to this day, apart from a few repairs and some maintenance work on the enclosure wall carried out at Napoleon's command during his campaign in Egypt in 1798/99. Before turning to the monastic age we must grope our

Fig. 42: Saint Catherine's Monastery (after W. A. Bartlett, 1848).

way through the mists of the scarcely researched early period, a period veiled in a mass of legends. Historical facts, the actual events, are exceedingly difficult to reconstruct.

THE LEGENDARY ACCOUNTS OF AMMONIUS AND NILUS
Until the beginning of the 20th century the findings of scholars were thought to be reliable. Thus Stephan Schiwietz, in his three-volume work "Das morgenländische Mönchtum"[3], still believed that the two principal sources—the so-called "Ammonius account" and the "Nilus narratives" of the massacre of the monks on Mount Sinai (Latin: Narrationes de caede monachorum in monte Sinai")—were, apart from minor legendary embroideries, reliable accounts by two eye-witnesses who had actually survived the bloody Saracen raids on the hermits in the Sinai area proper and on the monastic colony of Rhaithou.
As regards the first-named eye-witness report by the Sinai pilgrim Ammonius, this source is undoubtedly based on a historical event. About the year 373 A.D. Ammonius was living with the "monks in the valley of the Burning Bush" in order to pray on the "Holy Mountain". Suddenly a group of Saracen robbers appeared and Ammonius, together with a few hermits, only just succeeded in escaping to the near-by fortified tower next to the Chapel of the Burning Bush. The robbers tried in vain to storm the bulwark. At that point God intervened with a miracle, sending down a terrifying thunderstorm; as in Moses' day, the summit of Mount Sinai was surrounded by bright flames, so that the enemies of God abandoned their camels and weapons and beat a hasty retreat. No one will blame the Sinai pilgrim Ammonius for embroidering with legendary additions the report of his deliverance. Yet the wanton destruction of the hermits' habitations and the murder of all the monks who were unable to reach the safety of the fortified tower are no mere legend. For instance, in the Letcha Valley (west of Mount Sinai) 38 hermits were killed and two more martyrs died of their wounds a few days later. "While the

monks of Sinai were still mourning the death of their brethren, an Ishmaelite brought them news that the monks of Raithu had been cut down by predatory Blemmyes [= Arab nomads].[4] According to Ammonius' account, this second massacre at Rhaithou on the Gulf of Suez had likewise cost the lives of 40 monks. The total of 40 monks each in Sinai and at Rhaithou inevitably calls to mind the "40 martyrs of Sebaste" (in Armenia), who died a martyr's death about 320 A.D. as Christian legionaries of the Roman Emperor Licinius and who were greatly venerated both in the Eastern and in the Western Church even in early Christian times. It may therefore be assumed that the numbers in Sinai were adjusted to those of Sebaste—without necessarily calling in question the eye-witness account of Ammonius concerning the murder of the helpless monks.

Matters are rather different in the "narratives of Nilus", which have been subjected to a detailed textural criticism by the Church historian Karl Heussi.[5] It seems certain now that the author of these accounts (Greek *diegémata*, Latin *narrationes*) of the murder of the monks of Mount Sinai and the captivity of his (Nilus') son Theodulos[6] is not identical with the author of the extensive body of Letters (Latin: "Sancti Nili epistolae") which presume an entirely different circle of readers and differ entirely from the Sinai stories in style and content. The so-called Nilus Letters are addressed to an audience at home in Byzantium (Constantinople) and indeed at the Imperial Court; they contain admonitions to the Emperor Arcadius (395–408 A.D.), who had previously asked Nilus to intercede for Constantinople because the capital of the Byzantine Empire had been sorely tried by earthquake and fire. However, the fearless Nilus replied to the Emperor:

"How can you demand to see Constantinople delivered from frequent earthquakes and from fire hurled down from heaven so long as a thousand iniquities are committed there and wickedness rules with such great licence that the blessed Bishop John Chrysostom, the pillar of the Church, the light of truth, the trumpet of Christ, was banished thence?"[7]

Who was this Nilus who thus defied the Emperor of Byzantium and pleaded that his friend John Chrysostom (from 398 A.D. Bishop of Constantinople, deposed by intrigue and banished in 403 A.D.) be rehabilitated? His collected letters, of which 1,062 have come down to us, are addressed to the Emperor and to bishops, to Byzantine officials and abbots, to monastic friars and desert hermits—suggesting, therefore, that the author resided not too far from the capital city and was well acquainted with the political and ecclesiastical situation in the Byzantine Empire. This could hardly have applied if he were that "Sinaitic Nilus", far away from Byzantium. Karl Heussi therefore distinguishes in his study of "Nilus the Ascetic" between a highly respected "Abbot Nilus" (Greek *Abbas Neilos*), with his home at Ankyra in Galatia (Ankara in present-day Turkey) and hence a likely candidate for the authorship of the epistolary collection mentioned, and a "Nilus Sinaïta", who was the probable author of the "Narration of the Massacre of the Monks of Sinai". What really complicates Heussi's argument is his persistent use of "Nilus the Ascetic" (Greek *Neilos Asketes*, Latin *Nilus Asceta* or *Nilus Monachus Eremita*) for the epistolary abbot from Ankyra—since we should tend to think the term "ascetic" more appropriate for a desert hermit in Sinai. However, Heussi uses the traditional name, the one he found in the writings of the Fathers, all of whom proceed from the assumption that the author of the famous collection of letters was the same early Christian ecclesiastical author of the account of the martyrdom in Sinai.

The idea which the Fathers of the Eastern Church had of the life of Nilus is revealed most clearly in the so-called "Synaxarion" (a synopsis of the life of a saint) of Constantinople. Under the date of 12th November in the Calendar of Saints we find the following short biography of Saint Nilus:

"This same day is the commemoration of our saintly father, Nilus the Ascetic. A man with the power of speech, he became known under the Emperor Theodosius the Great [379–395] as Eparch of Constantinople. He was married to a noble consort and fathered two children, one boy and one girl. He then persuaded his consort to leave Constantinople and to reside in the abbeys of Egypt; they would share the children between them, he would take the son Theodulos, she should take the daughter. And this they did and parted from one another.

When Saint Nilus with his son had come to the Mount [Sinai] and lived together with the fathers, barbarians suddenly fell upon them and like savage beasts seized the son Theodulos with a great many others, taking them captive . . ."⁸

Since the "Synaxarion" or "Menologion" (Calendar of Saints) of Constantinople contains no further information on the subsequent fate of Nilus' abducted son, we shall quote instead from the more extensive "Greek Patrology", which reproduces the above-mentioned "Narratives" (of Nilus concerning the murder of ten Sinai monks and the capture of Theodulos). We find here an exceedingly strange story, but one which, from the point of view of religious history, is highly instructive for the early history of Sinai. Nilus here speaks of human sacrifices which were occasionally offered by the pre-Islamic "Blemmyes", as the Saracens are called in that account—sacrifices just before sunrise to the goddess Venus, i. e. the bright morning star. Let us see how Theodulos describes his own sacrifice and his last-minute deliverance:

"As thou knowest [Theodulos reported to his father] the Saracens had determined to sacrifice me and Magathon's slave to their detestable goddess. The altar had been erected, the sacrificial knife sharpened, the sacrificial cup, incense and garlands had been prepared, the hour before sunrise, when the morning star is brightest, chosen for the sacrifice. I expected only death unless God prevented it by a deed of his omnipotence . . . At last Venus appeared on the horizon. I rose from the ground, sat down, with my hands embraced my knees and continued to pray while allowing my tears to flow down my chest. Thus I spent the time until dawn. The Saracens, who had drunk much wine before falling asleep, did not wake until a short time after sunrise, ris-

ing noisily from their sleep. They were angry because they had not anticipated the great star of the day and now the hour of their sacrifice had passed".⁹

Theodulos was finally sold in the slave market of Suka to a merchant, who took pity on the terrified boy and handed him over, for a ransom, to the Bishop of Elusa (a town south of Beer-Sheba). Before long the father was embracing his lost son and the two, overjoyed, returned to the hermit colony on Mount Sinai.

As for the astral cult of the Saracens of the Sinai peninsula, which is confirmed also by the Father of the Church Hieronymus in the "Vita of Saint Hilarion"¹⁰, Nilus the Ascetic provides a few further details:

"They acknowledge no god, neither one imagined in the spirit nor one shaped by the hand, but instead adore the morning star and at its rising offer up to it whatever is best among their pillage, especially youthful slaves whom they butcher in the morning on an altar of stone, without their hearts being softened by their pleas or laments. If any such offering be lacking they will make a white and flawless camel lie down and make procession around it three times. A prince or an aged priest, who leads the procession and the chantin honour of the star, after the third circle strikes the beast at the nape of its neck with his sword and is the first man to taste its blood; thereupon the other members of the party cast themselves upon the sacrificial animal, cut it up with their swords, and consume it with hair and bone, so that the rising sun no longer shines upon any of it."¹¹

Who were those Blemmyes or Saracens? The Alexandrian geographer and astronomer, Claudius Ptolemaeus, or Ptolemy (87–165 A.D.), calls the nomadic people in the north of the Sinai peninsula "Sarakenoi", which probably means the "eastern ones". This evidently was an Arab tribe that had set out for the north and the west, and thus bound to clash with both the local population and the Roman occupying power in Palestine and in Sinai. As far as the the Sinai peninsula is concerned, one part of this Saracen tribe roamed about nomadically across the northern arid desert region, while another part settled in the well-watered mountain massif in the south. These semi-nomads in a certain sense entered upon the inheritance of the Nabataeans, who were also Arabs, and whose empire flourished from the second pre-Christian to the second post-Christian century and had its capital at Petra (in present-day Jordan) and who maintained lively trade relations with their neighbours in the north (Syria), in the west (Egypt) and in the south (Arabia). The numerous Nabataean rock inscriptions along the trade and pilgrims routes of the Sinai peninsula are mute witnesses to that efficient and peace-loving Arab people, whose empire was annexed to the Roman province of Arabia in the year 106 A.D. by the Syrian Legate on the orders of the Emperor Trajan. Still in the 3rd century, however, Nabataeans passed through southern Sinai, leaving their commemorative inscriptions. From the second post-Christian century onwards the Saracens are historically attested in the Sinai peninsula, but they had already been living there for a long time before that. They controlled the trade routes between east and west, and lived by exacting tolls and by pillage. Their occasional predatory raids and attacks on the monastic colonies in Sinai were probably due to the belief that the hermits received gifts from pious pilgrims. From the above-mentioned report of Ammonius concerning the bloodbath of Rhaithou we quote the following account:

"Thereupon the Superior Paulus stepped forth and delivered himself to them. Questioned where the money was hidden, he replied that he possessed nothing but the old hair-shirt that covered him. He died after he had been most horribly tortured by the savages for over one hour".[12]

There is no doubt that both Ammonius' account and the similar narrative of Nilus of Sinai are authentic eye-witness reports. What is legendary, on the other hand, is the hagiography of Saint Nilus the Ascetic—and we must not forget that we have to distinguish between Abbot Nilus of Ankyra, the author of the extensive collection of letters, and the desert hermit Nilus of Sinai, the author of the story of the martyr's death suffered by numerous monks.

THE CONVERSION OF THE SINAI SARACENS TO CHRISTIANITY The dictum of the Latin Church author Tertullian (who died about 223/225 A.D.) "Semen est sanguis Christianorum"—"the blood of Christians is a seed", viz., for the spread of Christianity (Apologia 50) proved to be true also with regard to the savage attacks on the Sinai monks. The innocent blood of the ascetics and their inflexible loyalty to the succession of Christ eventually led to the conversion of the Saracen Queen Mavia. Previously the armies of the warlike Mavia had constantly disturbed the peace of the Palestinian and Arab border regions of the Romano-Byzantine empire. Open war broke out between the Saracens and the Romans in the years 373–378 A.D. The Church historian Stephan Schiwietz assumes that the attacks reported by Ammonius also took place during that time. Following her husband's death, the royal widow, Queen Mavia, conducted peace negotiations with the Byzantine Emperor Valens (364–378 A.D.), whose headquarters were at Antioch in Syria. We do not know precisely when Mavia embraced Christianity. Tradition, however, has it that Mavia "had the Saracen monk Moses, who had his hermitage between Arabia and Palestine, ordained as a bishop for her people".[13] As his episcopal see he chose, "about the year 373" the oasis of Pharan (Feiran) between the Sinai mountains and the western gulf of the Red Sea. After his death, the monk Netra (Natera) succeeded the converted Saracen bishop.

THE PILGRIMAGE OF THE SPANISH NUN AETHERIA TO SINAI While our sparse reports on monastic settlements and on the appearance of the Saracens in the Sinai region during the first few centuries usually consist of a historical nucleus embroidered with various legends, the account of the travels of an Iberian nun (possibly an abbess) which now follows, contrasts refreshingly with the customary hagiographic records on account of its accurate topographical details and time-table. This sober, reliable and detailed account of a pilgrimage made in the fourth century has proved a mine of information for historians, archaeologists and geographers, as well as for theologians and liturgists concerned with the Holy Land during the early Christian period. The Spanish nun's travels took her through the entire Near East and gave rise to a diary-type record of her experiences in Palestine, Syria, the Taurus (southern Anatolia) and Mesopotamia, as well as of her pilgrimage to Egypt and Sinai, which she undertook with the intention of praying and, circumstances permitting, attending the celebration of a Mass at as many of the holy places as possible mentioned in the New and the Old Testaments.

Since the discovery of this informative account, in 1884, by the Italian scholar Gamurrini in a monastery library in Arezzo (Tuscany), a variety of datings have been proposed for this "Peregrinatio Aetheriae", written in Latin. It is now generally assumed that this noble Spanish lady, member of a religious order, embarked on her laborious expedition in 393 A.D. and completed it about 396 A.D.[14]

Let us allow the pilgrim Aetheria—some sources also call her Silvia—to speak for herself. This is her account of the strenuous climb to the summit of the Mountain of Moses and of her visit to the monks in the valley of the Burning Bush:

"But this I will say to you, venerable ladies, my sisters, that from the place where we stood... those mountains which previously we had climbed with very great effort... now seemed to lie below us as though they were but little hills, whereas in fact they were immensely high and I thought that I had never seen higher ones—with exception of one of them in their midst, which greatly towered above them [= the mountain of Moses]. Egypt, however, and Palestine, the Red Sea and the Parthenian Sea [= the eastern part of the Mediterranean], which extends towards Alexandria, and also the boundless territories of the Saracens we beheld from there below us... And when we had descended from the Mount of the Lord we arrived towards the tenth hour [from sunrise, i.e. 4 pm] to the bush... out of which the Lord spoke to Moses in fire; in that place many hermitages are situated and also the church [the so-called Chapel of the Burning Bush] at the end of the valley. In front of the church,

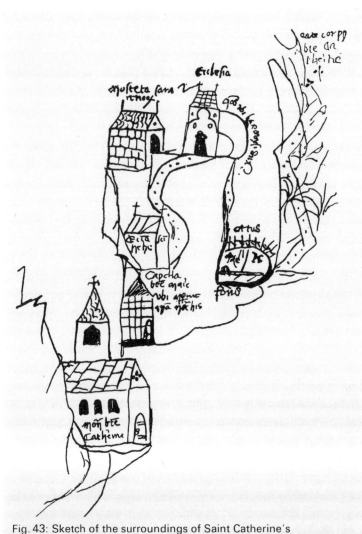

Fig. 43: Sketch of the surroundings of Saint Catherine's Monastery (Jacopo, 1335).

however, there is a dainty garden with sparkling richly flowing water, wherein that thorn bush stands...

On this [following] day we also came to the other most saintly monks who, however, because of their age and their debility, cannot go up on to the mount to offer up the sacrifice [of the Mass]; yet they were pleased, when we came to their hermitages, to receive us with exceeding friendliness.

When we had therefore seen all the holy places that we had wished for, and also all the places which the Children of Israel had touched on their way to and back from the Mount of God... we returned in the name of the Lord to Pharan [the Feiran oasis]".[15]

Aetheria also describes the places referring to the wanderings of the Children of Israel in the desert. Evidently in the fourth century A.D. there already existed memorials or chapels for pilgrims to visit: Aetheria names the place of the miraculous feeding with "quails and manna" (Exodus 16); she visited the place where Moses struck "water out of the rock" (Exodus 17); she saw the hill of the Golden Calf (Exodus 32) and describes "Elijah's cave on Horeb" (I Kings 19). Together with these early local traditions, the account of the pilgrimage contains the first confirmation of the existence of "a great many hermitages of holy men" (Latin: "monasteria plurima sanctorum hominum") and of "a chapel in the place where the bush is" (Latin: "ecclesia in eo loco, ubi est rubus").[16] In this context we have translated "monasterium" not with "monastery" but with "hermitage" in accordance with the original meaning of the word. Similarly we do not render "ecclesia" by "church" but, in accordance with its meaning and the situation in Sinai, by "chapel" (of the Burning Bush). It was not until 200 years later that the monastery of Saint Catherine and the Basilica were built by imperial command.

SAINT CATHERINE'S MONASTERY AND ITS ART TREASURES At the place where, according to early Christian tradition, Jahvé appeared to the shepherd Moses in the "burning bush" and where later, after the Exodus from Egypt, Moses gave to the people of Israel God's Ten Commandments, the Emperor Justinian I, about the middle of the sixth century, ordered his architect Stephanos to build the fortress-like Sinai monastery. For that purpose, 200 families from Wallachia on the Danube (present-day Rumania) were deported to Sinai, where the men had to do service as soldiers and to help in the monastery. With the militant expansion of Islam under the powerful Caliph Omar I (634–644 A.D.), Sinai also came under Muslim rule. The Christian Wallachians were forcibly converted to Islam; under the Arab dynasty of the Fatimids (909–1171 A.D.) they were given a mosque of their own, inside the monastery courtyard, so that a minaret now rises beside the bell-tower of the Basilica—a circumstance unique in the history of Christian monasteries. The monks of Sinai remained unmolested since they—unlike the "Gebalias" (i.e. the mountain people), as the former Wallachians or Rumanians are called today—were able to refer to a "safe conduct" of the Prophet Mohammed. Although its authenticity is questioned by historians, it certainly achieved its purpose—which was the most important thing.

A testimony to the diplomatic skill and linguistic prowess of the Sinai monks is contained in an interesting report by an anonymous pilgrim from the North Italian city of Piacenza, who visited the newly built monastery of Saint Catherine in 570 A.D. and who was later called "Pseudo-Antonius": "The monks of the monastery were highly educated. Three of them had mastery of the Latin, Greek, Syriac, Egyptian and Coptic tongues, so that they could act as interpreters in all fields".[17]

It is not therefore surprising that the educated members of the Sinai monastery should have laid the foundations of a library, which to this day contains, together with that of the Vatican, the most famous parchment manuscripts. Unfortunately the larger part of the most ancient manuscript belonging to the monastery, the 4th century so-called "Codex Sinaiticus", discovered in the monastery in 1859 by the Leipzig theology professor Konstantin von Tischendorf, is now no longer in the keeping of the monks but, by a roundabout route via Cairo, Leipzig and St. Petersburg (Leningrad), has come into the possession of the British Museum in London. In 1978, in the course of repairs to the monastery buildings, further sections of the Codex Sinaiticus were found; they are now in the Monastery Library. The Sinai monastery owns a unique treasure, consisting of the most ancient manuscripts in the Greek, Arabic, Syriac, Georgian and Ethiopian languages—some 3,400 manuscripts in all, many of them ornamented with beautiful cycles of paintings.

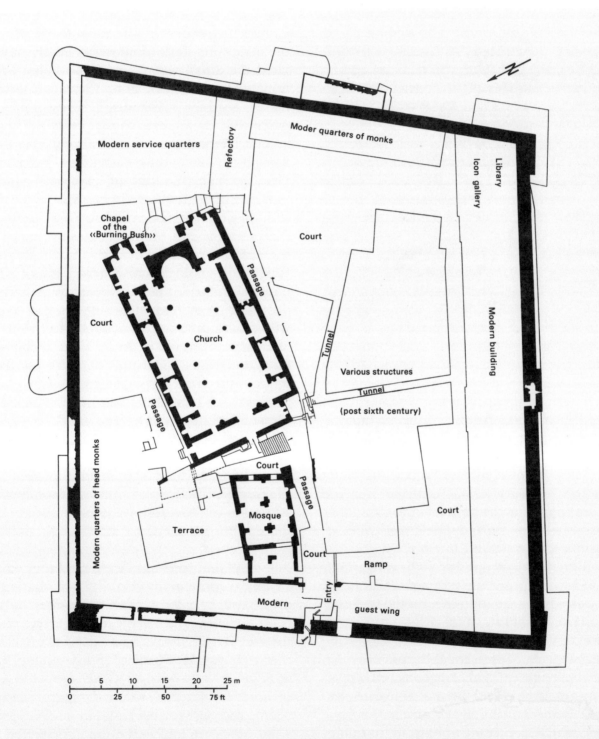

Fig. 44: Plan of Saint Catherine's Monastery; the architectural elements of the 6th century in bold outlines (after G. H. Forsyth / K. Weitzmann).

Fig. 45: Ritter (Knight) von Harff, kneeling before Saint Catherine (illustration of the late 15th century).

The collection of over 2,000 exquisite icons includes a few made by the ancient "encaustic" process, whereby the artist mixes his pigments with melted wax and applies them hot. These excessively rare "wax icons" date back to the 6th and 7th centuries. Of particular interest are the panel paintings from the period of the Crusades, characterized by a peculiar "mixed style", consisting of elements of Eastern and Western Church art.

The Transfiguration mosaic in the apse of the monastery Basilica is the most important early Byzantine work of art in Sinai. It dates from the founding period of Saint Catherine's Monastery (middle of the 6th century) and represents an ascetic Christ in a dark blue mandorla, surrounded by the law-giver, Moses, and the representative of Old Testament prophesy, Elijah. Kneeling or lying at the feet of the transfigured Christ are the three disciples James, Peter and John, showing their alarm at this pre-Easter epiphany, which, according to Eastern tradition, took place on Mount Tabor.

THE "LADDER OF PARADISE" The representation of Christ surrounded by the radiance of Mount Tabor in the mystically dark monastery church may have stimulated the Sinai hermit and later Abbot of Saint Catherine's Monastery, St. John Climacus, to write his tract on the "Ladder of Paradise". He owes his surname Climacus (Greek *ho tes klimakos* i.e. *he of the ladder*) to his ascetic instructions on how a man may gradually—as though by ascending a ladder—become worthy of Heaven. The "Ladder of Paradise" (also called the "Ladder of Virtue" or the "Ladder of Divine Ascent") of John Climacus (born before 579 A.D., died about 649 A.D.) was one of the best-known writings of monastic literature in the Middle Ages. In 30 chapters (steps or rungs)—in analogy with Christ's age of 30 years at his baptism in the Jordan at the hands of John the Baptist, the preacher of penitence—the text is concerned mainly with severe practices of penance and with ascetic regulations, pointing out to the monks a steep but practicable path to Heaven. The aim of these efforts is spiritual union with God, a "vision of God" in the uncreated "radiance of Tabor" the *unio mystica* on the highest step of the 30-rung ladder to Heaven.[18]

This ascetic work for the perfection of monastic life exerted a powerful influence throughout many centuries not only on the monks' practice of prayer but on that of the entire Orthodox community. It contains practical instructions on how to raise oneself out of the turmoil of the earthly existence to an "angelic life" (Greek *angelikos bios*)[19].

Although that spiritual ascent can be accomplished only by an exceptional effort of the will, the uppermost step of the heavenly ladder can be reached only "by grace" (Latin *gratis*). The "deification" (Greek *theopoiesis*) of the ascetic will always be a gift from Heaven; it is not a reward but an act of grace.[20] Subsequently the mysticism of Sinai spread above all to the "Holy Mountain" Athos in northern Greece, where Gregorius Sinaïtes (1255–1346) and Gregorius Palamâs (1296–1358), both by word of mouth and in writing, proclaimed the message of the "Tabor vision", i.e. the transfiguration through the divine light *(hesychamus)* in the spirit of St. John Climacus. But, in the final analysis, a mystical experience cannot be described in words. It remains ineffable for him who has received the gift and the grace of God. In the final chapters or "rungs" of his "Ladder of Paradise" John touches upon the secret of "mystical immersion" with the ambiguous Greek concepts of *hesychia* (spiritual tranquillity, heavenly peace) and *apatheia* (composure, imperturbality, the soul's state of freedom from emotion). All human striving towards perfection and proximity to God ultimately flows into God's love (Greek *agape*).

For this reason the legacy of the man who was probably the most important abbot of Sinai concludes with a song of praise to love:

"Love is the state of the angels and the state of perfection on this earth. Tell me, [o love,] which is the shortest way by which an eager disciple may raise himself to you in his heart, as though on the rungs of a ladder? The queen of virtues in heaven [love] descends and whispers these soft words to my soul: not until, dear friend, you are liberated from this sensual body can you comprehend my essential beauty. Let the ladder prove to you that there is a spiritual conjunction of the virtues, and on the summit thereof [on the 30th rung] I am enthroned, as he who has such great knowledge of the secrets of God [the Apostle Paul] says of me: And now abide faith, hope, love, these three; but the greatest of these is love [I Corinthians 13:13]".[21]

Paul Huber

Bibliographical Notes

[1] Marcel Viller and Karl Rahner: Aszese und Mystik in der Väterzeit; Freiburg i. Br. 1939. § 14. "Das Leben des hl. Anonius".

[2] Suso Frank: Angelikòs Bíos. Untersuchung zum "engelgleichen Leben" im frühen Mönchtum; Münster/Westfalen 1964, S. 64f.

[3] Stephan Schiwietz: Das morgenländische Mönchtum. Vol. 2: Das Mönchtum auf Sinai und in Palästina im vierten Jahrhundert; Mainz 1913, § 2. "Kritische Würdigung des Ammoniusberichtes über die sinaitischen Einsiedler". § 6. "Überfall der sinaitischen und raithunischen Mönche im oder um das Jahr 373". § 9. "Das Mönchsleben des heiligen Nilus auf Sinai". § 10. "Die Ermordung von elf sinaitischen Mönchen um das Jahr 400".

[4] Stephan Schiwietz: Loc. cit., p. 30.

[5] Karl Heussi: Untersuchungen zu Nilus dem Asketen; Leipzig 1917, § 9 bis § 16. "Die Briefsammlung". § 17 bis § 21. "Die Erzählung vom Überfall der Mönche am Sinai".

[6] Jacques-Paul Migne: Patrologia Graeca, Vol. 79; Paris 1865, Col. 583–694.

[7] Stephan Schiwietz: L. c., p. 57.

[8] Karl Heussi: L. c., p. 17.

[9] Stephan Schiwietz: L. c., p. 47.

[10] Jacques-Paul Migne: Patrologia Latina, Vol. 23; Paris 1883, Col. 42.

[11] Jacques-Paul Migne: Patrologia Graeca, Vol. 79; Paris 1865, Col. 612s.

[12] Stephan Schiwietz: L. c., p. 32.

[13] Stephan Schiwietz: L. c., p. 11s.

[14] "Die Pilgerreise der Aetheria (Peregrinatio Aetheriae)". Introduction and commentary by Hélène Pétré, translated by Karl Vretska; Klosterneuburg bei Wien 1958, p. 89–123: "Auf dem Sinai", Latin and German text. Dating of the pilgrimage account: p. 13.

[15] "Die Pilgerreise der Aetheria", L. c., p. 99s., 103 and 109.

[16] "Die Pilgerreise der Aetheria", L. c., p. 102/103 (Latin/German).

[17] Henri Leclercq: "Pèlerinages aux lieux saints". Article in: Dictionnaire d'archéologie chrétienne et de liturgie, Vol. 14, Pt. I: Paris 1939, Col. 144.—See also:
Anton Baumstark: Abendländische Palästinapilger des ersten Jahrtausends und ihre Berichte; Köln 1906, p. 6s. (Sinai pilgrim from Piacenza).

[18] Walther Völker: Scala Paradisi. Eine Studie zu Johannes Climacus und zugleich eine Vorstudie zu Symeon dem Neuen Theologen; Wiesbaden 1968, p. 278–290: "Der Hesychast als Höhepunkt mönchischen Daseins". — See also:
Klaus Wessel: "Himmelsleiter". Article in: Reallexikon zur byzantinischen Kunst, Vol. 3; Stuttgart 1978, Col. 1–13.

[19] Suso Frank: "Angelikòs Bíos". Untersuchung zum "engelgleichen Leben" im frühen Mönchtum; Münster/Westfalen 1964, p. 97–106: "Das Mönchsleben als Gemeinschaft mit den Engeln" and p. 106–119: "Das Mönchsleben als wiederhergestelltes Paradies."

[20] Paul Huber: Athos – Leben, Glaube, Kunst; Zürich und Freiburg im Breisgau 1969, p. 31–37: "Das ostkirchliche Mönchtum" and p. 38–42: "Der Hesychamus oder die jogaähnliche Mystik der Athosmönche" (Gregórios Sinaìtes and Gregórios Palamâs).

[21] "Die Leiter zum Paradiese, oder: Worte des Lebens, wodurch eifrige Seelen zur christlichen Vollkommenheit geleitet werden, von dem heiligen Kirchenvater Johannes Climacus, Abt auf dem Berge Sinai". Neu aus dem Griechischen übersetzt von einem katholischen Geistlichen [anon.]. Leitstern auf der Bahn des Heils. Vol. 7. new issue Vol. 1 (2nd ed.): Regensburg 1874, p. 328–348: *hesychia* (27th rung of the Ladder of Heaven), p. 362–367: *apatheia* (29th rung) and p. 368–374: *agape* (30th rung). Quotation p. 373s.

106 The famous mangrove *(Avicennia marina)* colony of Ras Muhammad on the southern tip of the Sinai peninsula.
107 Detail of the coral reef off the coast of Ras Muhammad.
108 Coral of the species *Dendronephthya* in the water of the Gulf of Elat-'Aqaba.
109 Pipe-fish *(Syngnathus),* a relative of the seahorse, in the coral reef of the Gulf of Elat-'Aqaba.

110 Ophira—the new town near Sherm el Sheikh, built by the Israelis after 1967.
111 El Tor, the ancient coastal town on the Gulf of Suez. It has an ancient Christian monastery (Rhaithou), now guarded by a solitary monk.
112 The deep blue of the sea at Ras Muhammad. The coast is here a reef uplifted by recent geological movements.
113 Satellite photograph of the Sinai peninsula, seen from the south.

Battlefields and Roads
From Romano-Byzantine Days to the Present

THE ROMAN SYSTEM Rome's conquest of the eastern Mediterranean was the achievement of Pompey, Caesar's opponent. In 30 B.C. Augustus added Egypt to this eastern province. The fertile Nile region and the rich harbours of Syria are separated by the Sinai desert. But anyone holding the Asian and African provinces was bound to concern himself with communications across this sparsely populated and arid area. To the Romans, and to subsequent masters of the eastern Mediterranean, Sinai never meant anything more than a transit region. Neither the copper mines nor the turquoise deposits, much less the nomadic Bedouin tribes, but only the transit routes roused Roman interest. That is why Sinai has no history so far as the classical Graeco-Roman world is concerned. The territory was important because of the adjacent cultivated regions—an idea inherited also by modern Western historians. Sinai nevertheless exhibits native trends of development and forces that ethnographers and archaeologists have only just begun to interpret. The desert tribes, who appear to the traveller to be a timeless people, have their own history, which was largely independent of that of their great neighbours, Egypt and Syria. Moreover, metal mining and working with precious stones, which gave rise to a local industry, have left historical traces which must also be taken into account in connection with Nabataean history. Finally, the Emperor Justinian's fortified monastery has also led a life of its own through the centuries, even though the monks intended to establish their place of refuge far from all human history. All these traces should make it possible to write a history of Sinai—but so far this task has not been attempted. It is to be hoped that it will be a subject of future research and is touched upon here simply because it seems unfair to deny an almost inaccessible territory its own history merely because the sources are still not accessible to us today.

The expositions which follow will deal with Sinai purely as a transit land. Most of the communication roads between Palestine/Syria and Egypt are ancient caravan routes and desert tracks which were already used in prehistoric times. The same ancient routes along which the Pharaohs led their armies eastwards ever since the third millennium B.C. were used in the opposite direction by the troops of the Persian Kings, Alexander the Great, the Hellenistic Kings and the Romans. Still today, on account of the mountain ranges and impassable expanses of sand, the passage through the desert is channelled into a few much-used routes:

1. The coastal road from the Nile delta to Gaza and to the Syrian ports was the main artery from Egypt to the east in the Pharaonic period. During the Graeco-Roman period this link between Africa and Asia was developed into a major overland highway; the Roman emperors equipped it with rest-houses and relay stations for horses. The road does not follow exactly the line of the coast but runs a short distance inland near the present-day railway line.

2. In antiquity a desert track led from present-day Nitzana to Ismailiya on the Suez Canal. This route could be chosen only by experienced caravans, as for some 200 km (120 miles) it led through a waterless desert. Today this track has been developed into a modern motor-road.

3. The Elat desert track from the Gulf of 'Aqaba via Nakhl and the Mittla Pass to Suez was used in antiquity chiefly by Nabataean traders. In the Islamic era this track became a "pilgrim's way" from Egypt to Mecca and Medina. Pious Islamic rulers used to build rest-houses, guard posts and draw-wells along the route.

4. Only recently, B. Rothenberg has identified traces of a Roman road from Elat to Suez, by-passing the Sinai mountains in the south and linking the ore mines with Egypt and Palestine (see p. 168/169). This route is possibly marked on the late-antique map known as the Tabula Peutingeriana, but the topographical details do not yet seem to have been clarified.

Concern for their communications also influenced the Romans when they were fixing the frontiers of their newly established province of Egypt. Although the trench of the Red Sea, with its continuation in the Bitter Lakes, had been regarded since Hellenistic times as the frontier between Asia and Africa, which meant that Sinai be-

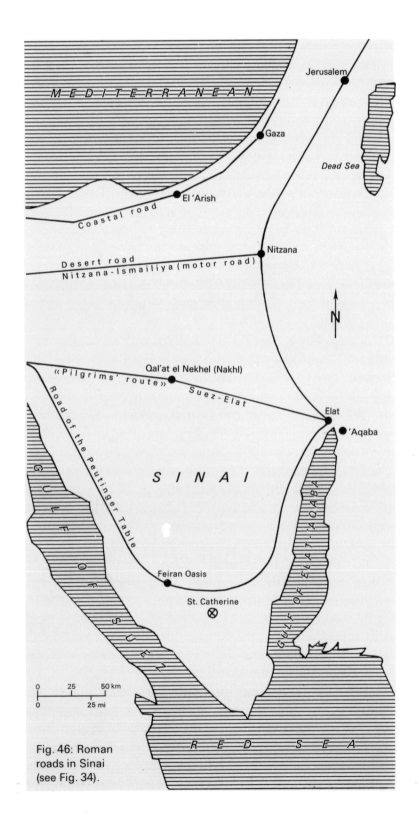

Fig. 46: Roman
roads in Sinai
(see Fig. 34).

longed to Asia, Augustus annexed to Egypt a strip of the peninsula, bounded by the El 'Arish–Suez line. The traveller from Asia therefore set foot on Egyptian soil on the coastal road shortly after leaving Gaza; as the first Egyptian station, the El 'Arish Oasis even in later times preserved its name of "the key to Egypt". Augustus thus gave the new province the most important gateway from the east. Similarly, the waterway from the Gulf of Suez to the Mediterranean, the forerunner of the Suez Canal, did not become the frontier, but Egyptian property. This Asian district of Egypt was called Augustamnica (Augusti amnis = River of Augustus); under the reorganization of Diocletian it became a sub-province of its own and continued to exist as such even under Byzantine administration. Safeguarding communications with Egypt called for a special arrangement under the Roman administration. As it was Rome's principal granary, Augustus withdrew the Nile region from normal provincial administration by senatorial governors and instead had it administered by special imperial officials.

As for the major part of the Sinai peninsula (apart from the coastal road), neither the Egyptian nor the Syrian provincial administration gave it a second thought under the early Roman emperors. The desert territory could not be used for agriculture, and the Bedouin of the coastal hinterland did not represent a threat to communications. Formal occupation by Rome was first introduced by the Emperor Trajan in 106 A. D. in connection with the foundation of the province of Arabia. This comprised the territory of the Nabataean empire on the soil of present-day Jordan and the south of Sinai as far as the Red Sea; it therefore had nothing in common with present-day Saudi Arabia except the name. The Nabataeans, a Hellenized Arab tribe, appear to have continued, even as Roman subjects, to engage in their trade along the Sinai roads and between Damascus and the Gulf of Elat-'Aqaba. The Roman governor first had his residence in the Nabataean capital of Petra but later moved further north to Bostra, where the occupying legion was also stationed. Soon after the annexation, the Roman engineers constructed a new and well-built road

from Damascus to Elat, of which numerous milestones
have survived. To protect their southern sea communications through the Red Sea to India, the Romans set up
a naval base at Elat (in Latin: Aila).

The rise of the Sassanid dynasty on the Roman frontier
on the Euphrates led to tedious complications between
the eastern provinces and the "New Persians", who repeatedly advanced from Mesopotamia towards the Syrian coast. In connection with these operations, the provincial boundaries of Syria and Arabia were changed on
several occasions. In the 5th century this reorganization
gave rise to a new province, Palaestina Tertia, which
comprised southern Sinai and the ancient Nabataean
land up to the latitude of the Dead Sea. The Roman
governor's residence was in Petra.

The Bedouin tribes in the interior of Sinai and in the
Arabian desert were never subjugated by the Romans.
However, the richer the trading-posts on the edge of Sinai became, the more pressing grew the need for military
protection against pillage by these desert horsemen. A
few words are therefore necessary concerning the Roman military organization in Palestine and Egypt. During the first three centuries of the imperial era, the Roman army consisted of a relatively small number of highly paid legions, recruited only from the citizens of Rome,
stationed as the occupation force in the provinces. These
garrisons were permanent barracks at important road in-
tersections to ensure that, in the event of war, the units
could be sent rapidly, by the network of roads, to any
threatened border region. In order to safeguard frontiers, harbours and relay-posts, the Romans used a widely ramified network of small garrison units levied from
among the local non-Roman population. It was such
auxiliary units *(auxilia)* that manned the defences
which, in Palestine and Egypt, separated the cultivated
land from the desert. For example, we know from inscriptions of the *Limes Palaestinae* between the Mediterranean coast near Gaza and the Dead Sea. Within the
area of this chain of relay-posts there were extensive imperial domains, protected against the incursions of nomadic tribes with their flocks by these Limes fortresses.

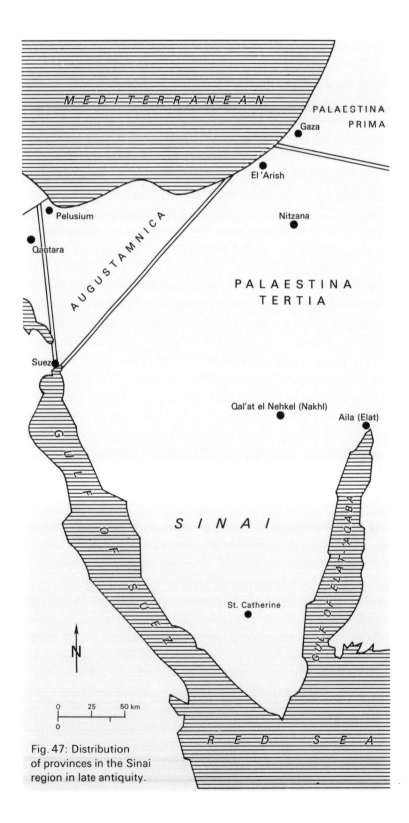

Fig. 47: Distribution
of provinces in the Sinai
region in late antiquity.

A similar chain of posts, the *Limes Arabicus*, protected the line of communication between Bostra and Aila (Elat) against the Bedouin of the Arabian desert. In the second century A.D. the *Legio III Cyrenaica* had its headquarters at Bostra in the province of Edumaea, but part of its forces was working in the 'Araba and far into Sinai in the ore mines. Under Diocletian, the *Legio X Fretensis* was transferred from Jerusalem to Aila (Elat) and there guarded the ports and the roads of the region until the later period of antiquity. We also know the identity of numerous units of the local auxiliary forces in the neighbourhood of Sinai: for instance, a detachment of the *Ala II Ulpia Afrorum* (= Trajan's 2nd African regiment of horse) was stationed along the Suez–Port Said road; and the *Ala I Herculia* garrison was stationed at Gerra (between Pelusium and Kasion on the coastal road).

The *Limes* fortifications in Palestine were maintained even during the Byzantine period. They proved incapable of halting the victorious advance of the forces of Islam, which erupted from the Arabian desert in the 7th century. The provinces of Palestine were the first part of the Byzantine Empire to fall to the Muslims.

THE ARAB CONQUEST   That the Arabs, advancing from the desert, were able to occupy the densely populated and well-fortified Palestine so quickly was largely due to the religious intolerance of the Byzantine rulers. The Emperor Justinian I (527–565 A.D.) had already suppressed Jewish religious practice in Jerusalem. His successors so consistently continued that policy that, when the Persians attacked the frontiers of the province, the Jews revolted and went over to the enemy. Jerusalem was conquered by the Persians (614 A.D.) and then handed over to the Jews.

A large number of Christians were carried off into exile in Persia. A decade later the Byzantine Emperor once more gained the upper hand and in 629 A.D. forced the Persians to evacuate Palestine. The Jews of Jerusalem were tried and punished, and the Emperor Heraklios ordered them to be evicted from the city. It is understandable that they viewed the approach of a new religion from the Arabian desert with interest and hope.

The first attack of the Islamic horsemen, still under the personal leadership of the Prophet Mohammed, was directed against the Hijaz town of Tebuk (630 A.D.). In the face of the mighty Islamic army, the Byzantine garrison of Aila (Elat) offered its submission. Shortly afterwards, the victorious army rode through the Negev towards the Mediterranean coast and there encountered the army of the Governor of Palaestina Prima, Sergios, who was killed on the battlefield. The surrender of the garrison of Bostra followed, and soon afterwards Tiberias and Galilee fell into Arab hands. A major Byzantine relief force suffered a crushing defeat in the Yarmuk Valley on 20th August 636 A.D. After stubborn resistance, Jerusalem surrendered to Caliph Omar's army of horsemen in the spring of 638 A.D. In accordance with the teachings of the Prophet, the new rulers displayed tolerance towards "the people of the Book", i.e. Jews and Christians, provided they submitted and paid a poll tax. The Byzantine administration with Greek scribes continued under Arab supervision; the provincial organization of Palaestina Prima and Palaestina Secunda also continued, though under Arabic names (Jund Filistin and Jund Urdun). Only the province of Palaestina Tertia with the Sinai peninsula ceased to be an administrative unit and was handed over to the Sinai Bedouin.

Within two years of the fall of Jerusalem, the Arab assault on Egypt was launched from Palestine. Omar's columns advanced towards the Nile estuary along the coastal road through Gaza. Pelusium held out for a time, but its local garrison consisted of Coptic Christians, who were therefore not eager to fight for the emperor of a State Church which, for many years had opposed their own faith. The only opposition encountered by the Arab generals was at Heliopolis, near present-day Cairo, where the imperial army in Egypt was deployed. But the Byzantine legions were no match for the desert horsemen, especially since the religious quarrels had isolated them from the local population. In 604 A.D. the victory of Omar's general 'Amr set the seal on the Byzantine defeat. The harbour of Alexandria fell to the conquerors without a single blow being dealt, as they had offered freedom of religion and internal freedom of administration. The bloody quarrels between the Christian confessions did in fact come to an end during the early Islamic era. The Coptic national Church, with its native Church language, which had also been dogmatically opposed by the Byzantines, has been preserved by the Arabs to our own day. Administratively, the new rulers of Egypt made few changes in the Romano-Byzantine pattern. After Mu'awiya, the founder of the Omayyad dynasty, had won the dispute concerning the Prophet's succession, Egypt, Palestine and the link between the two countries—the Sinai peninsula—were governed by the Caliphs in Damascus. The administration of the Islamic provinces lay in the hands of governors appointed by the Caliph, frequently a princely member of the Caliph's family.

In terms of world history, the most important change from the Romano-Byzantine period was no doubt in the economic sphere. Egypt and Palestine were lifted out of the ancient trade system of the Mediterranean. Egypt's rich grain yield no longer flowed to Byzantium but to Arabia. The Indian trade ended in the Arab sphere, and it took several centuries for the West's trade with the East to be resumed. The caravan routes in the Sinai peninsula, which had served the Romano-Byzantine trade, fell into Bedouin hands as the imperial troops withdrew. Sinai became a kind of political no-man's-land, of interest to the caliphs only because of the pilgrimage routes to Mecca. For such pilgrims from Egypt to Mecca, therefore, the Sinai route from Suez via Nakhl to Elat continued to be of importance. This route was continued along the Gulf of Elat-'Aqaba and the coast of the Red Sea. The Syrian pilgrimage route, on the other hand, circumvented the Sinai territory in the east and from Amman turned straight through the Arabian desert to Medina.

FROM CALIPHATE TO OTTOMAN PROVINCE The succession of Islamic dynasties in Egypt and Palestine from the 7th to the 16th century had little impact on conditions in the Sinai peninsula. As before, the territory remained a transit region between the Nile area and Palestine. Along the coastal road between the Nile delta and the ports of Palestine countless armies marched in the name of Allah—from west to east whenever the rulers of Egypt were in a position to reach out towards the Palestinian-Syrian coast. The intervention by the knights of Europe at the time of the Crusades had no impact whatsoever. That strange mixture of religious fanaticism and down-to-earth greed may have given rise to a few short-lived relations of predominance, but the system of Islamic territorial administration, resting as it did upon earlier traditions, was scarcely affected. In their attempt to seize Egypt, the Crusaders marched five times from their ports of disembarkation in Palestine towards the west along the Sinai coastal road. At the same time the Islamic defenders of the Nile delta received support from Damascus along the pilgrimage route from Elat via Nakhl to Suez. Elat, as a staging-post for pilgrimages to Mecca and Medina, was held with special care by the Muslims. To protect Islamic shipping in the Gulf of Elat-'Aqaba, the Ayyubid rulers fortified the Ile de Graye (Geziret el Fara'un) off Elat. Although the Crusaders succeeded in taking this island fortress, the European knights lacked the strength to develop this success either into control of the Islamic pilgrimage route to Suez or for an invasion of the Hijaz against Medina and Mecca. Thus the Crusades remained only an episode in oriental history, attested now only by some castle ruins around the eastern Mediterranean. In 1291 Akko, the last "Franconian" (= European) crusaders' fortress, reverted to the Mameluke Sultan el Ashraf-Khalil. The dynasty ruled in Cairo until 1361.

It was succeeded by another Mameluke dynasty, named the Circassian after its founder, and this succeeded in keeping Egypt and Syria under the same administration for another two centuries. The advance of the Ottomans about the middle of the 16th century put an end to the line of rulers in Egypt. In 1517, the year that Martin Luther nailed his theses to the Castle Church of Wittenberg, Cairo was stormed by the Turks and the last Mameluke Sultan was deposed. From then on Egypt was part of the Ottoman empire and became a Turkish province (Pashalic).

The administration of the Ottoman Empire was characterized by a high degree of local independence in the provinces. The governor of the Porte (Pasha) depended for his decisions on the regional princes (Beys); in Egypt, 24 such Beys collected the taxes, commanded the local troops and merely paid tribute to the Pasha of the Ottoman Sultan. Thus it came about that certain Beys with their troops seized power over the entire country. In 1771 'Ali Bey rebelled against the Porte (the Turkish imperial government), with the aid of his Mameluke troops prevailed against the other Beys, invaded Syria and made the Sherif of Mecca proclaim him Grand Sultan of Egypt and Ruler of Both Seas (i.e. the Mediterranean sea and the Red Sea). Following his assassination, two further Beys divided the rule over Egypt between them—a development which the Sultan in Istanbul was unable to prevent. This Egyptian military regime, however, was rejected not only by the Porte; the European powers were showing interest in the principal trading ports of the eastern Mediterranean so that, in March 1798, the French Directorate, with the secret connivance of Istanbul, decided upon military intervention in Egypt. The operation was conceived by Napoleon as a blow against Britain and at the same time, as an attempt to bar the way to India. In the summer of 1798 the French fleet arrived off Alexandria. The city was stormed on 2nd July. On the advance against Cairo the Mameluke army under its 23 Beys was scattered. While Napoleon was busying himself with the re-organization of the country, the British fleet appeared off the coast of Abukir and sank the French naval transports. This weakening of the French expeditionary force was an opportunity for the Porte to change its attitude towards Napoleon and on 1st September it declared war on France. At the same time, the Pasha of Syria was instructed to march into Egypt. Bonaparte, however, anticipated the Turkish counter-attack and at the beginning of 1799 advanced towards Gaza along the coastal road with 13,000 men. On 21st February the French occupied El 'Arish, on 5th March they stormed the fortress of Jaffa, and on 17th March they began their siege of Akko. Then Napoleon's military fortunes turned. He failed to capture Akko. Turkish opposition was stiffening, and the French were compelled, with heavy losses, to withdraw to Egypt along the coastal road. On 20th March 1800 developments at home forced Napoleon to return to France. The French army remained in Egypt under Kléber, but by then the British fleet was landing major Turkish relief units. The war went on into the summer of 1801 and ended with a disastrous defeat of the French. The last remnants of the expeditionary corps surrendered on 31st August 1801—at Alexandria, where the invasion had started.

Fighting the French was a young Turkish officer of Albanian origin, from Kavalla in Greece, Muhammad 'Ali, who particularly distinguished himself as a leader of an Albanian corps. He was proclaimed Pasha in 1805 and confirmed by the Porte. After the withdrawal of the French he turned against the British garrisons in Alexandria and Rosetta, defeated them in several engagements, and in the autumn of 1807 achieved the departure of the British fleet. He thereupon rid himself of his rivals, the Mameluke Beys, by having all 480 dignitaries massacred by his Albanians during "a night of long knives" on 1st March 1811. With great vigour Muhammad 'Ali thereupon pursued the goal of Egypt's independence: he initiated economic reforms to improve agriculture and recruited an army of fellahin on the European model. Muhammad 'Ali exploited the severe defeat suffered by the Turkish fleet at Navarino at the hands of the European powers by openly breaking with the Porte. In December 1831, with 60,000 men, he invaded Syria across the Sinai land bridge, drove out the Syrian Pasha and annexed the province. When the Egyptian troops marched into Anatolia and when even the Turkish fleet deserted to the rebel, the Sultan in Istanbul was compelled to appeal to the Great Powers for help. The latter had no interest in seeing Muhammad 'Ali on the Sultan's throne and therefore, by means of a great naval demonstration off the Syrian coast, enforced the withdrawal of the Egyptians. An agreement was reached between the Porte and Muhammad 'Ali and this was guaranteed by Britain, France, Russia, Prussia and Austria. Unter this arrangement, the rebellious vassal was installed as the hereditary liegeman of the province of Egypt. Muhammad 'Ali's successors continued his policy of independence, together with the modernization of the country in a European spirit. One of its aspects was the development of the Suez Canal.

HISTORY OF THE CONSTRUCTION OF THE CANAL   The Suez Canal intersects the African-Asian land bridge at its narrowest point, where the Mediterranean and a spur of the Indian Ocean approach to within 112 km (70 miles) of each other. Geographically the isthmus, which at its highest point reaches a mere 16 m (53 ft) above sea level, is the boundary between Africa and Asia. As a result of political history, however, the Sinai peninsula has, ever since the Ottoman Empire, belonged to Egypt, i. e. to Africa. The present boundary, running from the Mediterranean between El 'Arish and Gaza to Elat on the Gulf of 'Aqaba, dates back to Ottoman times. When Muhammad 'Ali reorganized the administration of the country, the territory east of the Suez trench was subdivided into the two governorships of El 'Arish (with an urban population) and Sinai (with the seven Bedouin tribes of the Tawara).

The idea of cutting through the isthmus in order to provide a link between the Mediterranean and the Red Sea goes back to the second millenium B. C. Pharaohs of the New Kingdom embarked on the attempt to drive a ship canal from the Red Sea through the Bitter Lakes and the Wadi el Tumelat to the easternmost arm of the Nile. This project was resumed by Pharaoh Necho (590–573 B. C.), as was accurately described by the Greek historian Herodotus (Book II, 158):

"Psamtik's son and his successor in Egypt was Necho. He first conceived the idea of building a navigation canal to the Red Sea, an idea taken up later and carried out by the Persian King Darius. In length one sails along it for

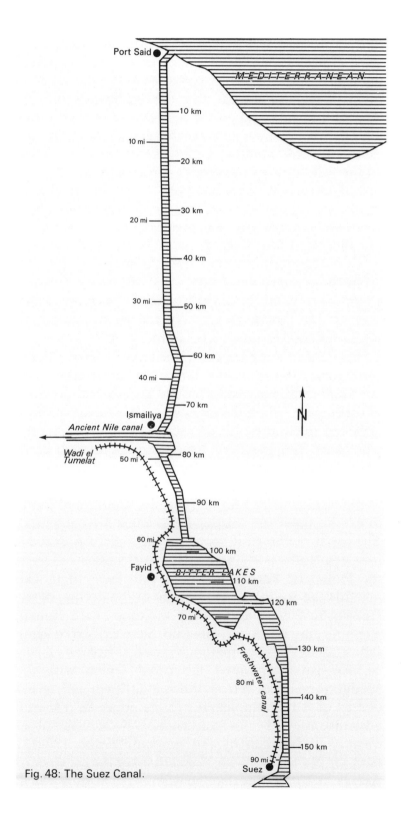

Fig. 48: The Suez Canal.

four days, and it was built so wide that two triremes can move alongside one another. The water is led into it from the Nile, a little above the city of Bubastis, not far from the Arab city of Patumos, and it drains towards the Red Sea. At first the canal on the Arabian side runs through the Egyptian plain, above which rise the mountains that extend towards Memphis and wherein are the quarries. At the foot of these mountains it runs for a while in an easterly direction; then, however, it turns through a gap in the mountains towards the south and the Arabian Gulf. The shortest way from the northern to the southern so-called Red Sea, from the Kasion mountains on the border of Egypt and Arabia to the Arabian Gulf is exactly one thousand stadia. That is the shortest way. The canal, however, is much longer because it has many windings. Of the Egyptians who worked on it under King Necho 120,000 lost their lives in the work."

To the Persian King Dareios (Darius, 522–486 B.C.), the construction of the canal meant a link between the eastern Mediterranean and India, the easternmost province of his empire. The Indian route round Arabia had been explored for him by his admiral, Skylax of Karyanda, who came from southern Asia Minor. A number of inscriptions have come down to us from the Persian canal construction project, in the multilingual style customary in the Achaemenid Empire (Persian, Elamic and Babylonian in cuneiform writing, Egyptian in hieroglyphics). The canal remained in use until the time of Alexander the Great and was maintained by his successors in Egypt, the Ptolemaic kings, and fitted with locks at its exit towards the Red Sea. At the time of the decline of the Hellenistic Powers and during the time of the Roman Republic, the waterway silted up, but was cleared again following Egypt's occupation by the first Roman emperor. Augustus separated the canal region with the Mediterranean coast from the rest of Egypt and, as the district of Augustamnica, it was placed under a special administration. Major construction work was subsequently undertaken by the Emperor Trajan (97–117 A.D.) in connection with his conquest of the province of Arabia. It is probable that the Roman naval units which, from that time onwards, were stationed in the Gulf of Elat-'Aqaba near Aila (Elat) reached their base from the Mediterranean through Trajan's Canal (amnis Traianus). In late antiquity the waterway once more fell into disrepair, since it is not shown on the Peutinger Table. When the Arabs conquered Egypt they immediately realized the importance of a direct waterway between their new capital of Cairo (then still called Fustat, from Latin *fossatum* = surrounded with a wall or fortifications) and Arabia. It is believed that Caliph Omar's general, 'Amr Ibn el 'As, repaired the canal in 641 A.D. and used it for consignments of grain from Egypt via Suez to Arabia. After the 8th century, however, the canal again fell into disrepair. From the period of the Ottoman Empire, a number of plans are known for the re-opening of the ancient waterway or for digging straight through the isthmus towards the Mediterranean. The Venetians were anxious to have shipping traffic with the Red Sea, the philosopher Leibniz sent a memorandum on the subject to Louis XIV (1671), and Sultan Mustafa II (1757–1774) had plans prepared for a new canal. None of these plans was ever put into execution.

Only when Napoleon went to Egypt with a large number of French scientists and engineers did the canal project receive a new stimulus. Bonaparte's engineer, Lepère, on behalf of the Directorate, surveyed the section from the Mediterranean to Suez in 1799 but had the misfortune to calculate a difference of roughly 10 m (over 30 ft) in the levels of the two seas. This mistake—the two water-levels are approximately equal—would have required a complicated system of locks, and this caused the building plans to be shelved. Only after another survey ordered by Metternich in 1847 had revealed the true state of affairs, did an international working party, composed of Egyptian, French and Austrian engineers, draw up modern plans for the reconstruction of the canal. For a long time there was much dispute about one project aiming directly at Port Said and another using the old Nile line. Eventually the brilliant diplomat, Ferdinand de Lesseps (1805–1894), who went to Cairo in 1836 as French Consul, submitted a finished project to the Egyptian Viceroy Zaid in 1854 and also raised an initial construction fund of 200 million francs. On 5th January 1856 the Khedive signed the deed of concession. Construction work did not begin until April 1859, since Palmerston's Cabinet in London viewed with great suspicion the opening of a new route to India paid for by the French. One of the chief constructional difficulties was the supply of drinking-water for the 25,000 Egyptian workmen. This was eventually overcome by the construction of a freshwater canal from the eastern arm of the Nile to Ismailiya and Suez (partly following the line of an ancient conduit). On 16th November 1869 the Suez Canal was opened with great ceremony. The costs of construction, which had rapidly exceeded the initial fund in the course of the work, were largely met by the Khedive, in consequence of which the Egyptian exchequer was heavily in debt. In 1875, therefore, the British Government took over a major block of shares of 4,000,000 pounds sterling. Britain's interest in the Suez route, which shortened the length of the voyage from London to Bombay by 44% compared with the Cape route, was reflected also in passenger statistics: in 1893, 2,400 of the total of 3,300 passages were accounted for by British ships; in 1910 the figure was 2,780.

BRITISH HEGEMONY IN SINAI   Since the beginning of the 19th century, Egypt's foreign policy had fluctuated between a striving for independence and dependence upon the Great European Powers. It needed considerable financial sacrifices to induce the Porte to grant to the Egyptian Pasha the title of Khedive (Viceroy) with the right of succession for his son. Other concessions, such as autonomy of administration and justice, and the right to enlarge the army, further increased the annual tribute payable to the Porte. Added to this there was an exacting programme of modernization of public life (schools, factories, railway, Post and Telegraph) which brought the public treasury (exchequer) to the verge of bankruptcy. The budget could be saved only by means of French and British loans; France and Britain therefore insisted that their representatives should be taken into the Ministry.

This financial dependence on foreign countries roused national susceptibilities. The Minister of War, 'Arabi Bey, became their spokesman from 1880 onwards. There were pogroms against Europeans in Alexandria, so that Britain and France had to send in units of their navies to protect their citizens. Thereupon 'Arabi Bey entrenched himself in a fortified camp near Tell el Kebir. British troops stormed the camp, took 'Arabi prisoner and deported him to Ceylon. Since that landing in 1882, British troops never again left Egypt until the middle of the 20th century. From 1883 onwards, Sir Evelyn Baring, subsequently Lord Cromer, virtually ruled Egypt as British Consul-General in Cairo. The main interest of that British presence was the Suez Canal, which—though joint French and British property—was guarded solely by British troops.

Although Egypt was still part of the Ottoman Empire, the British government felt a need for fixed and definitive frontiers in the Suez Canal zone. Therefore, after prolonged negotiations with the Porte, Egypt's new eastern frontier was laid down in 1906 along the Rafa–Elat line. This line still represents the frontier between the State of Israel and Egyptian Sinai. At the beginning of the First World War the line of demarcation between the Central Powers and the Allies in the Middle East ran along Egypt's eastern frontier. The Turkish High Command attempted, immediately after the British declaration of war in November 1914, to gain possession of the Suez Canal. By order of the Turkish Commander-in-Chief, Gamal Pasha, Turkish troops advanced westwards along the coastal road and on 10th November occupied El 'Arish. A second column shortly afterwards reached 'Aqaba along the Negev road. The British government thereupon placed on the alert its positions in Egypt (a garrison of five divisions, predominantly Indian and New Zealand troops) and on 18th December 1914 declared Egypt a British Protectorate. In February 1915 the Turks renewed their attack on the Canal but failed to capture either Qantara or Ismailiya. Gamal Pasha's troops had to withdraw into the Sinai desert. With the help of German technicians they then tried to bring their forces nearer to the front by the construction of a Sinai railway. That project, however, did not proceed beyond Beer-Sheba, and fighting between the British troops and the Turkish died down during the years 1915/16. Not until the end of 1916 did the British mount a major counter-offensive from the Suez Canal in the direction of Palestine. With superior forces they advanced along the coastal road towards the east, took El 'Arish and Rafa and built a railway-line from Qantara to west of Gaza. Several battles raged about the fortress of Gaza in February and April 1917, but the British did not achieve a break-through. At the same time an appeal by the Grand Sherif of Mecca, Hussein, mobilised the Bedouin tribes of Sinai against the Turkish rule. But it was not until the great offensive of the new British Commander-in-Chief in the east, Allenby, that the capture of Gaza was accomplished on 7th November, 1917, followed shortly afterwards by an advance to Jaffa and Hebron. The reorganization of the Turkish defences following the dismissal of Gamal Pasha and the appointment of the German General von Falkenhayn could not save the position of the Central Powers in the Middle East. On 9th December 1917 the British army captured Jerusalem; on 1st October 1918, with the help of the Arab desert horsemen (under Feisal and Lawrence) they took Damascus, and when the armistice was signed, Allied troops were standing at the Taurus. The peace treaty of Sèvres, which the new Turkish government was forced to sign on 10th August 1920, confirmed British rule over Egypt and Palestine.

Even during the war, the nationalist movement of the Wafd Party had been working towards Egypt's complete break with Britain. Nominally, the British Protectorate came to an end on 28th February 1922, and the successor of the last Khedive, Sultan Fuad, assumed the title of King. The British High Commissioner merely retained certain rights for the protection of the Suez Canal and a British presence in the event of war. These stipulations were the occasion for years of conflict between London and Cairo, a conflict eventually settled by the conclusion of a treaty of alliance and military aid between Egypt and Britain in 1936. Shortly afterwards Egypt became a member of the League of Nations. The consequence of the military alliance was that Egypt, at the outbreak of the Second World War, broke off diplomatic relations with Germany as early as 3rd September 1939. The Suez Canal and Sinai were firmly in British hands at the beginning of the war, especially since the neighbouring territory in the east—the legacy of Turkish Syria—was administered by the British as a mandated territory. The British position on the Suez Canal was never seriously threatened from the east during the Second World War; on the other hand, the German Afrika Korps under Rommel advanced from Cyrenaica as far as El Alamein in 1942 and was only halted by the British 100 km (60 miles) before Alexandria. Fighting for this access to Egypt went on for three months. Montgomery's counter-offensive in October 1942 and the landing of major American forces in North-West Africa eventually stabilized the British position in Egypt.

After the end of the war, the bulk of the British troops again left Egypt and the Suez Canal, the British presence being confined to the prerogatives laid down in the military treaty of 1936. However, the nationalist movement increasingly challenged those British prerogatives and demanded the total withdrawal of the British troops from the country. In 1947 the issue was submitted to the United Nations, which, however, declined to come out in favour of either party. It was the developments in Palestine which suddenly caused the Egyptian-British problem to become acute. In November 1947 the General Assembly of the United Nations approved the establishment of an independent State of Israel, and on 14th May 1948 the British officially gave up their mandate over Palestine. That decision resulted in open military intervention by all the neighbouring Arab states against Israel. On 15th May two Egyptian columns, advancing along the Sinai road, invaded Israeli territory. The Israeli war of independence which thereupon developed ended with a severe defeat for the aggressors. The armistice with Egypt was concluded on 29th February 1949, but the Egyptian Army was unable to get over its defeat. Under the leadership of General Nagib it staged a *coup d'état* in 1952, deposed King Faruk and proclaimed a Republic (1953). The following year, Nagib's successor, Lieutenant-Colonel Nasser, revoked the British treaties and nationalized ownership of the Suez Canal. This measure led to military intervention by the British and French fleets, but before war could in fact break out over the Suez Canal, a peremptory command by America and intimidation by the US Mediterranean Fleet brought all military movements to a halt. British influence in Egypt and in the Sinai region came to an end in 1956.

SINAI—BATTLEFIELD OF CONTEMPORARY HISTORY
During the years from 1948 to 1973 military movements across the Sinai peninsula succeeded each other more rapidly than at any previous period. Not only did the intervals between the numerous advances from Egypt to Palestine become shorter and, in the opposite direction, from Palestine towards Egypt, but the campaigns themselves completely changed their character—in terms of speed of movement, mass of troops in motion and nature of the materials of war—even though the character of the country, its roads and distances had remained the same. Alexander the Great, who had had at his disposal the best-equipped army of his day, had been delayed for two months on his advance towards Egypt by the resistance of the fortress of Gaza. From Gaza to Pelusium, on the estuary of the easternmost arm of the Nile, he took seven days for an unopposed march. For a modern mobile unit, on the other hand, the distance from Gaza to the Suez Canal has now shrunk to one day.
While Alexander had 32000 men for the conquest of Egypt, the Israelis had an army of 50000 men on the Sinai front alone in the Yom Kippur War, all of them recruited in that small country. For his siege of Tyre and Gaza, Alexander moved up an array of heavy siege apparatus (catapults, battering rams, mobile turrets) which his contemporaries regarded as irresistible. In the year 332 B.C., therefore, a few dozen machines may have decided the outcome of a war; in October 1973 some 800 Egyptian and 600 Israeli tanks faced each other on the Suez front alone, between Port Said and the Great Bitter Lake.
Military operations between Egypt and Israel are divided into four successive campaigns, all of them based on the same pattern: thrust by Egyptian columns from the Suez Canal region eastwards through Sinai, containment of the Egyptian movements by the Israelis, and counter-thrust by the Israeli Army in the direction of the Suez Canal. In the wars of 1956 and 1967 the Israelis anticipated the Egyptian advance to the Sinai and took preventive action. As for their axis of advance, both parties used the traditional roads and tracks through the Sinai Desert, the only innovation being that caterpillar vehicles now enjoyed increased mobility even in trackless terrain. Owing to modern artillery and the use of aircraft, the troop movements covered greater areas and were less massed than in the past. Moreover, modern guns are effective over a greater range, so that battles between opposing tank forces now resemble the naval battles of the past.

THE ISRAELI WAR OF INDEPENDENCE 1948/49 The response to the withdrawal of the British Palestine Army was the invasion of Israel by Arab troops on 15th May 1948. Egypt, Transjordan and Syria, with the help of the other Arab states, intended to apply a military solution to the problem of Palestine, which had been the object of negotiations at international conferences for several decades—in other words, to liquidate the State of Israel set up in 1947 by the United Nations' decision. After initial losses, the Israelis succeeded in holding their own on all fronts. In the south, on 15th May, two Egyptian brigades attacked from Sinai in the direction of Gaza and Beer-Sheba. The first column, moving along the coast road, reached Ashdod on 11th June; the Negev column took Beer-Sheba on 20th May and shortly afterwards also Hebron and Bethlehem; on 11th June, at the beginning of the first armistice, it stood south of Jerusalem. Fighting went on throughout the summer of 1948 along these routes of advance as the Egyptian thrust had by-passed many intact Israeli pockets of resistance. In the course of the autumn, Israeli resistance stiffened, and on 22nd December the Israeli High Command mounted an exceedingly vigorous counter-offensive on the southern front. By 27th December the road to Beer-Shaba had been cleared. From the Negev, the Israeli attack then developed towards the coast—the Egyptians being unable to oppose it by any fresh forces on account of their extended lines of supply. By the beginning of January 1949 the Israelis had reached El 'Arish and were about to capture the Egyptian frontier fortress. In that situation the European Great Powers, determined not to tolerate an Israeli advance into Egyptian territory, intervened. The armistice of 7th January 1949 froze the fronts along the Israeli state frontier from Rafa to Elat, the coastal positions of Rafa and Gaza remaining in Egyptian hands.

THE SINAI CAMPAIGN OF 1956 The Israeli Sinai offensive in the autumn of 1956 was closely connected with the nationalization of the Suez Canal by the revolutionary Head of State, Gamal 'Abd el Nasser. Since the armistice of 1949 the Egyptians had considerably reinforced their troops in the Canal and Sinai regions: in the Gaza strip there was one division (the 8th Palestine Division), another was in Sinai, with headquarters at El 'Arish (3rd Division) and in the Canal zone stood the 2nd Division (Ismailiya). The roads across Sinai were guarded by bases, depots and permanent fortifications; the Egyptian Air Force and Tank Force had been greatly strengthened by help from the Soviet Union. The blockade of the Strait of Tiran was the decisive factor in an Israeli preventive action designed, on the one hand, to remove the latent threat of an Egyptian deployment in Sinai and, on the other, to restore free access to Elat from the sea. Israel, at the same time, hoped for the success of the British-French operation against the Suez Canal. The Israeli offensive began at dawn on 29th October 1956 with a surprise occupation of the Mittla Pass outside Suez by a paratroop battalion. Egypt's reply consisted of fierce air attacks against the deployment of the Is-

raeli troops and in an attack on Haifa by a destroyer. By 31st October, however, the Israeli Air Force had proved superior and the destroyer was forced to surrender. Supported by Israeli superiority in the air, the advance of the ground forces was so rapid that Israeli tanks reached the Suez Canal on 2nd November.

The war reports named the following routes of advance: one infantry brigade on 2nd/3rd November captured the Gaza strip; a combat group consisting of one armoured brigade and one infantry brigade advanced along the coastal road as far as the flood area of Qantara between 31st October and 2nd November; the strongest combat group, consisting of one armoured brigade and two infantry brigades, covered the 200 km (120 miles) of desert track from Nitzana via Abu Ageila—Bir Gafgafa to a point opposite Ismailiya between 30th October and 2nd November; paratroops and infantry advanced from Kuntilla to Themed on the pilgrimage route on 29th and 30th October and from there to the Mittla Pass; finally, from the Mittla Pass and from Elat, the tip of the peninsula at Sherm el Sheikh was reached by difficult coastal tracks on 5th November.

At that time, on the morning of 5th November, British and French forces opened their attacks on Port Said and the Suez Canal. That same day the Soviet Government announced its military intervention (threat of rockets) and the USA joined in that pressure; as a result, the Armistice came into effect in the war-zone on 6th November. During the following weeks and months, an international police force of the United Nations took over the control of the Canal Zone. Israel had to pull its troops back, but at least it had free access to the port of Elat guaranteed by the U.N.

THE SIX-DAY WAR OF 1967 The Israeli victory in the Sinai war had so damaged Arab prestige that Egypt, as the strongest partner in the Arab League, openly aimed at a war of revenge. From 1956 to 1967 the Egyptian government systematically equipped its defeated army, chiefly with Russian material. The units stationed in the Sinai territory were increased to seven armoured and in-

233

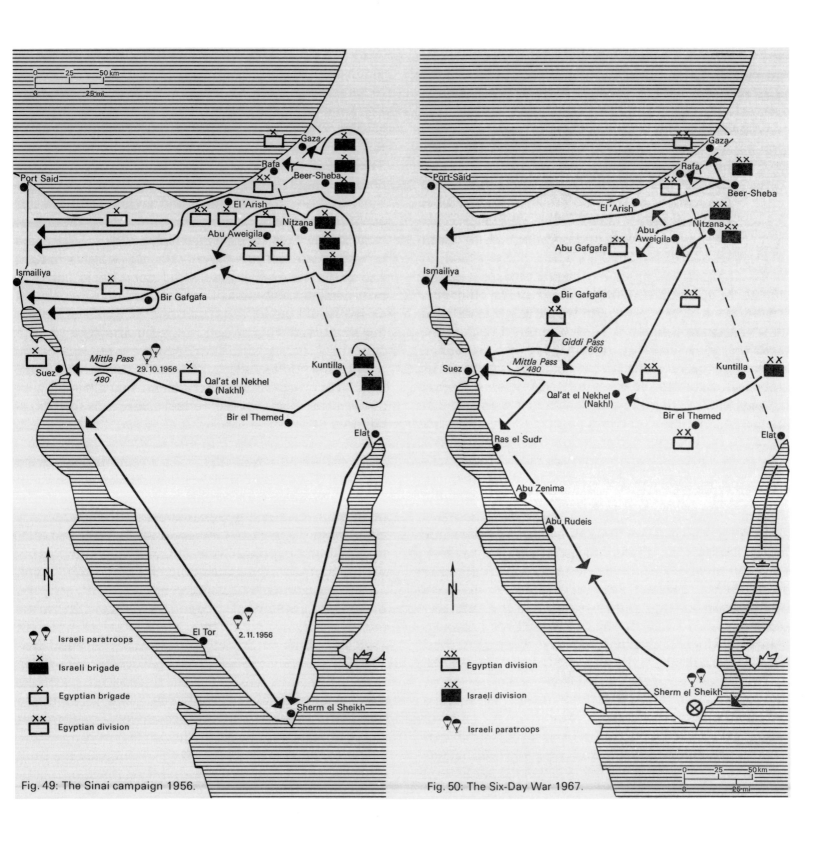

Fig. 49: The Sinai campaign 1956.

Israeli paratroops

Israeli brigade

Egyptian brigade

Egyptian division

29.10.1956

2.11.1956

El Tor

Mittla Pass
480

Suez

Ismailiya

Port Said

Bir Gafgafa

Qal'at el Nekhel
(Nakhl)

Bir el Themed

Kuntilla

Elat

Sherm el Sheikh

Gaza

Rafa

Beer-Sheba

El 'Arish

Abu Aweigila

Nitzana

Fig. 50: The Six-Day War 1967.

Egyptian division

Israeli division

Israeli paratroops

Port-Said

Ismailiya

Suez

Giddi Pass
660

Mittla Pass
480

Ras el Sudr

Abu Zenima

Abu Rudeis

Bir Gafgafa

Abu Gafgafa

El 'Arish

Abu
Aweigila

Gaza

Rafa

Beer-Sheba

Nitzana

Qal'at el Nekhel
(Nakhl)

Bir el Themed

Kuntilla

Elat

Sherm el Sheikh

fantry divisions. Of these, one division each was in a forward position right up against the Israeli frontier, in the Gaza strip and at Rafa; three divisions were in the Sinai desert close to Israel, and two armoured divisions were at Themed and Bir Gafgafa. The Egyptians increased their Air Force to 500 units. On 18th May 1967 in assurance of this strength, President Nasser demanded from the U.N. Secretary-General U Thant the withdrawal of the U.N. policing force from Gaza, Sinai and Sherm el Sheikh. That withdrawal of the U.N. troops was completed by 22nd May, whereupon Nasser had the Strait of Tiran closed to Israeli ships and the tip of Sinai at Sherm el Sheikh occupied by Egyptian troops. On 31st May there followed the conclusion of an Egyptian-Jordanian military agreement, and Iraqi troops were placed under Egyptian command. In view of this threat of war, the Israeli government again decided to take preventive action. On the morning of 5th June 1967, the Israelis launched a concentrated air offensive against enemy airfields, and during the first few hours destroyed 374 aircraft. At the same time they succeeded in putting the enemy radar network out of action. This Israeli superiority in the air explains the rapid advance of the Israelis in spite of the massive reinforcement of the Egyptian garrisons in Sinai. The offensive virtually followed the route of advance of the Sinai campaign, i.e. the roads and tracks which, since time immemorial, had made movement possible through the desert:

On 5th June one infantry division reinforced with tanks advanced from the Beer-Sheba region towards the coast, occupied Gaza, Rafa and El 'Arish, and the same day continued its advance along the coastal road towards Qantara, which it reached two days later. A second division advanced from Nitzana towards Abu Ageila, and after some heavy tank combat crossed the desert by the road through Bir Gafgafa, and on 8th June reached the Canal opposite Ismailiya.

A third division from the Nitzana area thrust southwards towards Nakhl, forced major Egyptian formations against the high Sinai range and reached the Suez Canal by way of the Mittla Pass.

A fourth Israeli column moved from the Kuntilla area along the Elat–Suez pilgrimage road and linked up with the advancing third column outside Suez. Finally, as in the Sinai war of 1956, the Israelis occupied Sherm el Sheikh with paratroops and mobile units on the third day of operations.

Their rapid advance to the Suez Canal between 5th and 8th June enabled the Israelis to switch a large part of their Sinai troops to the Jordanian and Syrian fronts as early as 9th June. The Egyptian formations, their lines of retreat having been cut off by the Israeli advance, retreated towards their western bases, with heavy losses in men and material. As the Israelis did not wish to take any prisoners, the remnants of the defeated divisions sought safety by making for the Canal and the Red Sea. During the months and years following the armistice of 10th June 1967, the Israelis developed the east bank of the Suez Canal into a solid line of defence, the Bar-Lev Line. This barred the occupied Sinai peninsula against Egypt and was intended to protect Israel against any further retaliatory attack.

THE YOM KIPPUR WAR 1973 The years following the Six-Day War of 1967 were characterized, for victor and vanquished alike, by further re-armament. While the Israelis were developing the Sinai peninsula as a military glacis against Egypt and increasing the mobility of their troops, the Egyptians were strengthening their army with modern equipment supplied by the Soviet Union. Large consignments of tanks, combat aircraft, artillery, rockets and anti-aircraft weapons, together with instructors, were landed at Egypt's Mediterranean ports. In 1970 the corps of Soviet military advisers numbered 12 000. The Arab leadership took particular care to keep their war preparations secret. The Egyptian attack on the Bar-Lev Line on the 6th October 1973 therefore took the Israeli and all foreign intelligence services by surprise. It was deliberately timed for the Jewish Day of Atonement, a time at which the men would be absent from the front on leave, and headquarters would be manned on a holiday basis.

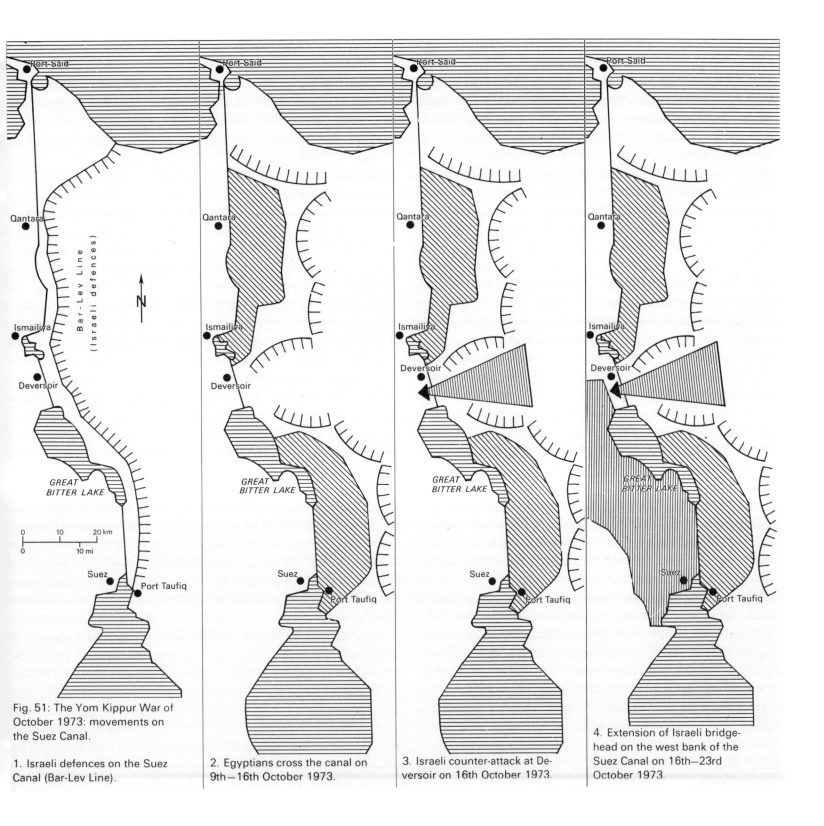

Fig. 51: The Yom Kippur War of October 1973: movements on the Suez Canal.

1. Israeli defences on the Suez Canal (Bar-Lev Line).

2. Egyptians cross the canal on 9th–16th October 1973.

3. Israeli counter-attack at Deversoir on 16th October 1973.

4. Extension of Israeli bridgehead on the west bank of the Suez Canal on 16th–23rd October 1973.

The Egyptian operations began with the landing of commando-troops on the east bank of the Suez Canal at five points between Qantara and Suez. Under the protection of a massed artillery barrage (from 1650 guns) the Egyptians succeeded, during the first 24 hours of the war, in establishing a number of pontoon bridges across the Canal and in ferrying over several hundred tanks. The Israeli Air Force, which had decisively impeded the Egyptian deployment in 1956 and 1967, was now effectively kept away from the Suez Canal by Russian Sam missiles. By 9th October the Egyptians had succeeded in breaking through the chain of strongpoints of the Bar-Lev Line on a broad front, and the two attacking armies—the Second Army in the Qantara sector north of the Great Bitter Lake (km 45—km 90 of the Canal), the Third Army adjoining it in the Bitter Lakes—Suez sector (km 90—km 160)—were able to deploy for their advance into Sinai. By the fourth day of operations, the east bank of the Suez Canal was in Egyptian hands to a depth of 10 to 20 km (6 to 12 miles); the Israelis had pulled back the remainder of their 3000-strong garrison of the Bar-Lev Line. Egyptian attacks against the Mittla Pass did not bring success, as the effectiveness of the Egyptian Sam missiles decreased with increasing distance from the Canal.

In retrospect, the Bar-Lev Line, even though relatively rapidly broken through by the enemy, proved a vital investment to the war-effort. The fact that the Egyptian army was held up among the Suez Canal obstacles for four days enabled the Israelis to accomplish the undisturbed mobilization of their army and an effective preparation for all-round defence. On the southern front, from which the strongest enemy forces had always attacked, and which was always of the greatest importance for Israel, Israeli units were re-forming for a counter-attack, benefiting from their exact knowledge of the terrain from earlier Sinai campaigns. The main problem was to make it possible to employ the Israeli Air Force along the Canal front, still not very deep, by the elimination of some of the Egyptian Sam batteries.

That objective was achieved by Israeli commandos on 16th October 1973, the 11th day of the war. The Canal crossing was effected north of the Great Bitter Lake, near the village of Deversoir, at the exact junction of the sectors of the Second and Third Egyptian Armies. Within an astonishingly short time, that bridgehead was enlarged. Three days after the crossing of the Canal, the Sam missiles captured by the Israelis were transported to the eastern bank and on the following day the advance of Israeli tanks on African soil began. This operation appreciably upset the supply and deployment of the Egyptian Third Army and forced it to fight on two sides—in the west and in the east. The Israeli General Staff quickly realized its opportunity and sent major forces through the gap in the Egyptian front at Deversoir. These troops thrust towards Suez behind the Egyptian lines, and, in a joint action with the units attacking on the eastern side, by 23rd October 1973 succeeded in completely encircling the Egyptian Third Army on both banks of the Canal. That encirclement of the Egyptian Third Army of 20,000 men decided the outcome of the war. The Great Powers, above all the Soviet Union, would not tolerate an annihilation of the enclosed army group as they feared incalculable political reactions on the part of the defeated Arab side. Thus, under the guidance of the United Nations, negotiations began for an armistice, initially aiming at a disentanglement of Israeli and Egyptian forces, but intended later to create the basic requirements needed for a more lasting settlement.

The surprise visit of the Egyptian President Sadat to Jerusalem in 1977 gave the willingness for peace of both sides a great impetus. In the Egyptian-Israeli Peace Treaty of 1979 the Sinai area was handed back to Egypt.

Gerold Walser

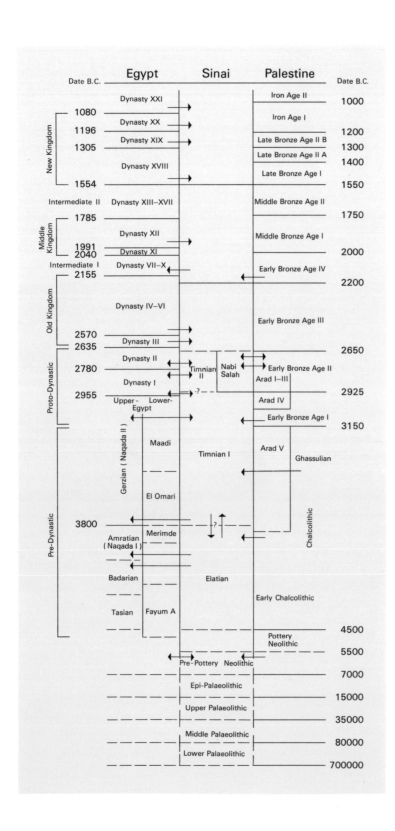

Date B.C.	Egypt		Sinai	Palestine	Date B.C.
		Dynasty XXI		Iron Age II	1000
1080	New Kingdom	Dynasty XX		Iron Age I	
1196		Dynasty XIX		Late Bronze Age II B	1200
1305				Late Bronze Age II A	1300
		Dynasty XVIII			1400
				Late Bronze Age I	
1554					1550
Intermediate II		Dynasty XIII–XVII		Middle Bronze Age II	
1785	Middle Kingdom				1750
		Dynasty XII		Middle Bronze Age I	
1991		Dynasty XI			2000
2040					
Intermediate I		Dynasty VII–X		Early Bronze Age IV	
2155					2200
	Old Kingdom	Dynasty IV–VI		Early Bronze Age III	
2570		Dynasty III			
2635					2650
2780	Proto-Dynastic	Dynasty II	Timnian II · Nabi Salah	Early Bronze Age II · Arad I–III	
		Dynasty I			
2955		Upper- Lower- Egypt	?—	Arad IV	2925
				Early Bronze Age I	
					3150
	Pre-Dynastic	Maadi	Timnian I	Arad V · Ghassulian	
		Gerzian (Naqada II)			
		El Omari			
3800			—?—		
		Merimde · Amratian (Naqada I)		Chalcolithic	
		Badarian	Elatian		
		Tasian · Fayum A		Early Chalcolithic	
					4500
				Pottery Neolithic	5500
			Pre-Pottery Neolithic		
					7000
			Epi-Palaeolithic		15000
			Upper Palaeolithic		35000
			Middle Palaeolithic		80000
			Lower Palaeolithic		700000

Comparative chronology of the Sinai peninsula, Egypt and Palestine (table on left)

Sinai, the desert triangle suspended between Africa and Asia, naturally reflects the cultural epochs of the territories in its immediate neighbourhood. The relations of the Sinai population both with Egypt and with Palestine (to be understood here as a geographical, cultural and historical and not as a political concept) were not only decisive for the emergence of local native Sinaitic cultures but are today an important criterion for dating. For this reason it seems important to us to present the chronology of Sinai in parallel tables with that of Egypt and of Palestine.

For the Egyptian chronology we have used the chronological table of J. v. Beckerath in his "Abriss der Geschichte des alten Ägypten", Munich 1971, and for that of Palestine the chronological table of the "Encyclopedia of Archaeological Excavation in the Holy Land", Jerusalem 1978.

Until the Neolithic Age, the terminology of the Stone Age cultures of Africa and the Levant were applicable; from about 4500 until about 2650 B.C., however, there existed in the Sinai region some local native cultural developments which demand a terminology of their own. During that period of nearly 2000 years there were two native cultures in Sinai which could be defined archaeologically by their specific flint industries, pottery and architecture—Beno Rothenberg: "New Researches in Sinai" (in preparation)—and which, according to the areas where they were first discovered and identified, Elat and Timna, are called "Elatian culture" and "Timnian culture".

About 2650 B.C. the local native cultural development in Sinai came to an end and from then onwards central and southern Sinai was a land of nomads "with no history", to which only the Egyptian chronology applies.

In Palestinian archaeology the "correct" designation of the cultural period from about 2200 to 2000 B.C. is being intensively discussed and concepts as "Middle Bronze Age I", "Early Bronze/Middle Bronze Age", "Early

North Sinai	Egypt	Palestine	Date B.C. (approximate)
North central, Northwest ●● 20–50 sites	Persian Conquest 525 B.C. Dynasty XXVI	Iron Age III	800– 525
Northeast, Northwest ● 1–20 sites	Third Intermediate Dynasty XXI–XXV	Iron Age I–II	1200– 800
Northeast, North central, Northwest ●●● 50–100 sites	New Kingdom Dynasty XVIII–XX	Late Bronze Age I–III	1550–1200
	Second Intermediate Dynasty XIV–XVII	Middle Bronze Age II B + C	1750–1550
Northeast, North central, Northwest ● 1–20 sites	Middle Kingdom Dynasty XII–XIII	Middle Bronze Age II A	1900–1750
Northeast, North central ●●● 50–100 sites	First Intermediate Dynasty VII–XI	Middle Bronze Age I Early Bronze Age IV	2000–1900 2250–2000
	Old Kingdom Dynasty III–VI Dynasty II (Proto-dynastic)	Early Bronze Age III A + B Early Bronze Age II B	2700–2250 2800–2700
Northeast, North central, Northwest ●●●● 100–200 sites	Proto-dynastic Dynasty I	Early Bronze Age I B + II A	3000–2800
Northeast, North central, Northwest ●● 20–50 sites	Pre-dynastic	Early Bronze Age I A Chalcolithic	4th millenium

Bronze Age IV" have been proposed. For cultural, historical and archaeological reasons we have decided in favour of "Early Bronze Age IV".

In order to indicate the principal emphasis in the relations between Sinai and the neighbouring cultures we have used arrows to represent such contacts—conquest, infiltration, new settlers, trade, mining expeditions, etc.

Beno Rothenberg

Distribution and chronology of archaeological sites in the northern coastal strip of Sinai (table on right)

To ensure the understanding of the importance which attaches to the northern coastal strip of Sinai it is essential to indicate the settlement density at various historical periods in an overall survey. The distribution statistics published here for the first time show the number of ancient northern Sinai settlements at different cultural periods of Egypt and Palestine.

Eliezer D. Oren